Without Criteria

Technologies of Lived Abstraction
Brian Massumi and Erin Manning, editors

Relationscapes: Movement, Art, Philosophy, Erin Manning, 2009

Without Criteria: Kant, Whitehead, Deleuze, and Aesthetics, Steven Shaviro, 2009

Without Criteria: Kant, Whitehead, Deleuze, and Aesthetics

Steven Shaviro

The MIT Press   Cambridge, Massachusetts   London, England

© 2009 Massachusetts Institute of Technology

All rights reserved. No part of this book may be reproduced in any form by any electronic or mechanical means (including photocopying, recording, or information storage and retrieval) without permission in writing from the publisher.

For information about special quantity discounts, please email special_sales@mitpress.mit.edu

This book was set in Garamond and Rotis semi-sans by Binghamton Valley Composition in Quark.

Printed and bound in the United States of America.

Library of Congress Cataloging-in-Publication Data

Shaviro, Steven.
Without criteria : Kant, Whitehead, Deleuze, and aesthetics / Steven Shaviro.
   p. cm.
Includes bibliographical references.
ISBN 978-0-262-19576-8 (hardcover : alk. paper)
1. Whitehead, Alfred North, 1861–1947. 2. Aesthetics. 3. Deleuze, Gilles, 1925–1995. 4. Heidegger, Martin, 1889–1976. 5. Kant, Immanuel, 1724–1804. I. Title.
B1674.W354S44   2009
192—dc22
                         2008041142

10 9 8 7 6 5 4 3 2 1

Contents

Series Foreword   vii

Preface: A Philosophical Fantasy   ix

1 Without Criteria   1

2 Actual Entities and Eternal Objects   17

3 Pulses of Emotion   47

4 Interstitial Life   71

5 God, or The Body without Organs   99

6 Consequences   143

References   163

Index   171

Technologies of Lived Abstraction

Erin Manning and Brian Massumi, editors

"*What moves as a body, returns as the movement of thought.*"
        Of subjectivity (in its nascent state)
        Of the social (in its mutant state)
        Of the environment (at the point it can be reinvented)
"*A process set up anywhere reverberates everywhere.*"

The Technologies of Lived Abstraction book series is dedicated to works of transdisciplinary reach inquiring critically but especially creatively into processes of subjective, social, and ethical-political emergence abroad in the world today. Thought and body, abstract and concrete, local and global, individual and collective: the works presented are not content to rest with the habitual divisions. They explore how these facets come formatively, reverberatively together, if only to form the movement by which they come again to differ.

    Possible paradigms are many: autonomization, relation; emergence, complexity, process; individuation, (auto)poiesis; direct perception, embodied perception, perception-as-action; speculative pragmatism, speculative realism, radical empiricism; mediation, virtualization; ecology of practices, media ecology; technicity; micropolitics, biopolitics, ontopower. Yet there will be a common aim: to catch new thought and action dawning, at a creative crossing. The Technologies of Lived Abstraction series orients to the creativity at this crossing, in virtue of which life everywhere can be considered germinally aesthetic, and the aesthetic anywhere already political.

    "*Concepts must be experienced. They are lived.*"

Preface: A Philosophical Fantasy

This book originated out of a philosophical fantasy. I imagine a world in which Whitehead takes the place of Heidegger. Think of how important Heidegger has been for thinking and critical reflection over the past sixty years. What if Whitehead, instead of Heidegger, had set the agenda for postmodern thought? What would philosophy be like today? What different questions might we be asking? What different perspectives might we be viewing the world from?

The parallels between Heidegger and Whitehead are striking. *Being and Time* was published in 1927, *Process and Reality* in 1929. Two enormous philosophy books, almost exact contemporaries. Both books respond magisterially to the situation (I'd rather not say the crisis) of modernity, the immensity of scientific and technological change, the dissolution of old certainties, the increasingly fast pace of life, the massive reorganizations that followed the horrors of World War I. Both books take for granted the inexistence of foundations, not even fixating on them as missing, but simply going on without concern over their absence. Both books are antiessentialist and antipositivist, both of them are actively engaged in working out new ways to think, new ways to do philosophy, new ways to exercise the faculty of wonder.

And yet how different these two books are: in concepts, in method, in affect, and in spirit. I'd like to go through a series of philosophical questions and make a series of (admittedly tendentious) comparisons, in order to spell out these differences as clearly as possible.

1 *The question of beginnings* Where does one start in philosophy? Heidegger asks the question of Being: "Why is there something, rather than nothing?" But Whitehead is splendidly indifferent to this question. He asks, instead: "How is it that there is always something new?" Whitehead doesn't see any point in returning to our ultimate beginnings. He is interested in creation

rather than rectification, Becoming rather than Being, the New rather than the immemorially old. I would suggest that, in a world where everything from music to DNA is continually being sampled and recombined, and where the shelf life of an idea, no less than of a fashion in clothing, can be measured in months if not weeks, Whitehead's question is the truly urgent one. Heidegger flees the challenges of the present in horror. Whitehead urges us to work with these challenges, to negotiate them. How, he asks, can our culture's incessant repetition and recycling nonetheless issue forth in something genuinely new and different?

2 *The question of the history of philosophy*   Heidegger interrogates the history of philosophy, trying to locate the point where it went wrong, where it closed down the possibilities it should have opened up. Whitehead, to the contrary, is not interested in such an interrogation. "It is really not sufficient," he writes, "to direct attention to the best that has been said and done in the ancient world. The result is static, repressive, and promotes a decadent habit of mind." Instead of trying to pin down the history of philosophy, Whitehead twists this history in wonderfully ungainly ways. He mines it for unexpected creative sparks, excerpting those moments where, for instance, Plato affirms Becoming against the static world of Ideas, or Descartes refutes mind–body dualism.

3 *The question of metaphysics*   Heidegger seeks a way out of metaphysics. He endeavors to clear a space where he can evade its grasp. But Whitehead doesn't yearn for a return before, or for a leap beyond, metaphysics. Much more subversively, I think, he simply *does* metaphysics in his own way, inventing his own categories and working through his own problems. He thereby makes metaphysics speak what it has usually denied and rejected: the body, emotions, inconstancy and change, the radical contingency of all perspectives and all formulations.

4 *The question of language*   Heidegger exhorts us to "hearken patiently to the Voice of Being." He is always genuflecting before the enigmas of Language, the ways that it calls to us and commands us. Whitehead takes a much more open, pluralist view of the ways that language works. He knows that it contains mysteries, that it is far more than a mere tool or instrument. But he also warns us against exaggerating its importance. He always points up the

incapacities of language—which means also the inadequacy of reducing philosophy to the interrogation and analysis of language.

5 *The question of style*   A philosopher's attitude toward language is also embodied in his style of writing. Heidegger's contorted writing combines a heightened Romantic poeticism with the self-referential interrogation of linguistic roots and meanings. It's a style as portentous and exasperating as the mysteries it claims to disclose. Whitehead's language, to the contrary, is dry, gray, and abstract. But in this academic, fussy, almost pedantic prose, he is continually saying the most astonishing things, reigniting the philosophic sense of wonder at every step. The neutrality of Whitehead's style is what gives him the freedom to construct, to reorient, to switch direction. It's a kind of strategic counterinvestment, allowing him to step away from his own passions and interests, without thereby falling into the pretense of a universal higher knowledge. Whitehead's language exhibits a special sort of detachment, one that continues to insist upon that from which it has become detached: particulars, singularities, and perspectives that are always partial (in both senses of this word: partial as opposed to whole, but also partial in the sense of partiality or bias).

6 *The question of technology*   Heidegger warns us against the danger of technological "enframing," with its reduction of nature to the status of a "standing reserve." He demonizes science, in a manner so sweeping and absolute as to be the mirror image of science's own claims to unique authority. But you can't undo what Whitehead calls the "bifurcation of nature" by simply dismissing one side of the dichotomy. Whitehead's account of science and technology is far subtler than Heidegger's, in part because he actually understands modern science, as Heidegger clearly does not. For Whitehead, scientific and technical rationality is one kind of "abstraction." This, in itself, is not anything bad. An abstraction is a simplification, a reduction, made in the service of some particular interest. As such, it is indispensable. We cannot live without abstractions; they alone make thought and action possible. We only get into trouble when we extend these abstractions beyond their limits, pushing them into realms where they no longer apply. This is what Whitehead calls "the fallacy of misplaced concreteness," and it's one to which modern science and technology have been especially prone. But all our other abstractions—notably including the abstraction we call language—need to be approached in the same spirit of

caution. Indeed, Whitehead's reservations about science run entirely parallel to his reservations about language. (By rights, Heidegger ought to treat science and technology in the same way that he treats language: for language itself is a technology, and the essence of what is human involves technology in just the same way as it does language).

7 *The question of representation*   Heidegger mounts an incessant critique of representationalist thought. As we busily represent the world to ourselves, he says, we do not allow it to stand forth in its Being. Whitehead similarly criticizes the way that Western philosophical thought, from Descartes onward, has excessively privileged "clear and distinct" conscious perception (what Whitehead calls "presentational immediacy"), ignoring the ways that this perception is always already grounded in our bodies, and in the inheritance of the present from the past (through the process of what Whitehead calls "causal efficacy"). But there's a big difference here of emphasis. For Heidegger, representation is *the problem*: one finds it everywhere, and one must always be vigilant against it. For Whitehead, this concern is exaggerated and misplaced. In everyday life (if not in post-Cartesian philosophy) representation plays only a minor role. Even when we do represent, we are also *feeling our bodies*, and *feeling with our bodies*. The Heideggerian (and deconstructionist) critique isn't wrong so much as it isn't all that interesting or important. Rather than insisting on critique, therefore, Whitehead shows us how the world is *already* otherwise.

8 *The question of subjectivity*   Heidegger polemically questions the rampant subjectivism of the humanist tradition. He seeks to undo the illusion of the autonomous, essentialized ego, with its voracious will-to-power. Of course, this aggressive questioning is the flip side of Heidegger's ontological privileging of Man as the "shepherd of Being," and as the site where Language manifests itself. The subject must be understood as an effect of Language, because Language is what calls to us and interrogates us. Now, nothing could be more foreign to Whitehead than this whole polemic. As before, this is not because Whitehead is concerned to defend what Heidegger is attacking, but because his interests lie elsewhere. Whitehead does not see the subject as an effect of language. Rather, he sees subjectivity as embedded in the world. The subject is an irreducible part of the universe, of the way things happen. There is nothing outside of experience; and experience always happens to some subject or

other. This subject may be human, but it also may be a dog, a tree, a mushroom, or a grain of sand. (Strictly speaking, any such entities are what Whitehead calls "societies," each composed of multitudes of "actual occasions," which themselves are the subjects in question.) In any case, the subject constitutes itself in and through its experience; and thereupon it perishes, entering into the "objective immortality" of being a "datum" for other experiences of other subjects. In this way, Whitehead abolishes the *ontological* privileging of human beings over all other subjectivities. This doesn't mean, of course, that the differences between human beings and other sorts of beings are irrelevant; such differences remain pragmatically important in all kinds of situations, and for all sorts of reasons. But in undoing the ontological privilege of being human, Whitehead suggests that the critique of the subject need not be so compulsive a focus of philosophical inquiry.

If Whitehead were to replace Heidegger as the inspiration of postmodern thought, our intellectual landscape would look quite different. Certain problems that we have been overly obsessed with would recede in importance, to be replaced by other questions, and other perspectives. What Isabelle Stengers calls a "constructivist" approach to philosophy would take precedence over the tasks of incessant deconstruction. Whitehead's thought has a kind of cosmic irony to it, which offers a welcome contrast both to the narcissistic theorizing to which the heirs of Heidegger are prone, and to the fatuous complacency of mainstream American pragmatism. Whitehead's metaphysics is a ramshackle construction, continually open to revision, and not an assertion of absolute truths. It stands outside the dualities—the subject or not, meaning or not, humanism or not—with which recent theoretical thought has so often burdened us. Whitehead both exemplifies, and encourages, the virtues of speculation, fabulation, and invention. These may be opposed both to the dogmatism of humanistic or positivistic certitudes *and* to the endless disavowals, splitting of hairs, and one-upmanship that has characterized so much recent academic "theory."

Without Criteria is an experiment; it is an attempt to rethink "postmodern" theory, and especially the theory of aesthetics, from a point of view that hearkens back to Whitehead instead of Heidegger. I do this largely by reading Whitehead in conjunction with Gilles Deleuze. Deleuze wrote only briefly about Whitehead; it is unclear how familiar he was with Whitehead, or to what degree he was influenced by Whitehead. Nevertheless, as I will try to show, there are important affinities and resonances between the work of Whitehead and that of Deleuze. In this book, I have tried to establish a sort of relay between the two thinkers, so that each of them helps to resolve difficulties in the work of the other. I started this book reading Whitehead from a Deleuzian perspective; by the time I was finished, I found myself, instead, reading Deleuze from a Whiteheadian perspective. This reversal of perspectives is one of the effects that reading Whitehead, and writing about him, has had on me. Critical writing should always be a transformative experience. As Michel Foucault put it many years ago: "what would be the value of the passion for knowledge if it resulted only in a certain amount of knowledgeableness and not, in one way or another and to the extent possible, in the knower's straying afield of himself?" (Foucault 1986, 8).

Deleuze's affinity with Whitehead lies, above all, in his focus on affect and singularity, as a way of working toward a nondialectical and highly aestheticized mode of critique. Deleuze's aestheticism, rooted in his readings of Kant and Nietzsche, is the most misunderstood aspect of his work. It remains a scandal for those few commentators who are willing to acknowledge it at all. One of the aims of *Without Criteria* is to argue for what can be best described as a *critical aestheticism*. I am well aware that aesthetics and aestheticism have had a bad name for quite some time. But perhaps we have reached the point today, in our post-everything world, where we can take a fresh look at aesthetics. Not the least scandalous of Whitehead's assertions are his maxims that "Beauty is a wider, and more fundamental, notion than Truth," and even that "Beauty is . . . the one aim which by its very nature is self-justifying." I would like to explore these claims—in deliberate contrast to the ethical focus of so much recent academic discourse.

In working through the ideas of Whitehead and Deleuze, I have found it necessary, again and again, to revert to Kant—or at least to a certain dimension of Kant. Whitehead and Deleuze are not usually thought of as Kantian or "critical" thinkers. They seem much more attuned to pre-Kantian philosophers like Spinoza and Leibniz; when they do refer to Kant, it is most often in a disparaging way. Deleuze even says that his own book on Kant approaches Kant as an "enemy." Nevertheless, I argue that certain crucial aspects of Kant's thought pave the way for the philosophical "constructivism" embraced by both Whitehead and Deleuze. I am thinking particularly of Kant's aesthetics (above all, his "Analytic of the Beautiful" in the Third Critique), of his transcendental argument in the First Critique (with what Whitehead calls its "conception of an act of experience as a constructive functioning"), and of his Transcendental Dialectic in the second half of the First Critique (which offers an alternative to, and an anticipatory criticism of, the Hegelian dialectic).

In the words of Michel Foucault, Kant in these texts made an "opening" in Western thought because he "articulated, in a manner that is still enigmatic, metaphysical discourse and reflection on the limits of our reason" (Foucault 1998, 76). It is perfectly true that Kant himself does very little to explore this opening; most of the time, he closes it down again, returning us to what Foucault calls "the confused sleep of dialectics and of anthropology" (ibid.). Nonetheless, this opening is there, in the margins of Kant's texts, which overflow with suggestions and possibilities that still await their proper elaboration. Whitehead and Deleuze explore certain of these alternative possibilities. Their encounters with Kant (or better, their corrections and revisions of Kant) make for an important dimension of their texts. These encounters also allow us to see Kant himself in a new light. The Kant with whom we are most familiar is the thinker who stands behind Jürgen Habermas's project of establishing norms of communicative action. But the Kant revealed by Whitehead and Deleuze puts this project most radically into question, by problematizing the very idea of such norms. As Deleuze and Guattari put it, "Kant's *Critique of Judgment* is an unrestrained work of old age, which his successors have still not caught up with: all the mind's faculties overcome their limits, the very limits that Kant had so carefully laid down in the works of his prime" (1994, 2).

In the course of its readings of Kant, Whitehead, and Deleuze, *Without Criteria* seeks to address a range of issues that are crucial to cultural theory today. The critical aestheticism that I discover in the conjunction of Kant, Whitehead, and Deleuze helps to illuminate contemporary art and media practices (especially developments in digital film and video), contemporary scientific and technological practices (especially the recent advances in neuroscience and in biogenetic technology), and controversies in cultural theory and Marxist theory (such as questions about commodity fetishism, about immanence and transcendence, about the role of autopoietic or self-organizing systems, and about the ways that "innovation" and "creativity" seem to have become so central to the dynamics of postmodern, or post-Fordist, capitalism). For the most part, I do not address these matters directly here—that will be a task for another book. But my interest in them has largely shaped my selective readings of the texts of Kant, Whitehead, and Deleuze.

No book is ever written in a vacuum; and my intellectual indebtedness in the case of *Without Criteria* is especially great. My book is largely written in the margins of Isabelle Stengers's magnificent *Penser avec Whitehead*. With this text, Stengers both made Whitehead accessible to me for the first time, and opened up the question of Whitehead's affinity with Deleuze. Erin Manning and Brian Massumi encouraged me to write this book, nurtured it throughout the stages of its preparation, and invited me a number of times to their seminars and forums in research creation, where I was able to present portions of this text, and which provided me with the intellectual stimulus that I needed to complete it. Among the many other people with whom I discussed my work, or who read and commented on portions of the manuscript, I particularly wish to thank Keith Robinson, Charles Stivale, Daniel Smith, Tim Clark, Sha Xin Wei, William Flesch, Robert Gooding-Williams, and Barrett Watten, as well as the anonymous readers of my manuscript for MIT Press, the members of the Sense Lab at Concordia University in Montreal, and the readers of my blog the Pinocchio Theory (http://www.shaviro.com/Blog).

Some sections of this book have previously been published elsewhere. An earlier version of chapter 1 appears in *Sensorium: Aesthetics, Art, Life*, edited by Barbara Bolt, Felicity Colman, Graham Jones, and Ashley Woodward (London: Cambridge Scholars Press, 2007). A portion of chapter 2 appears in *Secrets of Becoming: Negotiating Whitehead, Deleuze and Butler*, edited by Roland Faber (New York: Fordham University Press, 2009). A version of chapter 3 appears in *The Affect Reader*, edited by Greg Seigworth and Melissa Gregg (Durham: Duke University Press, 2008). A portion of chapter 4 appears in *Deleuze, Guattari, and the Production of the New*, edited by Simon O'Sullivan and Stephen Zepke (New York: Continuum, 2008). Another portion of chapter 4 appears in *Deleuze, Science, and the Force of the Virtual*, edited by Peter Gaffney (Minneapolis: University of Minnesota Press, 2009).

1
Without Criteria

"There is no science of the beautiful [*das Schöne*], but only critique," Kant says in the *Critique of Judgment*, "and there is no fine [*schön*] science, but only fine art" (1987, 172). Most recent discussions of Kant's aesthetics have concentrated on his analysis of the sublime (which is seen as prefiguring modernist—or postmodernist—concerns and practices), rather than on his analysis of the beautiful (which is generally regarded as rather conservative and old-fashioned). In what follows, I endeavor to suggest, against this common wisdom, that Kant's account of beauty is quite radical in ways that have not yet been sufficiently recognized. For Kant's theory of the beautiful is really a theory of affect and of singularity; and it implies an entirely new form of judgment. In the "Analytic of the Beautiful" in the Third Critique, Kant steps back from the legitimizing and universalizing projects of the first two Critiques, in order to problematize universalization and legitimation themselves. Beauty cannot be judged according to concepts; it is a matter neither of empirical fact, nor of moral obligation. This is why there is no science of the beautiful. For Kant, aesthetics has no foundation, and it offers us no guarantees. Rather, it throws all norms and values into question, or into crisis. Even if Kant himself ultimately shrinks from the more radical implications of his theories, a certain *critical aestheticism* still haunts his texts, and especially the Third Critique. My aim in *Without Criteria* is to unearth this subterranean dimension of Kant's argument, and to track its crucial role in the metaphysical speculations of Alfred North Whitehead and Gilles Deleuze.[1]

---

1. My starting point for these readings and speculations is an article I wrote quite some time ago: "Beauty Lies in the Eye" (Shaviro 2002). In that text, I argued for the continuing relevance of the beautiful, rather than the sublime, for a contemporary or "postmodern" aesthetics;

Beauty, Kant says, is not cognitive, not conceptual. "A judgment of taste is not based on *determinate* concepts"; that is to say, the concept behind such a judgment (if it can be called a "concept" at all) "does not allow us to cognize and prove anything concerning the object because it is intrinsically indeterminable and inadequte for cognition" (Kant 1987, 213). There is no objective or scientific way to determine whether an object is beautiful, and—if it is—to explain why. This is because of the strange status of aesthetic judgment. I may judge a flower to be beautiful, yet I know that "beauty is not a property of the flower itself"; the flower is beautiful "only by virtue of that characteristic in which it adapts itself to the way we apprehend it" (145). So beauty is not objectively *there*, in the world. It is not *in* nature; it is rather something that we attribute *to* nature. An aesthetic judgment, therefore, is one "whose determining basis *cannot be other* than *subjective*" (44).

Yet at the same time, beauty isn't *merely* subjective. It isn't just something that we project upon whatever it is that we see, hear, feel, touch, or taste. The attribution of beauty is not an arbitrary imposition. There is nothing about it that is special, or particular, to the person who happens to be making the judgment. It is not even "universally" subjective; for, in contrast to an empirical judgment of the understanding, a judgment of taste does not involve the mind's active impressing of its own Categories upon a passive external world. Rather, a judgment of taste involves an uncoerced *response*, on the part of the subject, to the object that is being judged beautiful. Aesthetic judgment is a kind of *recognition*: it's an appreciation of how the object "adapts itself to the way we apprehend it," even though, at the same time, it remains indifferent to us.

I'm inclined to read "adapt" here in a Darwinian sense (even though, of course, Kant could not have intended it this way). Deleuze and Guattari

---

I explored the ramifications of Kant's claim that a judgment of taste is nonconceptual; I suggested that there was a close affinity between Kant's notion of beauty and Deleuze's notion of singularity; and I proposed that a radicalization of Kant's "Antinomy of Taste" (1987, 210ff.) could lead to the transformation of Kant's *sensus communis* into a "cultivation and sharing of the highest possible degree of singularity" (Shaviro 2002, 17), or into what today we should call a *dissensus* (Ranciere 2004) rather than a consensus. All these points are pursued further, and expanded on, in the course of *Without Criteria*.

(1987) use the familiar scientific example of the orchid and the wasp. The orchid "adapts itself" to the way the wasp apprehends it; as a result, the wasp finds the orchid beautiful. The orchid isn't beautiful in and for itself; it is only beautiful *for* the wasp (and perhaps, too, for us). The orchid's interests, however, have nothing in particular to do with the wasp; the orchid only uses the wasp as a vector for its own pollination. It suits the plant just as well if a human being, having been seduced by the flower's beauty, pollinates it instead. Thus the orchid is indifferent even to the existence of the wasp; the exchange between the two organisms is what Deleuze and Guattari, quoting Rémy Chauvin, call "the *aparallel evolution* of two beings that have absolutely nothing to do with each other" (1987, 10).

You might say that the beauty of the orchid is what Whitehead, in *Process and Reality*, calls "a lure for feeling" (1929/1978, 25 and *passim*). Whitehead prefers to speak of *propositions*, rather than judgments, because the notion of judgment tends to imply, wrongly, that "the one function" of propositions and theories "is to be judged as to their truth or falsehood" (184). Whitehead insists, rather, that "at some point" in the entertainment of a proposition "judgment is eclipsed by aesthetic delight" (185). Sometimes, of course, what supervenes is aesthetic repulsion rather than delight. But in any case, whether true or false, delicious or repugnant, a proposition points to a *potentiality* (186, 196–197). That is to say, propositions are neither actual nor fictive; they are "the tales that might be told about particular actualities," from a given perspective, and that enter into the construction (or what Whitehead calls the *concrescence*) of that very perspective (256). As such, propositions are possible routes of actualization, vectors of nondeterministic change. The "primary role" of a proposition, Whitehead says, is to "pave the way along which the world advances into novelty. . . . A proposition is an element in the objective lure *proposed for feeling*, and when admitted into feeling it constitutes *what is felt*" (187). The orchid is not beautiful in itself: but something *happens to* the wasp, or to the gardener, who encounters the orchid and feels it to be beautiful.[2]

---

2. Whitehead does not ignore the question of judgment; but he regards *judgment* as a much narrower term than *proposition*. Any proposition that is admitted into thought is thereby felt, and

Though Kant refers to "judgments of taste" rather than to "propositions," he is in accord with Whitehead at least to this extent: he says that aesthetic judgments have nothing to do with determinations of truth and falsehood. (They also have nothing to do with moral determinations of good and evil.) This is because a judgment of beauty is affective, rather than cognitive. More precisely, it is a feeling entirely divorced from objective knowledge. "A judgment of taste," Kant says, "is merely *contemplative*, i.e., it is a judgment that is indifferent to the existence of the object: it [considers] the character of the object only by holding it up to our feeling of pleasure and displeasure." Such a judgment "is neither *based* on concepts, nor directed to them as *purposes*" (Kant 1987, 51). In an aesthetic judgment, I am not asserting anything about what is, nor am I legislating as to what ought to be. Rather, I am being lured, allured, seduced, repulsed, incited, or dissuaded. And for Whitehead—if not explicitly for Kant—this is part of the process by which I *become* what I am.

Beauty is therefore an *event*, a process, rather than a condition or a state. The flower is not beautiful in itself; rather, beauty *happens* when I *encounter* the flower. Beauty is fleeting, and it is always imbued with otherness. For although the feeling of beauty is "subjective," I cannot experience it at will. I can only find beauty when the object solicits me, or arouses my sense of beauty, in a certain way. Also, beauty does not survive the moment of the en-

---

becomes a feeling. But only some of these feelings are judgments. "In the realization of propositions, 'judgment' is at very rare component, and so is 'consciousness' " (1929/1978, 184).

More specifically, "the term 'judgment' refers to three species among the comparative feelings. . . . In each of these feelings the datum is the generic contrast between an objectified nexus and a proposition whose logical subjects make up the nexus" (ibid., 270). That is to say, a judgment involves a "felt contrast" between a state of affairs ("an objectified nexus") and a hypothesis (a "proposition") concerning that state of affairs. The three "species" of judgment are the affirmative ("the 'yes-form' "), the negative ("the 'no-form' "), and the uncertain ("the 'suspense-form' "). Thus, what Whitehead calls judgments are the feelings corresponding to the cognitions that Kant calls judgments of the understanding, or judgments "based on *determinate* concepts" (1987, 213). As for Kant's judgments of taste, or judgments based only on *indeterminate* concepts, Whitehead would regard their corresponding feelings as propositional, but not as involving judgment.

counter in which it is created. It cannot be recovered once it is gone. It can only be born afresh in another event, another encounter. A subject does not cognize the beauty of an object. Rather, the object *lures* the subject while remaining indifferent to it; and the subject *feels* the object, without knowing it or possessing it or even caring about it. The object *touches* me, but for my part I cannot grasp it or lay hold of it, or make it last. I cannot dispel its otherness, its alien splendor. If I could, I would no longer find it beautiful; I would, alas, merely find it useful.

This is why the apprehension of beauty is *disinterested*. The beautiful object is unconcerned with me; and in return, I have no actual interest in it. I don't care what benefit it can offer me, or what empirical "gratification" (Kant 1987, 47) it can give me, or even if it exists or not. I am only concerned with how it makes me feel; that is to say, with how it *affects* me. Outside of cognition or utilitarian interest, this is how the beautiful object allures me. In Whitehead's terms, "the basis of experience is emotional . . . the basic fact is the rise of an affective tone originating from things whose relevance is given." This *affective tone* is the "subjective form" through which "the experience constitutes itself" (Whitehead 1933/1967, 176–177).

In this way, the aesthetic experience is *intense* precisely to the extent that it is devoid of interest. "All interest," Kant says, whether empirical or rational, "either presupposes a need or gives rise to one"; only aesthetic judgment is detached from need. Kant notes that a starving person will eat just about anything; it is "only when their need has been satisfied," only when they are well fed and assured of remaining so, that people have the leisure to develop and express their *taste* with regard to food. It's only when I don't *need* something that my liking for it, my being affected by it, can be "disinterested and *free*" (Kant 1987, 52). The disinterested contemplation of beauty is a utopian conception, in that it requires and presupposes a world in which human needs have already been fulfilled.

Aesthetic disinterest may seem cold and detached, but it isn't neutral. From the indifference of the object to the disinterest of the subject—or from the former's superfluous self-exhibition to the latter's ungrounded reception—the experience of beauty is one of distance and separation. This distance is not a mere absence; it is something positively felt. When I contemplate something that I consider beautiful, I am moved precisely by that something's separation from me, its exemption from the categories that I would normally apply to it.

This is why beauty is a lure, drawing me out of myself. Aesthetic experience is a kind of *communication without communion* and *without consensus*. It can be shared, or held in common, without uniting the ones who share it. This is all because it is "a universal communicability that is indeed not based on a concept" (Kant 1987, 79). As pure, contentless communicability, beauty is also a pure effect, divorced from its rational and material causes. The painter Francis Bacon conveys this point well when he says that, in his paintings of "the human cry," he "wanted to paint the scream [itself] more than the horror" that provoked it (Sylvester 1987, 34, 48). Bacon's scream paintings are disturbingly beautiful, all the more so in that the situations to which they refer are not.[3]

A good synonym for Kantian aesthetic disinterest might well be *passion*. The scandal of passion is that it is utterly gratuitous: it has no grounding, and no proper occasion. In this sense, it is entirely free (though I am not free with regard to it). Passion has nothing to do with my actual needs, let alone with my self-interest, or with what is "good for me." It doesn't seem to be anything of mine. It moves me, drives me, takes possession of me; but it al-

---

3. Gilles Deleuze (2005, 34) cites this aphorism of Bacon's in the course of his discussion of the painter. The cry without the horror is the effect without the cause, or the event freed from the limits of its actualization in the depths of bodies: a configuration of the "virtual" to which I will return several times in the later chapters of this book.

Deleuze also implicitly invokes the Kantian notion of aesthetic disinterest in his discussion, in the second *Cinema* volume, of how films invoke "a pure optical and sound situation": one that "does not extend into action, any more than it is induced by an action." In such a situation, the sensory-motor circuits are paralyzed. Instead of allowing us to act, an optical and sound situation "makes us grasp, it is supposed to make us grasp, something intolerable and unbearable" (1989, 18). In this "visionary" state, the spectator is forcibly *disinterested*, in the sense that he or she is unable to act, unable to respond, unable to bring the vision in relation to himself or herself, unable to be equal to its extremity. The compulsion that Deleuze is describing might seem to be leagues away from the free exercise of the faculties that characterizes the aesthetic state according to Kant. But Deleuzian compulsion and Kantian freeplay alike are states in which the subject's "interests" play no part, because the subject experiences, and is brought into intimate contact with, something that is irreducibly distant from itself, something that exceeds any possibility of actualization.

ways remains *apart* from me, outside of my control. It is something superfluous and supplemental, yet inescapable. I pursue my passions without regard to my interests and needs, and even to their detriment.[4]

At the same time that passion is divorced from need, it also does not have the grandeur and seriousness that we commonly associate with desire. Kant is quite explicit about the difference between "the power of desire" (as theorized in the Second Critique) and the "feeling of pleasure and displeasure" that is the main topic of the Third (Kant 1987, 16). He defines desire as "the power of being the cause, through one's presentations, of the actuality of the objects of these presentations" (ibid.). This is a difficult formulation, but it is worth unpacking. Desire, for Kant, is what determines the will. It cannot be understood in terms of negativity and absence, for it is an active, autonomous power of the mind. The "object of desire" is not something that the subject lacks; to the contrary, it is what the subject imagines and creates. The act of desiring is the cause, and the existence of the desired object is the effect.

---

4. In thus relating passion and disinterest, I am drawing a parallel between the paralyzing vision of the intolerable described by Deleuze (see previous note) and Andy Warhol's self-described "affectless gaze" of "basically passive astonishment" (Warhol 1975, 10; cf. Shaviro 2004, 138). These might seem like opposites, but they both turn on the "aesthetic" suspension of ordinary self-interest. In other words, they both involve a "lure" which impinges on a previously constituted subject, and forcibly ejects it from its self-constituting, and self-confirming orbit. The ultimate form of aesthetic disinterest or passion would be the so-called Stendhal syndrome, in which the encounter with a beautiful work of art leads to swooning and hallucinations (cf. Dario Argento's film *The Stendhal Syndrome*, 1996).

Passion or disinterest is, of course, the dimension of human experience that is entirely left out of consideration by cognitive psychology, and by "rational choice" theory in economics and political science. If (neoclassical) economics is the "science" of how people make "choices" when faced with scarcity or limited resources, and if it is based on the assumptions that people "basically aim to fulfill their self-interests," and that they "are rational in their efforts to fulfill their unlimited wants and needs" (Investopedia 2008), then passion and aesthetic disinterest are excluded from economics *a priori* and by definition. They belong, rather, to what Georges Bataille calls *expenditure* (1985, 116–129), or the "accursed share" not reducible to the demands of utility (1988).

In short, *desire produces the real*.⁵ Kant insists that the empirical existence of failed and unfulfilled desires does not contradict this formulation. For even when a desire turns out to be "insufficient," so that the corporeal forces it calls on are unable to fully actualize its object, there is still a positive "causal relation" between the desire as a mobilization of force, and the effect toward which it was striving (ibid., 17). This is also what links desire to morality. In its pure form, the power of desire is Reason and universal Law: it legislates, and produces, the categorical imperative. Of course, just as empirical actions never fully conform to the categorical imperative, since they have other motivations than that of respect for the Law, so empirical desires are never pure, but always "pathological," or tinged with interest. Nonetheless, even the most limited and pathological desire, far from compromising the Law, bears witness to it, as a sort of "evidence of things not seen."

We can thus oppose desire to passion, reason to feelings of pleasure and displeasure, moral disinterest to aesthetic disinterest, the concerns of the Second Critique to those of the Third. Desire is autonomous, absolute, and universalizing, whereas passion is heteronomous, gratuitous, and singular. Reason transcends all interests; aesthetic feeling subsists beneath or before any interests. Desire is active and expressive: it comes out of the subject and legislates

---

5. Deleuze and Guattari (1983, 25) are rigorously Kantian when they assert that desire produces the real, in opposition to Hegelian and Lacanian definitions of desire as "lack." They are closer to Whitehead than to Kant, however, in that they place the subject not at the beginning of the productive process of desire, but at the end. "The subject is produced as a mere residuum alongside the desiring-machines . . . a conjunctive synthesis of consummation in the form of a wonderstruck 'So *that's* what it was!' " (ibid., 17–18). In this sense, the subject is defined as a supplemental torsion in the field of desiring production, a self-reflexive twist that produces self-enjoyment. "Even suffering, as Marx says, is a form of self-enjoyment" (ibid., 16). This accords with Whitehead's doctrine that the subject is always also a *superject* (1929/1978, 29), coming after the process of creation rather than before, and experiencing "satisfaction" (25–26), or "self-enjoyment" (145, 289), precisely to the extent that it is itself a product of this satisfaction. For both Whitehead and Deleuze and Guattari, this inversion implies a movement from the world to the self (rather than, as in Kant, from the self to the world), and implicitly privileges passion/disinterest over desire.

for the world. Passion, in contrast, emerges out of the world and approaches, or proposes itself to, the subject. More precisely, passion is not just passive (as its etymology suggests), but hyperbolically more-than-passive. The subject is not so much acted upon as it is incited to re-create itself. Desire is how the self projects itself into, and remakes, the world; aesthetic feeling is how the world projects itself into, and remakes, the self.

These differences correspond to Kant's doctrine of the faculties. "All of the soul's powers or capacities," he says, "can be reduced to three that cannot be derived further from a common basis: the *cognitive power*, the *feeling of pleasure and displeasure*, and the *power of desire*" (1987, 16). The doctrine of the faculties has little currency today; but even if it is just a fiction, it is a useful and illuminating one. For the doctrine of the faculties allows Kant to draw crucial structural distinctions. Whereas cognition and desire are powers (*Vermögen*), the aesthetic capacity is a feeling (*Gefühl*). Cognition and desire *go out from* the subject to the world, while the pleasure of beauty *comes into it*, from elsewhere. In desire, as in cognition, experience begins with the subject; in aesthetic feeling, experience begins outside, and culminates, or *eventuates*, in the subject.

All this can also be stated in terms of Kant's distinction between concepts of understanding and ideas; and among ideas between aesthetic and rational ones. "Ideas, in the broadest sense, are presentations referred to an object . . . but are such that they can still never become cognition of an object" (Kant 1987, 214–215). So many of our thoughts are not statements of matters of fact; so many of our utterances are not constative. And these noncognitive "presentations" are themselves of two sorts. *Aesthetic ideas* are "inner intuitions to which no concept can be completely adequate" (182–183); "an *aesthetic idea* cannot become cognition because it is an *intuition* (of the imagination) for which an adequate concept can never be found" (215). In contrast, "a *rational idea* can never become cognition because it contains a *concept* (of the supersensible) for which no adequate intuition can ever be given" (215). Aesthetic ideas are "*unexpoundable* presentations," whereas rational ideas are "*indemonstrable* concepts" (215). An aesthetic idea is a singular intimation of beauty; it "prompts much thought," but "no language can express it completely and allow us to grasp it" (182). A rational idea has to do, rather, with the sublime; it resists and subdues thought, yet thereby seems to prompt an excess of language. I cannot understand a sublime experience, but I am impelled to speak endlessly about my failure to understand it.[6]

Kant famously writes in the First Critique that "thoughts without content are empty; intuitions without concepts are blind" (1996, 107). This is supposed to mean that intuition and concept must always go together. But now, in the Third Critique, he discovers the actuality of contentless thoughts and blind intuitions. For rational ideas are precisely thoughts that no content can fill; and aesthetic ideas are intuitions that admit of no concept. Once we leave the realm of the understanding, we discover a fundamental asymmetry between concepts and intuitions, such that each of them exceeds the powers of the other. In the Second Critique, we are obliged to affirm—and indeed to live by—certain concepts, even though we know them to be undemonstrable. But at least we still have concepts, and the will that legislates these concepts is still, ultimately, our own. The Third Critique goes much further, as it dispenses with concepts altogether, as well as with an active, orginary self. Aesthetic ideas are no more moral than they are conceptual. Beauty is felt, rather than comprehended or willed. Intuition is decoupled from thought.

In *Process and Reality* Whitehead cites Kant's famous statement about intuitions and thoughts twice, in order to point up this disconnection. He ironically accepts "Kant's principle," only to apply it "in exactly the converse way to Kant's own use of it" (1929/1978, 139). Whitehead suggests that Kant's system is founded on the "suppressed premise" that "intuitions are never blind": that is to say, that all apprehension is, in principle and in fact,

---

6. This approach to the sublime would seem to be the strategy of deconstruction, which I largely regard as a footnote to Kant. Jacques Derrida's lifelong task as a philosopher was basically the Kantian one of critiquing what Kant calls *transcendental illusions*: "sophistries not of human beings but of pure reason itself. Even the wisest among all human beings cannot detach himself from them; perhaps he can after much effort forestall the error, but he can never fully rid himself of the illusion that incessantly teases and mocks him" (Kant 1996, 380–381). Derrida follows Kant's program in that he ceaselessly interrogates these illusions that are built into the very nature of rationality itself, and endeavors, patiently and carefully, to undo them, while remaining aware that such an undoing will never be definitive or final. In sum, Derrida is the great twentieth-century thinker of the Kantian sublime, whereas Whitehead and Deleuze are (more interestingly to my mind) thinkers of the Kantian beautiful.

already governed by concepts. But this premise must be rejected, once we have rejected Kant's "obsess[ion] with the mentality of 'intuition,' and hence with its necessary involution in consciousness" (ibid.). Some pages later, Whitehead accepts Kant's claim that "in every act of experience there are objects for knowledge," objects that, in principle, *can* be known. But Whitehead immediately adds that there is no reason to assume that these objects actually *are* cognized, or that cognition actually *is* involved, in any given experience. Most of the time, it is not. "The inclusion of intellectual functioning in th[e] act of experience" is in fact quite rare; "no knowledge" is by far the most usual case (155–156).

Whitehead describes the difference between his own philosophy and Kantian critique thus: "For Kant, the world emerges from the subject; for the philosophy of organism, the subject emerges from the world—a 'superject' rather than a 'subject' " (Whitehead 1929/1978, 88). Kant's greatness, Whitehead says, is that "he first, fully and explicitly, introduced into philosophy the conception of an act of experience as a constructive functioning." But the problem is that "for Kant the process whereby there is experience is a passage from subjectivity to apparent objectivity. The philosophy of organism inverts this analysis, and explains the process as proceeding from objectivity to subjectivity, namely, from the objectivity whereby the external world is a datum, to the subjectivity, whereby there is one individual experience" (156). Whitehead thus presents his own philosophy as the inversion, correction, and culmination of Kantian critique: "a critique of pure feeling, in the philosophical position in which Kant put his *Critique of Pure Reason*. This should also supercede the remaining *Critiques* required in the Kantian philosophy" (113). In this way, he performs a philosophical "self-correction" of the "initial excess of subjectivity" of Kant's own critiques (15).

Whitehead continues to ask the Kantian question of "constructive functioning," of how the subject arises in and through experience. Kant and Whitehead do not presuppose a subject existing outside of, and prior to, experience, as Descartes does; but neither do they dissolve the subject into the flux of experience, as Hume does. However, Kant assumes, in the First Critique, that experience is fundamentally conscious and cognitive. Whitehead says, to the contrary, that "in general, consciousness is negligible" in subjective experience (1929/1978, 308). Most of the time, even for human beings, let alone for other entities, experience is "implicit, below consciousness, in our physical feelings" (229). These "physical feelings" precede the subject; the latter is best described as the integration (in a quasi-mathematical sense), or as the "end" (both sequentially and causally), of the former. The subject is solicited by the feelings that comprise it; it only comes to be through those feelings. It is not a substance, but a process. And this process is not usually conscious; it only becomes so under exceptional circumstances. This is why Whitehead devalues knowledge, inverting the Kantian relation between subject and object, self and world.

This is also why Whitehead says that the subject is not self-perpetuating, but must be continually renewed. The subject does not outlive the feelings that animate it at any given moment. "The ancient doctrine that 'no one crosses the same river twice' is extended," Whitehead says; "no thinker thinks twice; and, to put the matter more generally, no subject experiences twice" (1929/1978, 29). Each new experience, even each repetition of what we think of as the "same" experience, implies a fresh creation, and a new subject. To say this is not to deny the sense of continuity that we actually feel from one moment to the next. Such a sense of continuity is easily explained, in Whitehead's terms, by inheritance. For the "datum" of any new experience is largely composed of the remnants of immediately past experiences, located in the same bodily mass, or in the same close neighborhood. But Whitehead's crucial point is that this sense of continuity is not self-evident, not given in advance. We cannot presuppose it, or take it for granted. It is rather what most urgently requires explanation. For the default situation of the subject, as of everything that exists in time, is to perish. Locke's phrase, that time is a "perpetual perishing," runs like a leitmotif through the pages of *Process and Reality* (e.g., 29, 147, 208ff.).

I have already mentioned that, for Whitehead, the subject is also a *superject*: not something that underlies experience, but something that emerges from experience, something that is superadded to it. This doesn't mean that Whitehead abolishes the subject, as "postmodern" thinkers are often accused of doing. Indeed, for Whitehead, just as much as for Kant, there is nothing outside of experience, and no experience without a subject. "The whole universe," Whitehead says, "consists of elements disclosed in the experiences of subjects" (ibid., 166). There is always a subject, though not necessarily a human one. Even a rock—and for that matter even an electron—has experiences, and must be considered a subject-superject to a certain extent. A falling rock "feels," or "perceives," the gravitational field of the earth. The rock isn't conscious, of course; but it is *affected* by the earth, and this *being affected* is its experience. What makes a subject-superject is not consciousness, but unity, identity, closure, and transcendence. Each subject is "something individual for its own sake; and thereby transcends the rest of actuality" (ibid., 88). It is different from everything else; nothing can be substituted or exchanged for it. "The term 'monad' also expresses this essential unity at the decisive moment, which stands between its birth and its perishing" (Whitehead 1933/1967, 177). In the moment of its actualization, a subject is entirely, irreducibly *singular*. Right afterward, of course, the moment passes, and the subject is "objectified" as a "datum" for other occasions; but that is another story.

I have been dwelling on Whitehead's self-proclaimed inversion of Kant, because I want to suggest that Kant himself already performs something like this inversion, or self-correction, in the Third Critique. For there, Kant proposes a subject that neither comprehends nor legislates, but only feels and responds. The aesthetic subject does not impose its forms upon an otherwise chaotic outside world. Rather, this subject is itself *informed by* the world outside, a world that (in the words of Wallace Stevens) "fills the being before the mind can think." Being thus informed, the aesthetic subject is *contemplative*: it is neither active nor quite passive, nor even really self-reflexive, but best described grammatically in the *middle voice* (which unfortunately doesn't exist in German or English). In aesthetic contemplation, I don't *have* particular feelings, so much as my very existence is suspended upon these feelings. The only "causality" of an aesthetic presentation, Kant says, is "to *keep* [us in] the state of [having] the presentation itself. . . . We *linger* in our contemplation of the beautiful, because this contemplation reinforces and reproduces itself" (1987, 68). It is a kind of auto-affecting short circuit. The contemplated object perpetuates itself in, and for, the contemplating subject; the subject subsists only to the extent that it resonates with the feelings inspired by that object. We can say, somewhat paradoxically, that the subject is *auto-affected by* the objectified "datum" that enters into it. The feelings cannot be separated from the subject for whom they exist; yet the subject itself can only be said to exist by virtue of these feelings, and in relation to them.

Expressed in this auto-affecting short circuit, and without any concept to determine it, beauty is always singular. An aesthetic judgment responds to a unique situation; it cannot be repeated, generalized, or codified into rules.

In Kant's terms, we are faced with "the universality of a singular judgment" (1987, 144): the claim to beauty is absolute, and yet at the same time limited to just this one instance. Each encounter with beauty is something entirely new; each aesthetic judgment responds to a contingency. This is why beauty is *incommunicable*: it cannot be copied and imitated, just as "it cannot be couched in a formula and serve as a precept" (177). Rather, Kant says, beauty is *exemplary* (175). An artwork of genius, for instance, "is an example that is meant not to be imitated, but to be followed by another genius. . . . The other genius, who follows the example, is aroused by it to a feeling of his own originality, which allows him to exercise in art his freedom from the constraint of rules" (186–187). That is to say, although we cannot mimic or replicate what we find beautiful, or explain it to others (or even to ourselves), it can inspire us to an act of emulation. And where we cannot communicate the inner sensations of beauty, or the grounds for any particular judgment of taste, the only things that do remain "universally communicable" (157) are "the subjective conditions for our employment of the power of judgment as such" (155). In short, there are no rules, methods, foundations, or criteria for the creation and appreciation of beauty. All we have are examples of what is beautiful, and the "subjective conditions" for striving to equal or surpass them.[7]

Kant's aesthetics is just one part of his system. He insists that aesthetic judgments are noncognitive, in order to differentiate them from judgments of understanding (which concern matters of empirical fact) and from moral judgments (which are categorical obligations or commands). This attempt to distinguish different sorts of judgment, and to circumscribe the powers and limits of each, remains crucial today. For it warns us against the totalitarianism of reason, or (to express the point more modestly) against the endeavor of scientists, philosophers, political despots, and religious fanatics to impose a unified field of assessment, in which the same fundamental critical standards

---

7. Derrida's frequent discussions of *exemplarity*, of the noncoincidence between the example and that of which it is an example, of the way that "an example always carries beyond itself" (1994, 34), are very much written in the margins of Kant's discussions of exemplarity in *The Critique of Judgment*.

would apply across all disciplines. Such an imposition could only have catastrophic consequences, for it would mean the end of any sort of novelty, creativity, or invention. Needless to say, this dream of totalizing reason is as incapable of realization as it is undesirable in principle. But it is also a dream that never goes away, since it is what Kant calls a "transcendental illusion," a self-deception built into the very nature of reason. Since we are always being lured by this illusion, like moths to a flame, we always need Kant to warn us against it. In the end, of course, the mania for reason, truth, foundations, and universally valid criteria is as singular, as gratuitous, and as intractable as any other passion. As Whitehead says, "the primary function of theories is as a lure for feeling" (1929/1978, 184); and we cannot do without such theories and such lures.

The *Critique of Judgment* might seem to play merely a marginal role in Kant's system. But when Whitehead says that philosophy should begin with a "critique of pure feeling," instead of reason, this amounts to putting the Third Critique first. For Whitehead, affect precedes cognition, and has a much wider scope than cognition. Understanding and morality alike must therefore be subordinated to aesthetics. It is only after the subject has constructed or synthesized itself out of its feelings, out of its encounters with the world, that it can then go on to understand that world—or to change it.

Such a revision or "correction" of Kant is more relevant today than ever. Kant was trying, among other things, to separate science from art, in order to define the proper limits of each. In practice, this meant preserving the arts and humanities from scientific encroachment, something that is still important today. But we also live in an age of astonishing invention and relentless innovation, when, as Fredric Jameson puts it, "aesthetic production" has become the "dominant cultural logic or hegemonic norm" (1991, 4–6). Even positivistic science finds itself approaching ever closer to the condition of aesthetics. Theoretical physics, for instance, seems to leave questions of empirical verification behind, as it pursues an ever-receding "final theory of everything," whose sole justification lies in the beauty of its theorems, the elegance and internal self-consistency of its mathematics.

Genetics and biotechnology are even more perplexing, since they are less about understanding the external world than they are about experimenting on—and thereby altering—ourselves. We are on the verge of developing the ability to clone ourselves, to tweak our genetic makeup, to hybridize ourselves through gene splicing, to incorporate silicon chips into our brains, to interface machinery directly with our nervous systems, and to reset our neurotransmitter and hormone levels at will. Such practices are inherently risky and unpredictable. How can we come to terms with forms of "knowledge" whose very effect is to change who "we" are? How do we judge these disciplines, when they undermine, or render irrelevant, the very norms and criteria that we use to ground our judgments? What will we do when advances in these practices force us to redefine, ever more radically, what we mean by such basic notions as self, life, humanity, and nature? The new biology, as much as any new work of art, requires us to abandon everything we think we know, and make singular judgments that cannot be subsumed under preexisting criteria. Aesthetics precedes cognition in such cases, because we are dealing with practices that can only be comprehended through the new categories that they themselves create. The question we should be asking, therefore, is not: How can we establish valid criteria and critical standards? but rather: How can we *get away* from such criteria and standards, which work only to block innovation and change?

2
Actual Entities and Eternal Objects

In a short chapter of *The Fold* that constitutes his only extended discussion of Alfred North Whitehead, Gilles Deleuze praises Whitehead for asking the question, "What Is an Event?" (Deleuze 1993, 76). Whitehead's work marks only the third time—after the Stoics and Leibniz—that events move to the center of philosophical thought. Whitehead marks an important turning point in the history of philosophy because he affirms that, in fact, everything is an event. The world, he says, is made of events, and nothing but events: happenings rather than things, verbs rather than nouns, processes rather than substances. As Deleuze summarizes it, "an event does not just mean that 'a man has been run over.' The Great Pyramid is an event, and its duration for a period of one hour, thirty minutes, five minutes . . . , a passage of Nature, of God, or a view of God" (ibid., 76). Becoming is the deepest dimension of Being.[1]

Even a seemingly solid and permanent object is an event; or, better, a multiplicity and a series of events. In his early metaphysical book *The Concept of Nature* (1920/2004), Whitehead gives the example of Cleopatra's Needle on the Victoria Embankment in London (165ff.). Now, we know, of course, that this monument is not just "there." It has a history. Its granite was sculpted by human hands, sometime around 1450 BCE. It was moved from Heliopolis to Alexandria in 12 BCE, and again from Alexandria to London in 1877–1878 CE. And some day, no doubt, it will be destroyed, or

---

1. My discussion of the affinities between Whitehead and Deleuze, both in this chapter and throughout *Without Criteria*, is deeply indebted to a number of recent studies comparing the two thinkers: most notably those by Keith Robinson (2006), James Williams (2005, 77–100), and Michael Halewood (2005).

otherwise cease to exist. But for Whitehead, there is much more to it than that. Cleopatra's Needle isn't just a solid, impassive object upon which certain grand historical events—being sculpted, being moved—have occasionally supervened. Rather, it is eventful at every moment. From second to second, even as it stands seemingly motionless, Cleopatra's Needle is actively *happening*. It never remains the same. "A physicist who looks on that part of the life of nature as a dance of electrons, will tell you that daily it has lost some molecules and gained others, and even the plain man can see that it gets dirtier and is occasionally washed" (ibid., 167). At every instant, the mere standing-in-place of Cleopatra's Needle is an event: a renewal, a novelty, a fresh creation.

That is what Whitehead means, when he says that events—which he also calls "actual entities" or "actual occasions"—are the ultimate components of reality. However, I am being a little sloppy here. In *Process and Reality* (1929/1978), Whitehead strictly distinguishes between *occasions* and *events*, and between *entities* and *societies*. He "use[s] the term 'event' in the more general sense of a nexus of actual occasions, inter-related in some determinate fashion in one extensive quantum. An actual occasion is the limiting type of an event with only one member" (73). At the limit, an event may be just one particular occasion, a single incident of becoming. But more generally, it is a group of such incidents, a multiplicity of becomings: what Whitehead calls a *nexus*. A nexus is "a particular fact of togetherness among actual entities" (20); that is to say, it is a mathematical set of occasions, contiguous in space and time, or otherwise adhering to one another. When the elements of a nexus are united, not just by contiguity, but also by a "defining characteristic" that is common to all of them, and that they have all "inherited" from one another, or acquired by a common process, then Whitehead calls it a society (34). A society is "self-sustaining; in other words . . . it is its own reason. . . . The real actual things that endure," and that we encounter in everyday experience, "are all societies" (1933/1967, 203–204). Whitehead sometimes also calls them *enduring objects* (1929/1978, 35, 109). Cleopatra's Needle is a society, or an enduring object; for that matter, so am I myself (1929/1978, 161).

To summarize, an "occasion" is the process by which anything becomes, and an "event"—applying to a nexus or a society—is an extensive set, or a temporal series, of such occasions. This contrast between individual becomings, and the progressive summation of such becomings, is crucial to Whitehead's metaphysics. An actual occasion is something like what Deleuze calls a *singularity*: a point of inflection or of discontinuous transformation. No actual occasion comes into being *ex nihilo*; rather, it inherits its "data" from past occasions. Yet each actual occasion is also self-creating, or *causa sui*, by virtue of the novel way in which it treats these preexisting data or prior occasions. Hence, no occasion is the same as any other; each occasion introduces something new into the world. This means that each occasion, taken in itself, is a *quantum*: a discrete, indivisible unit of becoming. But this also means that occasions are strictly limited in scope. Once an occasion happens, it is already over, already dead. Once it has reached its final "satisfaction," it no longer has any vital power. "An actual occasion . . . never changes," Whitehead says; "it only becomes and perishes" (1933/1967, 204). And a perished occasion subsists only as a "datum": a sort of raw material, which any subsequent occasion may take up in its own turn, in order to transform it in a new process of self-creation.

In contrast to the immediate becoming and perishing of actual occasions, change always involves a comparison. It can be understood as a passage *between* occasions, or as the "route of inheritance" (Whitehead 1929/1978, 279) from one incident of becoming to another. Therefore change is the mark of an event, understood in Whitehead's broader sense. "The fundamental meaning of the notion of 'change' is the difference between actual occasions comprised in some determinate event" (ibid., 73; cf. 80). This has an important consequence: it means that becoming is punctual and atomistic, and always needs to be repeated or renewed. There is "no continuity of becoming," Whitehead says, but only "a becoming of continuity" (35).[2]

---

2. Robinson (2007) argues that one major difference between Whitehead and Deleuze is precisely that "Deleuze is committed to a continuity of becoming but Whitehead is committed to the idea of a becoming of continuity." The problem for both thinkers is how to resolve the conflicting claims of unity and multiplicity, or how to achieve what Deleuze and Guattari (1987, 20) call "the magic formula we all seek—PLURALISM=MONISM." Deleuze, following Spinoza and Bergson, opts for radical continuity, and hence leans toward monism more than Whitehead, whose quantum theory of events puts more of an emphasis on irreducible plurality.

Becoming is not continuous, because each occasion, each act of becoming, is unique: a "production of novelty" that is also a new form of "concrete togetherness" (21), or what Whitehead calls a *concrescence*. Something new has been added to the universe; it marks a radical break with whatever was there before. For its part, continuity always has to *become*, precisely because it is never given in advance. The continuity implied by the existence of an enduring object—like Cleopatra's Needle, or like myself—is something that always needs to be actively produced. Nothing comes into being once and for all; and nothing just sustains itself in being, as if by inertia or its own inner force. Rather, an object can only endure insofar as it renews itself, or creates itself afresh, over and over again.[3]

At every moment, then, the continuing existence of Cleopatra's Needle is a new event. You can't bump into the same obelisk twice. All the more so, in that the same logic holds for me myself, as well as for my perception of the Needle. At any given instant, my encounter with the Needle is itself an event (Whitehead 1920/2004, 169). This encounter might take the form of my surprise at seeing the Needle for the first time; of my close scrutiny of its aesthetic features; of my barely conscious recognition of it as I walk negligently by; of the pain in my forehead, as I knock against it, without looking; of my vague

---

In any case, the advantage of Whitehead's "event epochalism," or atomism on the level of actual occasions, is—as George R. Lucas explains—that it allows him "to avoid the skeptical implications of an apparent 'paradox of becoming' common to Bergson and James. The paradox is that an undifferentiated continuity of becoming, since it neither begins nor ends, cannot itself be conceived of as determinate or concrete, nor can it meaningfully be said to give rise to a plurality of distinct existents" (Lucas 1990, 113).

For an attempt to revise Whitehead in the direction of a (more Bergsonian or Deleuzian) sense of the continuity of becoming, see Sha Xin Wei (2005).

3. This implies that Whitehead rejects Spinoza's basic principle of *conatus*, the claim that "each thing, in so far as it is in itself, endeavours to persist in its own being," and that this striving is "the actual essence of the thing itself" (de Spinoza 1991, 108: *Ethics*, Part III, propositions 6 and 7). For Whitehead, things strive not to persist in their own being, but rather to become other than they were, to make some alteration in the "data" that they receive. An entity's "satisfaction" consists not in persisting in its own being, but in achieving difference and novelty, in introducing something new into the world.

memory of having seen it years ago; or even, if I have never been to London, of my reading about it in Whitehead's book. Each of these encounters is a fresh event; and each of the selves to which it happens is also a fresh event. Perceiving the Needle is not something that happens to me as an already-constituted subject, but rather something that constitutes me anew as a subject. That is to say, whereas for Kant, and most post-Kantian thought, "the world emerges from the subject," in Whitehead's philosophy the process is inverted, so that "the subject emerges from the world—a 'superject' rather than a 'subject'" (Whitehead 1929/1978, 88). This superject is the remnant that the occasion leaves behind. I am not an entity that projects toward the world, or that phenomenologically "intends" the world, but rather one that is only born in the very course of its encounter with the world ("subject"), and that gets precipitated out of this encounter, like a salt precipitated out of a solution ("superject").[4]

For Whitehead, there is no *ontological* difference between what we generally call physical objects and what we generally call mental or subjective acts. Whitehead is in accord with William James in rejecting "the radical dualism of thought and thing" (James 1996, 28), and insisting rather that "thoughts in the concrete are made of the same stuff as things are" (37). The sheer material existence of Cleopatra's Needle is an event; and so is my perception of the Needle. Whitehead thus insists upon what Deleuze calls the "univocity" of Being: that "Being is said in a single and same sense of everything of which it is said," even when "that of which it is said differs" (Deleuze 1994, 36). Of course, my perception of the Needle is not the same thing as the Needle itself,

---

4. More needs to be said about the resonances between Whitehead's account of concrescence and the subject-superject, and Gilbert Simondon's (2005) notion of individuation. Simondon draws extensively on the example of a crystal being precipitated out of a solution, which I have borrowed as a metaphor here. In addition, Simondon's account of perception as *disparation*, a process whereby "individuation creates a relational system that 'holds together' what prior to its occurrence was incompatible" (Toscano 2006, 139), has close affinities with Whitehead's (1929/1978, 228) claim that "what are ordinarily termed 'relations' are abstractions from contrasts," and his description of the processes whereby entities strive toward a heightened "intensity of contrast" (ibid., 279), and ultimately toward the conversion of oppositions into contrasts (ibid., 348).

which stands there whether I look at it or not. Or, to put it more precisely, the event by which the Needle stands on the Victoria Embankment is different from the event by which I perceive the Needle standing on the Victoria Embankment. But these events are both of the same nature; they are both "spoken" or expressed in the same way; and they exist together in one and the same world.[5]

In order to speak adequately—which is to say, univocally—about events, Whitehead rejects the "subject-predicate forms of thought" (1929/1978, 7) that have dominated Western philosophy since Descartes. In subject-predicate thought, an underlying substance or subject is assumed to remain the same, no matter what "secondary qualities" are attributed to it, or predicated of it. Events are subordinated to the subjects to whom they happen, or to the substances upon which they supervene. Even at its best, as with Spinoza, classical thought still leaves us with a division between "one substance, *causa sui*," on the one hand, and the many affections of this substance, "its individualized modes," on the other. Whitehead declares that his own philosophy "is closely allied to Spinoza's scheme of thought." But he criticizes "the gap in [Spinoza's] system" that is due to "the arbitrary introduction of the 'modes'" (6–7). The trouble with Spinoza, in other words, is that he "bases his philosophy upon the monistic substance, of which the actual occasions are inferior modes"; Whitehead's philosophy "inverts this point of

---

5. Robinson (2007) questions the degree to which Whitehead is committed to univocity in Deleuze's sense of this term. Robinson sees "the persistence of the assumption of an analogical structure of being in Whitehead's thought"; whereas Deleuze's doctrine of radical univocity excludes analogical thought altogether. Analogy implies an underlying similarity; but Deleuze always insists on a primordial difference that subtends, and ruptures, any apparent similarities. For Deleuze, analogical reasoning necessarily implies a collapse back into dualist and representationalist thought. Whitehead's continuing use of analogy would therefore entail "an irreducible break with Deleuze." Be this as it may, and however much Whitehead may rely on analogical reasoning elsewhere in his work, nothing in Robinson's argument precludes Whitehead's committment to the univocity of how events are expressed, in the sense that I am noting here. And indeed, Robinson concedes that the differences he notices between Whitehead and Deleuze are matters of "balance" or emphasis, rather than fundamental incompatibilities.

view" (81). In altogether abolishing the distinction between substance and mode, Whitehead converts Spinoza from a logic of monism to one of pluralism (74). In *Process and Reality*, "morphological description is replaced by description of dynamic process. Also Spinoza's 'modes' now become the sheer actualities; so that, though analysis of them increases our understanding, it does not lead us to the discovery of any higher grade of reality" (7). For Whitehead, there is nothing besides the modes, no unified substance that subsumes them—not even immanently. Even God, Whitehead suggests, is *natura naturata* as well as *natura naturans*, "at once a creature of creativity and a condition for creativity. It shares this double character with all creatures" (31). In itself, every individual "actual entity satisfies Spinoza's notion of substance: it is *causa sui*" (222). The modes, affections, or actual occasions are all there is.[6]

There is therefore no stable and essential distinction, for Whitehead, between mind and matter, or between subject and object. There is also no stable and essential distinction between human and nonhuman, or even between living and nonliving. It's not that such distinctions are unimportant; often they are of the greatest pragmatic importance. I should not treat a human being the way that I treat a stone. But we need to remember that these distinctions are always situational. They are differences of degree, not differences of essence or kind. Whitehead seeks to produce a metaphysics that is nonanthropomorphic and nonanthropocentric. This means that he is a secular and naturalistic thinker, but one of a very special sort. He rejects supernatural explanations, holding to what he calls the *ontological principle*: the claim that "actual entities are the only *reasons*" (1929/1978, 24), that "the search for a reason is always the search for an actual fact which is the vehicle of that reason" (40). For "there is nothing which floats into the world from nowhere. Everything in the actual world is referable to some actual entity" (244). This means that empiricism is ultimately correct: all our knowledge comes from experience, and there is nothing outside experience,

---

6. Whitehead's rejection of Spinoza's monism in favor of William James's pluralism goes along with his rejection of Spinoza's *conatus* in favor of James's (and Bergson's) sense of continual change, becoming or process, or what he also calls *creativity*.

or beyond it. Even the concept of God needs to be secularized, explained in empirical terms, and located within phenomenal experience (207).

In this regard, it is important to note that Whitehead always seeks—as does Deleuze, after him—to conciliate his arguments with the findings of experimental science. Too many twentieth-century philosophers reject science and technology as abusive "enframings" of experience (Heidegger), or as exercises in "instrumental reason" (Horkheimer and Adorno). Whitehead, however, is positively stimulated by the science of his day: the theory of relativity, and to a lesser extent quantum mechanics. One of his goals is to create a metaphysics that frees itself from the outdated assumptions of classical (Cartesian and Newtonian) thought as thoroughly as twentieth-century physics does. This doesn't mean that philosophy is subsumed into science (as certain positivist and analytical philosophers would wish); Whitehead, no less than Deleuze, insists on the essential difference between the philosophical enterprise and the scientific one, and the irreducibility of the former to the latter. But Whitehead's metaphysics always presumes a respect for the findings of physical science. Today, Whitehead's thought (like that of Deleuze) can be brought into fruitful contact with such lively areas of contemporary scientific research and debate as complexity theory (Robinson 2005) and neurobiology (Pred 2005; Meyer 2005).

But Whitehead's ontological principle also implies that physical science—with its rejection of the "search for a reason," its separation of questions of *how* from questions of *why*—is not altogether adequate for comprehending reality. It is incomplete. As Isabelle Stengers (2005, 37ff) puts it, science is a necessary condition for understanding the world, but not a sufficient one. To stop at the level of scientific explanation would be to accept the "bifurcation of nature into two systems of reality," one the realm of "molecules and electrons," and the other that of mental phenomena (Locke's "secondary qualities") like "the greenness of the trees, the song of the birds, the warmth of the sun" (Whitehead 1920/2004, 30–31). To overcome this bifurcation, Whitehead, like Leibniz, seeks a "sufficient reason" for all phenomena. And as Deleuze (1993, 41) says, commenting on Leibniz, "a cause is not the reason being sought" here; or at least, the causality traced by physical science is not *enough* of a reason. As Deleuze further explains, Leibniz's principle of sufficient reason "claims that everything that happens to a thing—causations included—has a reason. If an event is called what happens to a thing, whether it undergoes the event or makes it happen, it can be said that sufficient reason is what includes the event as one of its predicates" (ibid.). We cannot ignore the physical chain of causality that is at work in a given event; but we do not want our explanation to stop there. We also "require to understand," as Whitehead says (cited in Stengers 2005, 42), the reason behind this chain of causality, the "decision" that makes of it what it is. Whitehead warns us that such " 'decision' cannot be construed as a casual adjunct of an actual entity. It constitutes the very meaning of actuality" (1929/1978, 43).

Whitehead's ontological principle thus makes the same metaphysical demand as Leibniz's principle of sufficient reason—except that Whitehead, once again, rejects the subject-predicate form of thought found in Leibniz. For Whitehead, events do not "happen to" things: rather, events themselves *are* the only things. An event is not "one of [the thing's] predicates," but the very thing itself.[7] Where Leibniz refers all final causes and sufficient reasons to God, the ground of being and the architect of a "preestablished harmony," Whitehead inverts this logic. In Whitehead's account, God is the *result* of the sufficient reasons, or final causes, of all finite entities, rather than their ground. In a world of process rather than predication, the sufficient reason for any actual occasion is "decided" by, and is entirely immanent to, the occasion itself. Each actual entity is the architect of its own private "preestablished harmony" (Whitehead 1929/1978, 27; cf. 224). In contrast to Leibniz's God, what Whitehead calls the "consequent nature of God" (345ff.) only works *ex post facto*, gathering these many little private harmonies, without exception, into a grand, public, and never-completed "conceptual harmonization" (346).

All this implies a new, modernist sort of "harmony": one that does not exclude dissonances, but encompasses them within itself as well. In dealing

---

7. As I have already noted, the things *to which* events happen are not actual entities or occasions, but societies and enduring objects. At the same time, these societies and enduring objects are themselves composed of nothing more than a set of actual occasions, together with the "historical routes" (Whitehead 1929/1978, 63) or "routes of inheritance" (180) that link them together.

with "antitheses," or "apparent self-contradictions," Whitehead's God neither selects among the alternative possibilities in the manner of Leibniz's divinity, nor "sublates" the oppositions into a higher, self-reflexive and self-differentiating unity in the manner of Hegel's Absolute. Rather, Whitehead's God operates "a shift of meaning which converts the opposition into a contrast" (1929/1978, 348).[8] Where Leibniz's God selects "the best of all possible worlds" by excluding incompossibilities, Whitehead's God affirms, without preference or restriction, the "discordant multiplicity of actual things" (349). Or, as Deleuze puts it: for Whitehead, in contrast to Leibniz, "bifurcations, divergences, incompossibilities, and discord belong to the same motley world. . . . Even God desists from being a Being who compares worlds and chooses the richest compossible. He becomes Process, a process that at once affirms incompossibles and passes through them" (Deleuze 1993, 81).[9]

What difference does this approach make to Whitehead's understanding of the world? How does his "philosophy of organism" compare to more conventional varieties of empiricism and naturalism? The most important difference, I think, is this. In rejecting the bifurcation of nature, and in

---

8. This merits more extended commentary than I am able to give it here. Whitehead's resolution of antitheses—by operating "a shift of meaning," and by converting conceptual oppositions into aesthetic "contrasts"—has a strong affinity with Kant's decidedly non-Hegelian (or anti-Hegelian in anticipation) treatment of antitheses, or "Antinomies," in the "Transcendental Dialectic" section of the First Critique.

9. Tim Clark (2002) questions Deleuze's reading of Whitehead as a thinker of disjunction, incompossibility, and "chaosmology." Closely reading Whitehead's account of God in *Process and Reality* and elsewhere, Clark concludes that Whitehead does not quite affirm difference, incompossibility, openness, and the "disjunctive synthesis" in the radical manner that Deleuze himself does. "Within Whitehead's system, the universe remains, in principle, only semi-open" rather than "radically open" (ibid., 202).

In other words, although Whitehead goes beyond the Baroque harmony of Leibniz, he doesn't quite move to the "dissipation of tonality," "polytonality," and (citing Boulez) "polyphony of polyphonies" that Deleuze finds in the modernist "neo-Baroque" (Deleuze 1993, 82). Harmony is more than just a metaphor here; but in looking at Whitehead's

requiring a sufficient reason for all phenomena, Whitehead necessarily challenges the founding assumption of modern scientific reason: that of a "split subject" (Lacan 1978, 138ff.), or a figure of Man as "empirico-transcendental doublet" (Foucault 1970, 318ff). For Whitehead, the experimenter cannot be separated from the experiment, because they are both present in the world in the same manner. I cannot observe other entities any differently from how I observe myself. There can be no formal, permanent distinction between the observing self (the self as transcendental subject, or subject of enunciation) and the self being observed (the self as object in the world, or subject of the statement). Therefore there can be neither phenomenology nor positivism, and neither cognitivism nor behaviorism. Whitehead underscores this point by using the same vocabulary to describe the biological world, and even the inorganic world, as he does the human world. He suggests that categories like will, desire, and creation are valid, not just for us, but for nonhuman (and even nonorganic) entities as well. He writes without embarrassment of the "feelings" and "satisfactions" of a plant, an inorganic object like Cleopatra's Needle, or even an electron. Every event or entity has what he calls both "mental" and "physical" poles, and both a "private" and a "public" dimension. In the vast interconnections of the universe, everything both perceives and is perceived.

Weird as this may sound, it is a necessary consequence of Whitehead's pursuit of univocity, or of what Manuel De Landa (2006) calls a *flat ontology*: one in which entities on different scales, and of different levels of reflexivity

---

aesthetics of "harmony," I think that we need to get away from Deleuze's implicit endorsement of the modernist narrative of the progressive expansion and liberation of harmony in Western concert music, culminating in the twelve-tone method of composers like Boulez.

I return to Clark's argument, and to the question of Whitehead's notion of god, in Chapter 5. But even granting Clark's interpretation, Whitehead is sufficiently open as regards God and the "chaosmos" as to not altogether exclude Deleuze's reading—at least in the way that I am citing it here. Overall, I am less concerned with reconstructing Whitehead's thought precisely than in delineating the outlines of the encounter between Whitehead and Deleuze, an encounter that changes our apprehension of both of them.

and complexity, are all treated in the same manner.[10] When Whitehead writes of the "mental pole" of an electron, or a monument, we must remember that "mental operations do not necessarily involve consciousness"; indeed, most often they happen entirely without consciousness (Whitehead 1929/1978, 85). Whitehead derives his terms from our ordinary language about human thought, feeling, and behavior; in this way, he signals his distance from any sort of positivism, or from what more recently has come to be called "eliminative materialism." But he also radically deanthropomorphizes these terms, in order to distinguish his position from any simple privileging of the human, or from the "panpsychism" of which he is sometimes accused. It is not the case that we human beings have some special essence of "mentality," whereas trees and rocks and electrons don't. But neither is our sentience just an illusion. The difference is rather one of degree. The "mental pole" of an occasion contributing to the existence of a tree or a rock or an electron is never entirely absent, but it is so feeble as to be "negligible." In contrast, the "mental pole" of an occasion that contributes to my consciousness, or to my identity, is intense, active, and largely dominant.

To avoid the anthropomorphic—or at least cognitive and rationalistic—connotations of words like "mentality" and "perception," Whitehead uses the term *prehension* for the act by which one actual occasion takes up and responds to another. Clear and distinct human sense perception, as it is conceived in

---

10. It is sometimes argued that Whitehead's distinction between actual entities and societies, or between occasions (which are atomistic) and events (which involve change), violates the dictum of a flat ontology and reintroduces the very "bifurcation of nature" that Whitehead is so concerned to overcome. As I have already suggested, Whitehead needs this distinction in order to affirm the actuality of meaningful change—or what he calls the "creative advance into novelty" (Whitehead 1929/1978, 28 and *passim*)—and to avoid reducing becoming to what Ernst Bloch, criticizing both Bergson and the endless alternation of fashions in capitalist consumer society, calls "sheer aimless infinity and incessant changeability; where everything ought to be constantly new, everything remains just as it was . . . a merely endless, contentless zigzag" (Bloch 1986, 140).

In any case, the dictum of a flat ontology at least applies to anything that we may encounter in lived experience, since everything from a neutrino to the cosmos as a whole is equally a "society" in Whitehead's definition of the term.

the classical philosophical tradition from Descartes to the positivists of the twentieth century, is one sort of prehension. But it is far from the only one. Our lives are filled with experiences of "non-sensuous perception" (Whitehead 1933/1967, 180–181): from our awareness of the immediate past (181), to the feelings we have of "the '*withness*' *of the body*" (Whitehead 1929/1978, 312). "We see the contemporary chair, but we see it *with* our eyes; and we touch the contemporary chair, but we touch it *with* our hands" (62). Or again, "we see *by our eyes*, and taste *by our palates*" (122). In the same way, "a jellyfish advances and withdraws, and in so doing exhibits some perception of causal relationship with the world beyond itself; a plant grows downwards to the damp earth, and upwards to the light" (176). These are all prehensions. For that matter, the earth prehends the sun that gives it energy; the stone prehends the earth to which it falls. Cleopatra's Needle prehends its material surroundings; and I prehend, among other things, the Needle. A new entity comes into being by prehending other entities; every event *is* the prehension of other events.[11]

All this applies, it should be noted, not only to the encounter between subject and object, but also to encounters between one object and another, as well as to what is commonly called the "identity" of the individual subject. Self-identity, the relation of a subject to itself, has the same structure as the relation of a subject to an object. They are both grounded in prehensions. I prehend Cleopatra's Needle afresh every time I pass it, or think about it. But also, I continually prehend myself; I renew myself in being, at every instant, by prehending what I was just a moment ago, "between a tenth of a second and

---

11. As Deleuze puts it: "Everything prehends its antecedents and its concomitants and, by degrees, prehends a world. The eye is a prehension of light. Living beings prehend water, soil, carbon, and salts. At a given moment the pyramid prehends Napoleon's soldiers (forty centuries are contemplating us) and inversely" (Deleuze 1993, 78). However, regarding Deleuze's summary, as well as my own, two precautions are in order. In the first place, as Didier Debaise notes, all these examples refer to what Whitehead calls *societies*, rather than—as would be more proper—to actual entities themselves (Debaise 2006, 73–75). Second, Deleuze fails to mention the temporal dimension of prehension. An actual entity does not prehend what is contemporaneous with it, but only what lies in its past (although this is usually its immediate past, so that the distinction is for the most part unnoticeable).

half a second ago." Such an immediate past "is gone, and yet it is here. It is our indubitable self, the foundation of our present existence" (Whitehead 1933/1967, 181). An "enduring object" can only persist through time, and retain a certain "identity" amid the becomings that it passes through, by virtue of "a genetic character inherited through a historic route of actual occasions" (Whitehead 1929/1978, 109). I am only the "same," only able to "sustain a character" (35), to the extent that I continually, and actively, take up this inheritance from the immediate past. My self-identity, or the manner in which I relate to myself, is the expression of such an inheritance: the process by which I receive it, reflect on it, and transform it, again and again.[12] And the same could be said, more or less, for Cleopatra's Needle. The only difference is that I take up my inheritance from the past on a higher and more reflexive level than does a plant, a stone, or an electron.

If Being is univocal, and everything is an event, and the human and the rational hold no special privileges, then epistemology must be demoted from the central role that it generally holds in post-Cartesian (and especially post-Kantian) thought. The whole point of Whitehead's philosophy is "to free our notions from participation in an epistemological theory of sense-perception" (Whitehead 1929/1978, 73). It no longer makes sense to separate the theory of *how* we know from the theory of *what* we know. Whitehead points out the unacknowledged ontological premises lying behind traditional philosophy's

---

12. In other words, I am continually caught up in what Foucault calls "the care of the self," or the practice of constructing and governing "the relationship of the self to itself" (Foucault 1997, 300). Much more needs to be said about this process of self-constitution, and how it differs from the ways that the subject is conceived in "subject-predicate forms of thought"—or for that matter, from the ways that it is conceived in forms of thought that critique or deconstruct the "subject-predicate" approach, but without proposing any alternative, constructivist account.

I think that Whitehead's understanding of subjectivity as process (and Foucault's account as well, for that matter) is best grasped in relation to Kant's discussions of time as "the form of inner sense," and of the constitution of the "I" as transcendental unity of apperception. Whitehead (1929/1978, 156) "inverts" the Kantian analysis—or, as I prefer to say, *converts* it from a cognitive to an experiential basis—by replacing Kant's abstract temporality with Bergson's "concrete duration," or better with what William James calls the "specious present."

epistemological investigations: Descartes's methodical doubt, Hume's skepticism, and Kant's transcendental deduction. In all these cases, continuity and causality are in fact already preassumed by the arguments that claim to put them into doubt (or, in the case of Kant, to ground and authorize them). Hume, for instance, questions causality by arguing that all we can really know of a necessary link between events is their constant conjunction in memory. Such a conjunction, Hume says, must be ascribed to our habits and associations; it is in our minds, rather than in the world. But Whitehead rejects this very distinction. He remarks that "it is difficult to understand why Hume exempts 'habit' from the same criticism as that applied to the notion of 'cause.' We have no 'impression' of 'habit,' just as we have no 'impression' of 'cause.' Cause, repetition, habit are all in the same boat" (ibid., 140).

In other words, habits and mental associations could not themselves be posited without the hidden assumption of what Whitehead calls *causal efficacy*: "the sense of derivation from an immediate past, and of passage to an immediate future" (ibid., 178). So where Hume separates subjective impressions from objective matters of fact, and argues that we cannot make inferences from the former to the latter, Whitehead notes that the logics, and the contents, of these two ostensibly separate realms are in fact entirely the same. There is no reason why mental events should be treated any differently than any other sort of events; they are all parts of the same stream of experience. If Hume were consistent, he would have to reject habit, memory, and mental association on the same grounds that he rejects causality. The lesson is that epistemological metaquestions ("how do we know what exists?"; "do we really know what we think we know about what exists?") have the same ontological status as the first-order questions to which they ostensibly refer ("what exists?"). Whitehead thus short-circuits the entire process of epistemological reflection. There is no metalanguage, and epistemology collapses back into ontology.

This rejection of epistemology is what leads Deleuze to praise "the list of empirico-ideal notions that we find in Whitehead, which makes *Process and Reality* one of the greatest books of modern philosophy" (Deleuze 1994, 284–285). Deleuze opposes Whitehead's proliferating list of categories—a list that includes "the Category of the Ultimate," together with eight "Categories of Existence," twenty-seven Categories of Explanation," and nine "Categoreal Obligations" (Whitehead 1929/1978, 20–28)—to the twelve fixed Categories of the understanding in Kant's *Critique of Pure Reason*. Kant's categories are logical and epistemological; they "belong to the world of representation" (Deleuze 1994, 284), and concern the ways in which we organize—and thereby present to ourselves—the data that we receive from the senses. Whitehead calls them "the ghosts of the old 'faculties,' banished from psychology, but still haunting metaphysics" (1929/1978, 18). Whitehead's own categories, to the contrary, are "generic notions inevitably presupposed in our reflective experience . . . [based] upon the most concrete elements in our experience" (ibid.). They do not *represent* that experience, nor do they explain how it is possible for us to *know* things in experience. They cannot be *applied to* experience, because they are already located *within* experience itself. Deleuze calls them "notions which are really open and which betray an empirical and pluralist sense of Ideas . . . Such notions . . . are conditions of real experience, and not only of possible experience" (Deleuze 1994, 284–285).

Kant's categories of understanding are universal and intrinsic to the mind that imposes them upon an otherwise inchoate external reality. But Whitehead's categories are not imposed by the mind. They are immanent to the "data"—the events or actual occasions—out of which they arise by a process of abstraction. "It is a complete mistake," Whitehead says, "to ask how concrete particular fact can be built up out of universals. The answer is, 'In no way.' The true philosophic question is, How can concrete fact exhibit entities abstract from itself and yet participated in by its own nature?" (1929/1978, 20).[13] Whitehead abstracts "empirico-ideal" categories from the events that participate in them, rather than imposing *a priori* categories upon phenomena that remain external to them. In analyzing events, he does not assume any priority of the subject, but rather traces its genesis alongside that of the world in which it finds itself. And he delineates the conditions of real experience, which determine concrete processes of emergence, rather than proposing apodictic conditions for all possible experience. Whitehead rejects Kant's "endeavor to balance the world upon thought—oblivious to the scanty supply of thinking." But he still agrees with Kant on the fundamental principle "that

---

13. Deleuze and Guattari (1994, 7) similarly remark that "the first principle of philosophy is that Universals explain nothing but must themselves be explained."

the task of the critical reason is the analysis of constructs; and 'construction' is 'process'" (ibid., 151). In this way, Whitehead is far from simply rejecting Kant; rather, he converts Kant's "transcendental idealism" into something like what Deleuze calls "transcendental empiricism."[14]

Deleuze's own "transcendental empiricism" centers on his notion of the virtual. I think that this much-disputed concept can best be understood in Kantian terms. The virtual is the transcendental condition of all experience. And Ideas in the virtual, which are always "problematic or problematizing," are Deleuze's equivalent of "regulative ideas" in Kant (Deleuze 1994, 168ff). For Kant, as Deleuze points out, "problematic Ideas are both objective and undetermined." They cannot be presented directly, or re-presented; but their very indeterminacy "is a perfectly positive, objective structure which acts as a focus or horizon within perception" (ibid.). The error of metaphysical dogmatism is to use these Ideas constitutively: to take their objects as determinate, transcendent entities. This is to forget that such objects "can be neither given nor known." The correlative error of skepticism is to think that, since the Ideas are indeterminate and unrepresentable, they are thereby merely subjective, and their objects merely fictive. This is to forget that "problems have an objective value," and that "'problematic' does not mean only a particularly important species of subjective acts, but a dimension of objectivity as such which is occupied by these acts" (ibid., 168). Against both of these errors, Kant upholds the regulative and transcendental use of the Ideas. A regulative idea does not determine any particular solution in advance. But operating as a guideline, or as a frame of reference, the regulative idea works *problematically*, to establish the conditions out of which solutions, or "decisions," can emerge. In positing a process of this sort, Kant invents the notion of the transcendental realm, or of what Deleuze will call the virtual.

---

14. As Robinson (2006, 72) forcefully puts it, "the key context for understanding . . . Whitehead is to refuse to read Whitehead as simply a pre-Kantian metaphysical realist. . . . Rather, Whitehead's pre-Kantianism plays much the same role in his thought as it does in Deleuze: a way of approaching and confronting the aporias of Kantianism as preparation for the laying out of an essentially post-Kantian philosophy of creativity and becoming. Whitehead is a deeply post-Kantian philosopher in much the same way that Deleuze is post-Kantian."

There are, of course, important differences between Kant's transcendental argument and Deleuze's invocation of the virtual. For one thing, Kant's stance is legislative and juridical: he seeks to distinguish legitimate from illegitimate uses of reason. Deleuze seeks rather (citing Artaud) "to have done with the judgment of God"; his criterion is constructivist rather than juridical, concerned with pushing forces to the limits of what they can do, rather than with evaluating their legitimacy. Also, Kant's transcendental realm determines the necessary form—but only the form—of all possible experience. Deleuze's virtual, in contrast, is "genetic and productive" of actual experience (Deleuze 1983, 51–52). Finally, Kant's transcendental realm has the structure of a subjectivity; at the very least, it takes on the bare form of the "I" in the "transcendental unity of apperception." But Deleuze's virtual is an "impersonal and pre-individual transcendental field" (Deleuze 1990, 102); it does not have the form of a consciousness. In making these corrections to Kant, Deleuze himself does what he credits Nietzsche with doing: he "stands [Kantian] critique on its feet, just as Marx does with the [Hegelian] dialectic" (Deleuze 1983, 89).

To convert Kant from transcendental idealism to transcendental empiricism, and from a juridico-legislative project to a constructivist one, is to move from the possible to the virtual, and from merely formal conditions of possibility to concrete conditions of actualization. Deleuze's transformation of Kant thus leads directly to his famous distinction between the virtual and the possible. For Deleuze, the possible is an empty form, defined only by the principle of noncontradiction. To say that something is possible is to say nothing more than that its concept cannot be excluded *a priori*, on logical grounds alone. This means that possibility is a purely negative category; it lacks any proper being of its own. Mere possibility is not generative or productive; it is not *enough* to make anything happen. It does not satisfy the principle of sufficient reason. This is why Deleuze says that "the possible is opposed to the real" (Deleuze 1994, 211). Something that is merely possible has no claim to existence, and no intrinsic mode of being. Its only positive characteristics are those that it borrows from the real that it is not. The possible "refers to the form of identity in the concept"; it "is understood as an image of the real, while the real is supposed to resemble the possible" (211–212). That is to say, the possible is exactly like the real, except for the contingency that it does not, in fact, exist. And the real is nothing more than the the working-out of what was already prefigured and envisioned as possible. In this mirror play of resemblances, there can be nothing new or unexpected. When a possibility is realized—when it *does* come into existence—no actual creation has taken place. As Deleuze says, "it is difficult to understand what existence adds to the concept when all it does is double like with like" (212).

The virtual, on the other hand, is altogether real in its own right; it "possesses a full reality by itself" (ibid. 211). It is just that this reality is not actual. The virtual is like a field of energies that have not yet been expended, or a reservoir of potentialities that have not yet been tapped. That is to say, the virtual is not composed of atoms; it doesn't have body or extension. But the potential for change that it offers is real in its own way. In the Proustian formulation so frequently used by Deleuze, the virtual is "real without being actual, ideal without being abstract" (208). One can in fact explain the virtual in entirely physicalist terms: as Gilbert Simondon (2005) did in work that greatly influenced Deleuze, and as Manuel De Landa (2002) has more recently done. But Deleuze most often describes the virtual as a transcendental field or structure, conditioning and generating the actual. The virtual is a principle of emergence, or of creation. As such, it does not prefigure or predetermine the actualities that emerge from it. Rather, it is the impelling force, or the principle, that allows each actual entity to appear (to manifest itself) as something new, something without precedence or resemblance, something that has never existed in the universe in quite that way before. That is why the virtual is entirely distinct from the possible. If anything, it is closer to Nietzsche's will-to-power, or Bergson's *élan vital*. All of these must be understood, not as inner essences, but as post-Kantian "syntheses" of difference: transcendental conditions for dynamic becoming, rather than for static being (see Deleuze 1983, 51–52).

The virtual works as a transcendental condition for the actual by providing a sufficient reason for whatever happens. This brings us back to the distinction—or better, the gap—between sufficient reason and ordinary causality. Linear causality, of the sort that physical science traces, is always, and only, a relation among bodies. It is a matter, as Deleuze puts it in *The Logic of Sense*, of "bodies with their tensions, physical qualities, actions and passions, and the corresponding 'states of affairs.' These states of affairs, actions and passions, are determined by the mixtures of bodies . . . all bodies are causes—causes in relation to each other and for each other" (Deleuze 1990, 4).

Everything in the world is determined by such physical causes; they consitute a necessary condition for every event—but as we have seen, not a sufficient one.

This linear causality, and this necessity, are what Kant seeks to guarantee against Hume's skepticism. But if we accept Whitehead's critique of Hume, then we can only conclude that Kant's very search for such a guarantee is superfluous. Causal efficacy is always already at work in the depths of bodies. Kant never questions Hume's initial dubious assumption: that causality cannot be found *out there*, in the world, and that consequently it can only be located *in here*, in the mind of the perceiver. Hume appeals to habit as the basis of the mind's ascription of causality to things; Kant's transcendental argument converts this empirical generalization into an *a priori* necessity. But Kant still accepts what Whitehead (1929/1978, 157) calls the *subjectivist* and *sensationalist* principles derived from Locke and Hume.[15] In consequence, Kant's transcendental deduction remains caught within "a logic of tracing and reproduction" (Deleuze and Guattari 1987, 12), "a tracing of the transcendental from the empirical" (Deleuze 1994, 143). Kant merely transfers the structure of causal efficacy from the world to the subject apprehending the world. The possible just doubles the real, without adding anything to it.

Deleuze converts Kant's argument from possibility to virtuality, and from the role of guaranteeing causal efficacy to one of providing sufficient reasons, by positing a different sort of transcendental logic. Alongside the actual, material "connection" of physical causes to one another, there is also a virtual relation, or a "bond," linking "effects or incorporeal events" among themselves (Deleuze 1990, 6). The virtual is the realm of effects separated from their causes: "effects in the causal sense, but also sonorous, optical, or linguistic 'effects'" (7), or what in the movies are called "special effects." Effects come after

---

15. As Whitehead (1929/1978, 157) specifies: "The subjectivist principle is, that the datum in the act of experience can be adequately analysed purely in terms of universals.

"The sensationalist principle is, that the primary activity in the act of experience is the bare subjective entertainment of the datum, devoid of any subjective form of reception. This is the doctrine of mere sensation."

causes, of course, in the physical world of bodies. But transcendentally, these incorporeal special effects establish a strange precedence. Considered apart from their physical causes, and independently of any bodily instantiation, they are something like the generative conditions—the "meanings" and the "reasons," or what Whitehead calls the final causes—for the very processes that physically give rise to them.

Deleuze (1990, 6) refers to such generative aftereffects as "quasi-causes." Quasi-causality is "an unreal and ghostly causality" (33), more an insinuation than a determination. It happens, not in the bodily density of the living present, but in an "instant without thickness and without extension, which subdivides each present into past and future" (164). The quasi-cause "is nothing outside of its effect"; but neither can it just be identified with, or reduced to, its effect. For "it haunts this effect . . . it maintains with the effect an immanent relation which turns the product, the moment that it is produced, into something productive" (95). In itself, the virtual quasi-cause partakes only of "extra-being"; it is "sterile, inefficacious, and on the surface of things" (7). But at the same time, by virtue of its infinite relations, and insofar as it "evades the present" (165), the quasi-cause is also a principle of creativity. Looking forward, it *induces* the process of actualization; looking backward, it is an *expression* of that process. Deleuze's transcendental realm is thus "an aggregate of noncausal correspondences which form a system of echoes, of resumptions and resonances, a system of signs—in short, an expressive quasi-causality, and not at all a necessitating causality" (170). Only in this ghostly, paradoxical way can Deleuze posit a transcendental that neither copies the actual, nor prefigures it.

What does all this have to do with Whitehead? As far as I know, Whitehead never uses the word *virtual*. But as Robinson notes, Whitehead's "distinction between the actual and the potential . . . resembles the Deleuzian distinction between the actual and the virtual" (Robinson 2006, 72). And potentiality, for Whitehead, is always something more, and other, than mere possibility. Alongside events or actual entities, Whitehead also posits what he calls "eternal objects." These are "Pure Potentials" (Whitehead 1929/1978, 22), or "potentials for the process of becoming" (29). If actual entities are singular "occasions" of becoming, then eternal objects provide "the 'qualities' and 'relations'" (191) that enter into, and help to define, these occasions. When "the potentiality of an eternal object is realized in a particular actual entity," it "contribut[es] to the definiteness of that actual entity" (23). It gives it a particular character. Eternal objects thus take on something of the role that universals (48, 158), predicates (186), Platonic forms (44), and ideas (52; 149) played in older metaphysical systems. But we have already seen that, for Whitehead, a "concrete particular fact" cannot simply "be built up out of universals"; it is more the other way around. Universals, or "things which are eternal," can and must be abstracted from "things which are temporal" (40). But they cannot be conceived by themselves, in the absence of the empirical, temporal entities that they inform. Eternal objects, therefore, are neither *a priori* logical structures, nor Platonic essences, nor constitutive rational ideas. They are adverbial, rather than substantive; they determine and express *how* actual entities relate to one another, take one another up, and "enter into each others' constitutions" (148–149). Like Kantian and Deleuzian ideas, eternal objects work regulatively, or problematically.[16]

To be more precise, Whitehead defines eternal objects as follows: "any entity whose conceptual recognition does not involve a necessary reference to any definite actual entites of the temporal world is called an 'eternal object' "

---

16. Whitehead's account of eternal objects thus has strong affinities with Kant's transcendental argument. Just as Kant sought to reject both idealism and empiricism by posing the transcendental in opposition to both the transcendent and the mere flux of sensations, so Whitehead argues against two opposed, but complementary, philosophical positions. On the one hand, to assert the objective reality of sensa or qualia is to reject mainstream empiricism and positivism. From Locke through Hume, and right on up to mid-twentieth-century positivism, sensa are regarded as "secondary qualities," not present in reality, but only in the mind. The doctrine of "private psychological fields" still remains a feature of our commonsense understanding of the world today, even though, as Whitehead (1929/1978, 326) wryly notes, it "raises a great difficulty in the interpretation of modern science." On the other hand, to insist that eternal objects exist only insofar as their "conceptual recognition" must be "an operation constituting a real feeling belonging to some actual entity" (ibid., 44) is to reject all forms of idealism (whether of the classical or the post-Hegelian variety). There can be no infinite spirit or absolute (such as that of Bradley, on whom Whitehead unfavorably comments at several points in *Process and Reality*). As I will discuss in chapter 5, even God, who is able to envision the totality of eternal objects, must be viewed as an empirical entity rather than as a transcendent one.

(1929/1978, 44). This means that eternal objects include sensory qualities, like colors (*blueness* or *greenness*) and tactile sensations (*softness* or *roughness*), conceptual abstractions like shapes (a *helix*, or a *dodecahedron*) and numbers (*seven*, or *the square root of minus two*), moral qualities (like *bravery* or *cowardice*), physical fundamentals (like *gravitational attraction* or *electric charge*), and much more besides. An eternal object can also be "a determinate way in which a feeling can feel. It is an emotion, or an intensity, or an adversion, or an aversion, or a pleasure, or a pain" (291).[17] "Sensa"—or what today are more commonly called "qualia"—are "the lowest category of eternal objects" (114). But there are also "complex eternal objects" that have the simpler ones as components. In this way, affects or emotions are eternal objects; and so are "contrasts, or patterns," or anything else that can "express a manner of relatedness between other eternal objects" (114). There is, in fact, "an indefinite progression of categories, as we proceed from 'contrasts' to 'contrasts of contrasts,' and on indefinitely to higher grades of contrasts" (22). The levels and complexities proliferate, without limit. But regardless of level, eternal objects are ideal abstractions that nevertheless (in contrast to Platonic forms) can only be encountered *within* experience, when they are "selected" and "felt" by particular actual occasions.

Whitehead's use of the word "eternal" might seem to be a strange move, in the context of a philosophy grounded in events, becomings, and continual change and novelty. And indeed, as if acknowledging this, he remarks that, "if the term 'eternal objects' is disliked, the term 'potentials' would be suitable" instead (1929/1978, 149). But if Whitehead prefers to retain the appellation "eternal objects," this is precisely because he seeks—like Nietzsche, Bergson, and Deleuze—to reject the Platonic separation between eternity and time, the binary opposition that sets a higher world of permanence and perfection ("a static, spiritual heaven") against an imperfect lower world of flux (209). The two instead must continually interpenetrate. For "permanence can be snatched only out of flux; and the passing moment can find its adequate intensity only by its submission to permanence. Those who would disjoin the

---

17. It is important to recall here that, for Whitehead, all entities feel and have feelings, and not just sentient ones.

two elements can find no interpretation of patent facts" (338). Actual entities continually perish; but the relations between them, or the patterns that they make, tend to recur, or endure. Thus "it is not 'substance' which is permanent, but 'form.'" And even forms do not subsist absolutely, but continually "suffer changing relations" (29). In asserting this, Whitehead converts Plato from idealism to empiricism, just as he similarly converts Spinoza, Leibniz, Hume, and Kant.[18]

When Whitehead says that forms as well as substances, or eternal objects as well as actual entities, must be accepted as real, he is arguing very much in the spirit of the *radical empiricism* of William James. For James, *experience* is the sole criterion of reality; we live in "a world of pure experience" (James 1996, 39–91). Classical empiricism has great difficulty in making sense of relations, as well as of emotions, contrasts and patterns, and all the other phenomena that Whitehead classifies as "eternal objects." Since these cannot be recognized as "things," or as direct "impressions of sensation," they are relegated to the status of mental fictions (habits, derivatives, secondary qualities, and so on). But James says that, in a world of pure experience, "relations" are every bit as real as "things": "the relations that connect experiences must themselves be experienced relations, and any kind of relation experienced must be accounted as 'real' as anything else in the system" (ibid., 42). Whitehead argues, by the same logic, that eternal objects must be accounted as real as the actual entities which they qualify, and which select them, include them, and incarnate them. Eternal objects are

---

18. The distinction between perishing substances and permanent forms is relevant to the way in which so much "postmodern" and "posthuman" thought—from cybernetics to complexity theory—is concerned with form rather than substance. As Katherine Hayles (1999, 27, *passim*) puts it, postmodernity is characterized by a dialectic of pattern and randomness, rather than one of presence and absence. Today, we are all still Platonists, to the extent that we believe in recurring patterns that can be instantiated indifferently in any number of material substrates. The same mathematical equations are supposed to describe the development of the weather, the changing balances between predators and prey in an ecosystem, the irregularities of a heart murmur, and the fluctuations of the stock market. Whitehead seeks both to acknowledge this inveterate Platonism and to indicate its limitations.

real, because they are themselves "experienced relations," or primordial elements of experience.¹⁹

But even though eternal objects are altogether real, they are not the same as actual entities. Like Deleuze's virtualities, they are precisely not actual. This is because, in themselves, they are not causally determined, and they cannot make anything happen. Eternal objects "involve in their own natures indecision" and "indetermination" (Whitehead 1929/1978, 29); they always imply alternatives, contingencies, situations that could have been otherwise. This patch of wall is yellow, but it might have been blue. This means that their role is essentially passive. "An eternal object is always a potentiality for actual entities; but in itself, as conceptually felt, it is neutral as to the fact of its physical ingression in any particular actual entity of the temporal world" (44). You might say that yellowness "in itself," understood as a pure potentiality, is utterly indifferent to the actual yellow color of this particular patch of wall. Yellowness *per se* has no causal efficacy, and no influence over the "decision" by which it is admitted (or not) into any particular actual state of affairs. Eternal objects, like Deleuze's quasi-causes, are neutral, sterile, and inefficacious, as powerless as they are indifferent.

At the same time, every event, every actual occasion, involves the *actualization* of certain of these mere potentialities. Each actual entity is determined

---

19. David Lapoujade (2000, 190) reads James as a transcendental empiricist. Where classical empiricism "begin[s] with an anarchic distribution of sensible *minima*—psychic atoms," James's "radical empiricism" instead posits what Deleuze calls a plane of immanence, or "an impersonal and pre-individual transcendental field." At the same time, in contrast to the transcendental reductions of Kant and Husserl, which posit the pure form of the "I" as the *a priori* condition for all experience, James's transcendental "pure experience" does not take the form of a subjectivity or a consciousness. It is rather a flux "pure of all form," and "free . . . from the categories with which it is traditionally partitioned" (ibid., 193).

For his part, Whitehead simply makes more fully explicit the transcendental argument that is implicit in the work of James. He follows James in positing "pure experience" as a fundamental category: "apart from the experiences of subjects there is nothing, nothing, nothing, bare nothingness" (Whitehead 1929/1978, 167). And amid all this experience, he says, "we find ourselves in a buzzing world" (ibid., 50)—deliberately echoing James's famous description of the "blooming, buzzing confusion" of the stream of consciousness.

by what Whitehead calls the *ingression* of specific eternal objects into it. "The term 'ingression' refers to the particular mode in which the potentiality of an eternal object is realized in a particular actual entity, contributing to the definiteness of that actual entity" (Whitehead 1929/1978, 23). Each actual entity creates itself, in a process of decision, by making a *selection* among the potentialities offered to it by eternal objects. The concrescence of each actual entity involves the rejection of some eternal objects, and the active "entertainment," or "admi[ssion] into feeling" (188), of others. And by a kind of circular process, the eternal objects thus admitted or entertained serve to define and determine the entity that selected them. That is why—or better, how—this particular patch of wall actually *is* yellow. By offering themselves for actualization, and by determining the very entities that select and actualize them, eternal objects play a transcendental, quasi-causal role in the constitution of the actual world.[20]

Whitehead also explains the difference, and the relation, between eternal objects and actual entities by noting that the former "*can* be dismissed" at any moment, whereas the latter always "*have* to be felt" (ibid., 239). Potentialities are optional; they may or may not be fulfilled. But actualities cannot be avoided. Indeed, "an actual entity in the actual world of a subject *must* enter into the concrescence of that subject by *some* simple causal feeling, however vague, trivial, and submerged" (ibid.). An actual entity can, in fact, be rejected or excluded, by the process of what Whitehead calls a *negative prehension*: "the definite exclusion of [a given] item from positive contribution to the subject's own real internal constituion" (41). But even this is a sort of backhanded acknowledgement, an active response to something that cannot just be ignored. Even "the negative prehension of an entity is a positive fact with its emotional subjective form" (41–42).[21] An actual entity has causal efficacy,

---

20. The actual and the potential thus reciprocally determine one another in Whitehead, much as the actual and the virtual are reciprocally determining in Deleuze. James Williams (2005, 77–100) rigorously examines "the concept of reciprocal determination" in both thinkers.

21. Strictly speaking, Whitehead uses the term "negative prehension" to designate both the exclusion of an actual entity and the exclusion of an eternal object. But although a negative prehension of an actual entity "may eliminate its distinctive importance," nevertheless "in some

because in itself it is entirely determined; it is empirically "given," and this "givenness" means Necessity (42–43). Once actual entities have completed their process, once the ingression of eternal objects into them has been fixed, they "are devoid of all indetermination.... They are complete and determinate... devoid of all indecision" (29). Every event thus culminates in a "stubborn matter of fact" (239), a state of affairs that has no potential left, and that cannot be otherwise than it is. An event consists precisely in this movement from potentiality (and indeterminacy) into actuality (and complete determination). The process of actualization follows a trajectory from the mere, disinterested (aesthetic) "envisagement" of eternal objects (44) to a pragmatic interest in some of these objects, and their incorporation within "stubborn fact which cannot be evaded" (43).

In the course of fully determining itself, an actual entity thus perishes, and subsists only as a "datum" for other entities to prehend in their own turn. An eternal object, on the other hand, is not exhausted by the event into which it ingresses, or which includes it; it "never loses its 'accent' of potentiality" (ibid., 239). It remains available for other events, other actualizations. This is another mark of the transcendental. As Deleuze similarly says, referring both to Kantian Ideas and to his own notion of the problematic virtual, "true problems are Ideas, and... these Ideas do not disappear with 'their' solutions, since they are the indispensible condition without which no solution would ever exist" (Deleuze 1994, 168). Eternal objects and problematic Ideas never disappear. They are "indispensible conditions" that cannot be grasped outside of the actualities that they condition, and that incarnate them. But they also cannot be reduced to those actualities, and cannot be contained within them. They are not actual, but they haunt the actual. They subsist, like

---

way, by some trace of causal feeling, the remote actual entity is [still] prehended positively. In the case of an eternal object, there is no such necessity" (1929/1978, 239). "All the actual entities are positively prehended, but only a selection of the eternal objects" (ibid., 219). Actual entities, you might say, can only be excluded via something like (psychoanalytic) repression whereas eternal objects can actually be dismissed, without residue, when subject to a negative prehension. This follows from the very nature of eternal objects: although they are real, they are not "facts," and they have no causal efficacy.

specters, outside of their ingressions and actualizations, and according to a different temporal logic than that of the "specious present of the percipient" (Whitehead 1929/1978, 169), the present in which things happen. This outside, this extra-being, this space without "simple location" (ibid., 137), this time in which "a future and past divide the present at every instant and subdivide it ad infinitum into past and future, in both directions at once" (Deleuze 1990, 164): all this is the realm of the transcendental.

Kant's transcendental deduction serves (at least) two purposes. It has both a juridical use, and a problematic or speculative use. The juridical use is to determine the legitimate conditions of rationality: to "make reason secure in its rightful claims and . . . dismiss all [its] baseless pretensions" (Kant 1996, 8). The problematic or speculative use of the deduction is to answer the three basic questions: "What can I know? What ought I to do? What may I hope?" (735). In converting Kant from transcendental idealism to transcendental empiricism, Whitehead and Deleuze refashion both of these uses. The juridical use of the transcendental deduction is displaced, as I have already suggested, from Kant's "tribunal" in which reason turns back upon and scrutinizes itself, into an evaluation according to immanent criteria.[22] And the problematic use of the transcendental deduction is transformed, because Whitehead and Deleuze ask different sorts of questions than Kant does. The fundamental questions that Whitehead and Deleuze ask, and seek to answer with their

---

22. I have already mentioned Deleuze's rejection of questions of legitimation, his desire "to have done with the judgment of God." But Deleuze's immanent and constructivist mode of thought also, in its own way, involves a kind of critical self-reflexivity, and thereby poses the transcendental question of the *limit*: "You never reach the Body without Organs, you can't reach it, you are forever attaining it, it is a limit" (Deleuze and Guattari 1987, 150). An experimental, constructivist practice seeks to affirm itself to the full extent of what it can do—a concept that Deleuze develops in his discussions of Spinoza's *conatus* (Deleuze 1988), and Nietzsche's doctrine of active forces (Deleuze 1983). But this means precisely pushing a force, or a practice, to its limits, and confronting the Body without Organs as ultimate limit. This is where we face the question of blockages and flows, "emptied bodies" and "full ones," accomplishments and further problematizations.

Whitehead, for his part, is always circumspect in his critiques. When he discusses other philosophical systems, he always recognizes their validity within limits, but criticizes the attempt

transcendental arguments about eternal objects and the virtual, are these: How is it that there is always something new? How are novelty and change possible? How can we account for a future that is different from, and not merely predetermined by, the past? And behind all these is the question with which I began: "What is an Event?"

The shift from Kant's questions to Whitehead's and Deleuze's questions is largely a historical one, deeply embedded in the progress (if we can still call it that) of our modernity. Kant, of course, is a great thinker of the Enlightenment, which he famously defines as "man's emergence from his self-imposed immaturity" into intellectual adulthood (Kant 1983, 41). Foucault, commenting on Kant's Enlightenment text some two centuries later, remarks that "the historical event of the Enlightenment did not make us mature adults, and we have not reached that stage yet" (Foucault 1997, 319). Nonetheless, he praises Kant's stance for providing "a point of departure: the outline of what one might call the attitude of modernity" (309). And he urges us to continue Kant's reflection in the form of "an attitude, an ethos, a philosophical life in which the critique of what we are is at one and the same time the historical analysis of the limits imposed on us and an experiment with the possibility of going beyond them" (319). This is the task that lies behind Whitehead's and Deleuze's renewals of the Kantian transcendental argument. As for the shift from foundational questions about knowing, obligation, and belief to pragmatic, constructivist questions about events, potentialities, and the process of actualizing them, this is not a betrayal of Kant, but an urgent and necessary renewal of his legacy, at a time when "all that is solid melts into air,"

---

to push beyond these limits: "the chief error in philosophy is overstatement. The aim at generalization is sound, but the estimate of success is exaggerated. There are two main forms of such overstatement. One form is what I have termed elsewhere the 'fallacy of misplaced concreteness.' . . . The other form of overstatement consists in a false estimate of logical procedure in respect to certainty, and in respect to premises" (Whitehead 1929/1978, 7–8). In many ways, this is very close to Kant's project of rejecting the dogmatic excesses of rationalism, but without adopting, in their place, a generalized (and eventually self-discrediting) skepticism. The difference, of course, is one of affect or temperament: Whitehead's genial and relaxed mode of critique is far removed from Kant's high seriousness and severity.

and when we are told that the grand narratives of modernity are dead (Lyotard 1984), and even that "we have never been modern" in the first place (Latour 1993). For, as Deleuze and Guattari suggest, "it may be that believing in this world, in this life, becomes our most difficult task, or the task of a mode of existence still to be discovered on our plane of immanence today" (Deleuze and Guattari 1994, 75). It is such a task, with the aim of converting ourselves to this kind of belief, that Whitehead envisions as "the use of philosophy," which is "to maintain an active novelty of fundamental ideas illuminating the social system" (Whitehead 1938/1968, 174).

3
Pulses of Emotion

Whitehead insists that "the basis of experience is emotional" (1933/1967, 176). In this chapter, I will work through Whitehead's "theory of feelings" (1929/1978, 219ff.), and show how this theory opens the way to an affect-based account of human (and not just human) experience. For Whitehead, the questions of how we feel, and what we feel, are more fundamental than the epistemological and hermeneutical questions that are the focus of most philosophy and criticism (including Kant's *Critiques*). This emphasis on feeling leads, in turn, to a new account of affect-laden subjectivity. Most broadly, Whitehead's affect theory places aesthetics—rather than ontology (Heidegger) or ethics (Levinas)—at the center of philosophical inquiry. Aesthetics is the mark of what Whitehead calls our *concern* for the world, and for entities in the world (1933/1967, 176).[1]

Whitehead characterizes his philosophy as taking the form of a "critique of pure feeling" (1929/1978, 113). As we have already seen, the reference to

---

1. In what follows, I will use the terms "feeling," "emotion," and "affect" pretty much interchangeably. This is in accordance with Whitehead's own usage. Nonetheless, I remain mindful of Brian Massumi's crucial distinction between *affect* and *emotion* (Massumi 2002, 27–28 and *passim*). For Massumi, affect is primary, nonconscious, asubjective or presubjective, asignifying, unqualified, and intensive, whereas emotion is derivative, conscious, qualified, and meaningful, a "content" that can be attributed to an already constituted subject. I think that this distinction is relevant for Whitehead as well, but he does not mark it terminologically. As I will argue, Whitehead's "feeling" largely coincides, in the first instance, with Massumi's "affect." Whitehead goes on, however, to give a genetic account of how, in "high-grade" organisms such as ourselves, something like "emotion" in Massumi's sense arises out of this more primordial sort of feeling.

Kant is by no means trivial or merely occasional. For Whitehead, the great accomplishment of Kant's Copernican Revolution in philosophy is its "conception of an act of experience as a constructive functioning" (156). That is to say, Whitehead credits Kant with originating philosophical constructivism.[2] Kant denies the possibility (or even the meaningfulness) of knowing "things in themselves," and points instead to the ways that we are always already constructively involved with whatever it is that we experience or observe. That is to say, Kant rejects the notion of representing, in our minds, a reality that would simply exist *out there*, by itself, independent of and prior to our experience of it. For our observation of the world, or of anything in the world, is a process that interacts with, intervenes in, and changes the nature of, whatever it is that we are observing. In this way, our subjective experience *of* the world is itself the reflexive process through which the world, including ourselves, gets constituted. For Whitehead, as for Kant, there is no possibility of knowing the world nonsubjectively or extraexperientially, *sub specie aeternitatis*. For "the whole universe consists of elements disclosed in the experiences of subjects," and nothing else (ibid., 166). As a constructivist, Whitehead is very

---

2. My sense of Whitehead as a constructivist philosopher comes from Isabelle Stengers' great book on Whitehead (Stengers 2002b). For Stengers, philosophical constructivism is nonfoundationalist: it rejects the notion that truth is already *there* in the world, or in the mind, independent of all experience and just waiting to be discovered. Instead, constructivism looks at how truths are *produced* within experience, through a variety of processes and practices. This does not mean that nothing is true, or that truth is *merely* subjective; rather, truth is always embodied in an actual process, and it cannot be disentangled from this process. Human subjectivity is one such process, but it is not the only one. Constructivism does not place human cognition at the center of everything, because the processes that produce and embody truth are not necessarily human ones. For Stengers, as for Bruno Latour (2005), the practices and processes that produce truth involve such "actors" as animals, viruses, rocks, weather systems, and neutrinos, as well as human beings. Constructivism also does not imply relativism; in a phrase that Stengers borrows from Deleuze and Guattari, constructivism posits "not a relativity of truth, but, on the contrary, a truth of the relative" (Stengers 2006, 170, citing Deleuze and Guattari 1994, 130). In insisting on the truth of the relative, and on nonhuman agents in the production of this truth, constructivism is ultimately a realism, in contrast to the anthropocentrism and antirealism of so much postmodern, and indeed post-Kantian, philosophy.

much a Kantian, or post-Kantian, thinker—rather than the pre-Kantian throwback that he is sometimes taken to be.

Even Kant's notorious doctrine of "things in themselves" is a consequence of his constructivism. For the very point of Kant's insistence upon the existence of "things in themselves" that we cannot know or describe, but whose unknowability and ungraspability we are nonetheless obliged to affirm, is that objects subsist beyond the limited and incomplete ways that we are able to grasp them. The given always exceeds our representations of it. Our constructions are always provisional and ongoing. Our thoughts and actions cannot shape the world all by themselves. Our mental processes or forms of representation are always limited, always compelled to confront their own limits.[3] Though Whitehead is not directly concerned with the question of limits, he similarly reminds us that no metaphysical system is ever complete. "In its turn every philosophy will suffer a deposition," he says—including his own (Whitehead 1929/1978, 7). More immediately, every prehension involves a particular selection—an "objectification" and an "abstraction" (160)—of the "data" that are being prehended. Something will always be missing, or

---

3. Kant refuses, as it were in advance, Hegel's intellectualizing move, which consists in shifting the ground "from epistemological obstacle to positive ontological condition," so that "our incomplete knowledge of the Thing [in itself] turns into a positive feature of the Thing which is in itself incomplete, inconsistent" (Žižek 2006, 27). For Hegel, Kant fails to see that, in positing limits, he is at the same time affirming the power of the mind, or Spirit, as that which performs this positing. But when Kant proclaims the limits of thought, he is precisely insisting on the radical exteriority of objects to the ways that we cognize them. He is not making an idealist claim about the supposed self-containment and perfection of things in themselves; rather, he is suggesting that even to posit things in themselves as radically incomplete and inconsistent is already to claim too much. Kant thereby disqualifies, in advance, the sort of self-aggrandizing, self-reflexive move that Hegel makes. The incompleteness of our understanding of the Thing cannot be posited as a feature of the Thing (in) itself. The limits of cognition cannot themselves be cognitivized. In positing limits in this radical sense, Kant opens the way (despite his own cognitive bias) toward a sense of relations that are precognitive and affective. But when Hegel transforms the pre- and noncognitive into negative cognition, and cognition of the negative, he leaves no room for affect. The relation of Kant to Hegel merits more extended discussion.

left out. There is nothing outside "experience as a constructive functioning"; but experience itself is always partial (in both senses of the word: *incomplete*, and *biased*).

Whitehead nonetheless criticizes Kant—as he criticizes other philosophers of the sixteenth through the eighteenth centuries—for exhibiting an "excess of subjectivity" (Whitehead 1929/1978, 15). Kant simply claims too much for the mind. He unduly privileges those particular sorts of abstraction that are peculiar to human beings and other "high-grade" organisms (172). According to Kant, our minds actively shape experience by structuring it according to what he calls the "concepts of understanding," or Categories. "There can be no doubt that all our cognition begins with experience," Kant writes. "But even though all our cognition starts *with* experience, that does not mean that all of it arises *from* experience" (Kant 1996, 43–44). For Kant, the Categories of the understanding cannot be *derived* from experience—even though they can only be legitimately applied *within* experience. In referring the Categories to "our *spontaneity* of cognition" (106), Kant in effect reaffirms the *cogito*: the Cartesian subject that is separated from, unconditioned by, and implicitly superior to the world that it only observes from a distance. Though Kant, in the "Paralogisms of Pure Reason," demolishes any substantive claims for the Cartesian ego, he nonetheless retains that ego in the ghostly form of the "transcendental unity of apperception" that accompanies every act of cognition. In this way, Kant risks limiting the scope of his own discovery of constructivism. "Experience as a constructive functioning" is reserved for rational beings alone. At the same time, those beings are not themselves vulnerable to the vagaries of such experience. Kant's subject both monopolizes experience, and exempts itself from immersion in that experience.

Whitehead, like many post-Kantians, rejects this exemption or separation.[4] For constructivism to be complete, the human or rational subject

---

4. As Deleuze puts it, the post-Kantians "demanded a principle which was not merely conditioning in relation to objects but was also truly genetic and productive. . . . They also condemned the survival, in Kant, of miraculous harmonies between terms that remain external to one another" (Deleuze 1983, 51–52). Deleuze, of course, credits Nietzsche as the thinker who most fully carried out this post-Kantian program. Whitehead shows little interest in Nietzsche, but he similarly radicalizes and revises Kant.

cannot be specially privileged. And the transcendental presuppositions of experience must themselves arise—immanently, contingently, and historically—from *within* experience. Even Kant's basic "form of intuition," Whitehead says, must be "derived from the actual world *qua datum*, and thus is not 'pure' in Kant's sense of that term" (Whitehead 1929/1978, 72). In line with this requirement, the transcendental presuppositions of experience must be processes, rather than fixed logical categories. And they cannot be attributed to the "spontaneity" of a subject that would already be in place. "For Kant," Whitehead says, "the process whereby there is experience is a process from subjectivity to apparent objectivity." But Whitehead's own philosophy "inverts this analysis, and explains the process as proceeding from objectivity to subjectivity" (ibid., 156). The subject emerges out of constructive experience, rather than being presupposed by it. Also, the "subjective unity" of any given act of experience does not preexist that experience, but is itself only produced in the course of its unfolding.[5] Whitehead thus replaces Kant's "transcendental idealism"—his "doctrine of the objective world as a construct from subjective experience" (ibid.)—with something more on the order of William James' "radical empiricism," or of what Deleuze will later call "transcendental empiricism."[6]

The important thing for Whitehead about Kantian "critique," therefore, is neither its determination of the limits of reason, nor its deduction of the concepts of understanding, but rather its constructivist account of the conditions of receptivity, or sensibility. That is to say, Whitehead rejects Kant's "Transcendental Logic," according to which "ordered experience is the result of schematization of modes of *thought*, concerning causation, substance, quality,

---

5. Whitehead, works this out in the form of what he calls "the Category of Subjective Unity" (1929/1978, 26, 223–225). More generally, all of Whitehead's Categories are "empirico-ideal" transformations of Kant's synthetic *a priori* notions. The entire question of "subjective unity" as a transcendental condition, and how Whitehead transforms it from a necessary presupposition into a "Categorial Obligation" (ibid., 26)—or what I would want to call a *postsupposition*—merits more extended discussion.

6. It is crucial to remember that, despite these critical revisions of Kant, Whitehead nonetheless maintains that "the order [from subjectivity to objectivity, or from objectivity to subjectivity] is immaterial in comparison with [Kant's] general idea" of experience as "constructive functioning," which is the really important thing (Whitehead 1929/1978, 156).

quantity" (Whitehead 1929/1978, 113). But he largely accepts the "Transcendental Aesthetic," in which Kant gives his "exposition" of space and time. This rendering of "the rules of sensibility as such" (Kant 1996, 107) is, for Whitehead, "a distorted fragment of what should have been [Kant's] main topic" (Whitehead 1929/1978, 113). Kant's great discovery in the "Transcendental Aesthetic" is that space and time are "constructs," in opposition to "the Newtonian 'absolute' theory of space-time" (Whitehead 1929/1978, 70–72); but also that space and time, *as* constructs, are acategorical and non-conceptual.[7] Space is "an a priori *intuition*, not a *concept*," Kant (1996, 79) reminds us. Time, similarly, "is not a discursive or, as it is called, universal concept; rather, it is a pure form of sensible intuition" (86). This is why time is "nothing but the form of inner sense . . . the formal a priori condition of all appearances generally" (88). Space and time are immanent conditions of sensible intuition: they indicate the *ways* in which we *receive* the "data" that objects provide to us, rather than being logical categories to which the objects providing such data are themselves compelled to conform. Because they are merely forms of reception, space and time are not adequate for cognition. Indeed, Kant says that space and time are "sources of cognition" (92), in that nothing can be cognized apart from them. But space and time still come *before* cognition; they are not in themselves enough to ground or authorize it.

This is why Kant, with his demand for adequate cognition, moves on from the "Transcendental Aesthetic" to the "Transcendental Logic." Kant's great mistake, according to Whitehead, is to accept Hume's founding assumption: a complete atomism of subjective sensations, or "the radical disconnection of impressions *qua data*" from one another (Whitehead 1929/1978, 113). For Hume, "the primary activity in the act of experience is the bare subjective entertainment of the datum, devoid of any subjective form of

---

7. Kant is often taken, even by Whitehead, as having sought to "save" Newtonian physics and Euclidean geometry by giving them an *a priori* grounding. But I agree with Kojin Karatani (2003, 63) that, in fact, "just the opposite is closer to the truth." As Karatani shows, the whole point behind Kant's discussion of time and space, and the mathematics of time and space, is to show that these are synthetic conditions, rather than analytic logical necessities, and hence that they actually need to be constructed, and cannot simply be taken for granted, or presupposed (ibid., 55–63).

reception" (157). Kant's aim, in the *Critique of Pure Reason*, is to avoid the skeptical consequences of this position. But Kant never questions the premise of starting out with the chaos of "*mere* sensation"; he only tries to show how this chaos can be ordered, and its elements connected, in a more satisfactory way than Hume was able to accomplish. Hume offers nothing but mere habit as an explanation for the basic stability of experience. In Kant's account in the "Transcendental Logic," the understanding, with its Categories, forcefully imposes a conceptual order on an otherwise disconnected and featureless flux of individual impressions. In resolving the matter in this way, Kant relies exclusively on "the higher of the human modes of functioning" and ignores the more "primitive types of experience" (113). He retains what Whitehead criticizes as "the overintellectualist bias prevalent among philosophers" (141).

By ordering experience as he does in the "Transcendental Logic," Kant remains within the tradition—stretching back at least to Aristotle—of what Gilbert Simondon calls *hylomorphism* (Simondon 2005, 45–60). This is the dualism of form and matter. Hylomorphism presumes that materiality, or the "sensible" (that which can be apprehended by the senses alone), is passive, inert, and intrinsically shapeless, and that it can only be organized by an intelligible form that is imposed upon it from outside, or from above. Simondon argues that hylomorphism, with its rigid dualism, ignores all the *intermediaries* that are at work in any actual process of formation or construction. In fact, matter is never entirely passive and inert, for it always contains incipient structures. Matter already contains distributions of energy, and potentials for being shaped in particular directions or ways. (It's easier to plane a piece of wood if you work in the direction of the grain, rather than across it—cf. Massumi 1992, 10.) For its part, form is never absolute, and never simply imposed from the outside, since it can only be effective to the extent that it is able to translate itself, by a process of "transduction," into one or another material. That is to say, form is energetic: it works by a series of transformations that transmit energy, and thereby "inform" matter, affecting it or modulating it in a process of exchange and communication. (The medium is the message, as Marshall McLuhan puts it; contrary to the hylomorphic assumptions of Shannon's theory of communication, no message, or formal structure, can be indifferent to the medium by and through which it is transmitted.)

In the Transcendental Aesthetic, in contrast to the Transcendental Logic, Kant does not altogther adhere to hylomorphism. He does indeed say that space and time are the "pure forms" of perception, and that "sensation as such is its matter" (Kant 1996, 95). But his discussion also bears the traces of a different logic, one that is more open to intermediaries. Because time and space are not categories or concepts, they do not relate to their objects in the way that the forms of logical intelligibility ("causation, substance, quality, quantity") do. They are not organizing principles actively imprinted upon an otherwise shapeless and disorganized matter. In Simondon's terminology, space and time are the media of a flexible, always-varying *modulation*, whereas the Categories are the principles of a rigid and always identical *molding* (Simondon 2005, 47).[8] Space and time have a certain flexibility, because they are modes of receptivity rather than spontaneity. Kant says that sensibility or receptivity "remains as different as day and night from cognition of the object in itself"; rather than being cognitive, sensibility has to do with "the appearance of something, and *the way we are affected by that something*" (Kant 1996, 96; italics added).

And that is the crucial point. Even though the "thing in itself" is unknowable, or uncognizable, nevertheless *it affects us*, in a particular way. And by conveying and expressing "the way we are affected," space and time establish immanent, noncognitive connections among objects, between the object and the subject, and between the subject and itself. These affective connections are intrinsic to the very course of any experience in space and time. Whitehead laments the fact that Kant "conceives his transcendental aesthetic to be the mere description of a subjective process" (Whitehead 1929/1978, 113) and reserves for the Transcendental Logic the more basic task of giving an account of the necessary conditions of all experience. But once we take the Transcendental Aesthetic in the more radical manner that Whitehead suggests, there is no problem of formlessness, or of disconnected, atomistic impressions;

---

8. As Deleuze—explicitly drawing on Simondon's terminology—puts it, traditional philosophy posits "a concept-object relation in which the concept is an active form, and the object a merely potential matter. It is a mold, a process of molding." But with Kant, thanks to his new treatment of time and space, everything changes: "The concept-object relation subsists in Kant, but it is doubled by the I-Self relation, which constitutes a modulation and no longer a mold" (Deleuze 1997, 30).

and therefore there is no need to impose the Categories of understanding from above, in order to give these impressions form, or to yoke them together. As Whitehead puts it, in such a *process of feeling* causality does not need to be established extrinsically, since "the datum includes its own interconnections" already (ibid.).

Understood in this way, Kant's Transcendental Aesthetic provides the basis for one of Whitehead's most important notions, that of "subjective form." In Whitehead's account, every prehension "consists of three factors: (a) the 'subject' which is prehending, namely, the actual entity in which that prehension is a concrete element; (b) the 'datum' which is prehended; (c) the 'subjective form' which is *how* that subject prehends that datum" (ibid., 23). Elsewhere, in another list of the same three factors, Whitehead defines subjective form as "the affective tone determining the effectiveness of that prehension in that occasion of experience" (1933/1967, 176). The first two of these factors—"subject," or "occasion of experience," and "datum" or "prehended object"—may stand in for the "subject" and "object" of traditional epistemology, though the parallels are not exact.[9] But the third factor, the *how* or the *affective tone*, is the really crucial one. Any given "datum," Whitehead says, is objective and entirely determinate. In itself, a datum is always the same. But this self-identity does not entirely determine, although it somewhat limits, the particular *way* in which a given entity receives (prehends or perceives) that datum. There is always some margin of indeterminacy, some room for "decision" (1929/1978, 43), with regard to "*how* that subject feels that objective datum" (221).

---

9. The differences include the fact that prehension is not necessarily conscious, and indeed most of the time is entirely unconscious; as well as the fact that the "subject" does not preexist its encounter with the "datum" or "object," but is only produced in the course of that encounter. In any encounter between entities, "subject and object are relative terms" (Whitehead 1933/1967, 176). Whitehead regards the "clear and distinct" perception privileged in seventeenth- and eighteenth-century epistemology as only a very special case of prehension, and not a typical one; generalizing from this case, as philosophers from Descartes through Kant tend to do, leads precisely to the sensationalist principle and the overvaluation of "the higher of the human modes of functioning."

This margin is what allows for *novelty*: "the essential novelty of a feeling attaches to its subjective form. The initial data, and even the nexus which is the objective datum, may have served other feelings with other subjects. But the subjective form is the immediate novelty; it is how *that* subject is feeling that objective datum" (Whitehead 1929/1978, 232). Every subjective form is different from every other; no subject feels a given datum in precisely the same manner as any other subject has done.[10] This means, among other things, that novelty is a function of *manner*, rather than of essence. The important question for Whitehead is not *what* something is, but *how* it is—or, more precisely, how it affects, and how it is affected by, other things. If Being is a substantive for the classical metaphysicians and a verb for Heidegger, then for Whitehead it is adverbial. "*How* an actual entity *becomes* constitutes *what* that actual entity *is*. . . . Its 'being' is constituted by its 'becoming' " (23).

This emphasis on "subjective form" as a manner of reception is what links Whitehead to Kant's Transcendental Aesthetic. For all that Kant privileges and foregrounds cognition, he is drawn into a movement that precedes it and that is irreducible to it. Time and space, the inner and outer forms of intuition, are modes of feeling *before* they are conditions for understanding. This follows from Kant's very definition of sensibility as "the capacity (a receptivity) to acquire presentations as a result of the way we are affected by objects"; Kant goes on to say that this is how "objects are *given* to us" (Kant 1996, 72). Whitehead retains a number of things from this formulation. First, there is Kant's insistence upon the sheer *givennness* of the external world, and upon the receptivity with which we encounter it. This parallels Whitehead's own

---

10. This is even the case when the "subjects" in question are successive instances of the same person or self. I do not feel a given datum in the same way that I did a minute ago, if only because the memory of my experience of a minute ago has added itself to what I am feeling now. This is what Whitehead means when he states that "no two actual entities originate from an identical universe; though the difference between the two universes only consists in some actual entities, included in one and not in the other" (1929/1978, 22–23). The difference between my universe of "between a tenth of a second and half a second ago" (Whitehead 1933/1967, 181) and my universe right now, in the present instant, is that my experience of the former is an "actual entity" that has been "objectified" and added to the "data" prehended by the latter.

insistence upon "stubborn fact which cannot be evaded" (1929/1978, 43), and "which at once limits and provides opportunity for the actual occasion" (129). Then, there is the fact that Kant phrases his account in terms of actual "objects," rather than in terms of sensa (Hume's bare sense impressions). This accords with Whitehead's appeal to "actual entities," or *res verae*, as the ultimate constituents of reality, and his insistence that the "ideas" of seventeenth- and eighteenth-century empiricism always already (despite the empiricists' own mentalist presuppositions) refer to "exterior things" (55), or are " 'determined' to particular existents" (138). Finally, there is Kant's implicit acknowledgment that these objects *affect* us, prior to any knowledge of them on our part, or to any formal process of cause and effect (since Kant only accounts for, or accepts, causality at a later stage, in his "deduction" of the Categories of understanding). This means that Kant, like Hume before him, implicitly (and in contradiction to his own premises) accepts the existence of relations of "inheritance" and influence, connecting entities to one another according to what Whitehead calls the mode of "causal efficacy" (168–183). In all these ways, Kant opens the door to Whitehead's "theory of feelings."

Through his analysis of "subjective form," Whitehead privileges feeling over understanding, and offers an account of experience that is affective rather than cognitive. Even if we restrict our focus, as Kant did, to "sensa" (qualia, the basic atoms of sense-perception in the mode of "presentational immediacy"), the "main characteristic" of these sensa "is their enormous emotional significance" (Whitehead 1933/1967, 215). The "affective tone" (176) that suffuses every experience of perception both determines and exceeds cognition. We do not first perceive what is before us, and then respond emotionally to these perceptions. Whitehead says that the order is rather the reverse. For "the direct information to be derived from sense-perception wholly concerns the functionings of the animal body" (215). Perception is first of all a matter of being affected bodily. Contact with the outside world strengthens or weakens the body, stimulates it or inhibits it, furthers or impairs its various functions. Every perception or prehension thus provokes the body into "adversion or aversion"—and this is already the "subjective form" of the prehension (Whitehead 1929/1978, 184). It is only later that (in "high-grade" organisms such as ourselves, at least) "the qualitative characters of affective tones inherent in the bodily functionings are transmuted into the characters of regions" in space (Whitehead 1933/1967, 215), so that sensa can be taken up into propositions and thereby be used to qualify (or to give us information about) objects of knowledge in the external world. We respond to things in the first place by feeling them; it is only afterward that we identify, and cognize, what it is that we are feeling.

Whitehead's account of perception as feeling is a refinement, and an extension, of William James's theory of the emotions. James claims "that we feel sorry because we cry, angry because we strike, afraid because we tremble, and not that we cry, strike, or tremble, because we are sorry, angry, or fearful, as the case may be" (James 1983, 1065–1066). Emotions do not cause bodily states; rather, the bodily states come first, and the emotions arise out of them. Strictly speaking, this is more an argument about expression than about causality. Our "perception" of an "exciting fact" takes the form of "bodily changes"; and "our feeling of the same changes as they occur *IS* the emotion" (1065). James's real point is not to reverse the order of causality, so that (contrary to what we usually think) the bodily state would be the cause and the mental state the effect. Rather, he asserts the *identity* of these conditions, in a radical monism of affect: "whatever moods, affections, and passions I have are in very truth constituted by, and made up of, those bodily changes which we ordinarily call their expression or consequence" (1068). There is no separating body from mind, or the (bodily) expression from what it (mentally) expresses. Perception is already, immediately,[11] an action/passion that takes the form of "bodily changes." The way that I receive a perception, or apprehend its "sensa," *is* the way that my body changes, or has changed. Perception or excitation, action or bodily changes, and emotion or response, are all one and the same event. It is only in subsequent reflection that we can separate them from one another (just as, for Whitehead, it is only in subsequent reflection, and by a process of abstraction, that we can separate the "subjective form" of a prehension from the datum being prehended, and both of these from the "actual entity" of which the prehension is a "concrete element").

---

11. "Immediately" here means in the same undecomposable present moment. Of course, James insists that such a "*present* moment of time," or what he prefers to call the "specious present," is never literally instantaneous, but always possesses a certain thickness of *duration* (James 1983, 573–574).

James describes emotion as a particular sort of experience. Whitehead radicalizes this argument, and expands its scope, by describing *all* experience as emotional. This includes bare sense-perception; it also includes modes of "experience" that are not conscious, and not necessarily human. Indeed, Whitehead's philosophy "attributes 'feeling' throughout the actual world" (1929/1978, 177). For Whitehead, "feelings" are identical with "positive prehensions" in general, which are all the ways in which entities interact with one another, or affect one another (220).[12] To feel something is to be affected by that something. And the *way* that the feeling entity is affected, or changed, is the very content of what it feels. Everything that happens in the universe is thus in some sense an episode of feeling: even the "actual occasions in so-called 'empty space' " discovered by modern physics (177). Of course, quantum fluctuations in the void do not involve anything like consciousness or sense-perception. But when we examine these fluctuations, "the influx of feeling with vague qualitative and 'vector' definition is what we find" (177). Overall, there is "a hierarchy of categories of feeling" (166), from the "wavelengths and vibrations" of subatomic physics (163) to the finest subtleties of human subjective experience. But in every case, phenomena are felt, and grasped as modes of feeling, before they can be cognized and categorized. In this way, Whitehead posits feeling as a basic condition of experience, much as Kant establishes space and time as transcendental conditions of sensibility.

This brings us back to the Transcendental Aesthetic. If time and space are the forms, respectively, of inner and outer intuition, then feeling is their common generative matrix. It is *by* the receptive act of feeling that I locate things in space and in time. In other words, feeling is the process by which all

---

12. To be more precise, Whitehead distinguishes between "physical prehensions," in which an actual entity feels, or interacts with, other actual entities, and "conceptual prehensions," in which an actual entity feels, or interacts with, "eternal objects" (potentialities, including qualities and concepts). And most prehensions are "hybrids" of both of these kinds. But in every case, a prehension is a process whereby an actual entity *feels* something.

There are also "negative prehensions," in which an actual entity *excludes* other entities (or eternal objects) from being felt, or from any such interaction. But Whitehead says that these "can be treated in their subordination to the positive prehensions" (1929/1978, 220).

entities get spatialized and temporalized. Whitehead thus agrees with Kant that "space represents no property whatever of any things in themselves" (Kant 1996, 81), and that "time is not something that is self-subsistent or that attaches to things as an objective determination" (87). Space and time are basic forms of affectivity; they cannot be preassumed, but need to be constructed in and through the process of experience. Whitehead is in accord, then, with Kant's contention that space "is the subjective condition of sensibility under which alone outer intuition is possible for us" (81), and that "time is nothing but the subjective condition under which alone any intuition can take place in us" (88). Whitehead's one crucial difference from Kant on this point is that, for Whitehead, such "subjective conditions" apply for all entities, and not just for human (rational) minds. Time and space are not epistemological necessities that we alone impose upon the world, but "subjective conditions" that all beings in the world effectively produce, in the course of their experiences.

In line with this assertion of the constructed, conditional nature of time and space, Whitehead denounces what he calls "the fallacy of simple location" (1929/1978, 137; citing 1925/1967, 49ff.). This fallacy consists in believing that a "bit of matter" can be located absolutely "in a definite finite region of space, and throughout a definite finite duration of time, apart from any essential reference of that bit of matter to other regions of space and to other durations of time" (1925/1967, 58). But so to posit "the individual independence of successive temporal occasions" (1929/1978, 137), and the correlative notion of "absolute places" in space (71), is to ignore the way that feeling is relational, and "essentially a transition" (221). Feeling always points from place to place; and feeling inherits from the past and projects toward the future. Through the process of feeling, different points in space "are united in the solidarity of one common world" (72). And every process of feeling produces time: both as the "perpetual perishing" of the entity that feels, and as "the origination of the present in conformity with the 'power' of the past" (210). This "power" of the past, which marks time as transition, and which forges relations from one point in space to another, is the force of *repetition*. Every "present" moment forcibly "inherits," and thereby repeats, what came before. "The notion of 'simple location' " is a fallacy, because it "is inconsistent with any admission of 'repetition,' " or of a time that intrinsically refers to another time (137). To establish a particular spacetime location is always, first of all, to affirm repetition, and thereby establish a difference by referring elsewhere and elsewhen, to other stretches of space and other periods of time.[13]

Actual entities, then, are not primordially located in space and ordered by time. Rather, spatial location and temporal sequence are themselves generated through the becoming of these actual entities. That is to say, an entity composes or creates itself by feeling the other entities that have influenced and informed it; and it feels them as being spatially and temporally distinct from itself. This self-distinguishing action of each new entity, and the consequent differentiation of time and space, is a necessary concomitant of the very process of feeling. Every "pulse of emotion" (Whitehead 1929/1978, 163) is both a fresh creation of spacetime and an immediate perishing, or "objectification." The "emotional continuity of past with present . . . is a basic element from which springs the self-creation of each temporal occasion. . . . How the past perishes is how the future becomes" (Whitehead 1933/1967, 238). It is only when an actual entity perishes—when it is no longer actively engaged in the process of feeling—that it is fully " 'spatialized,' to use Bergson's term" (1929/1978, 220; cf. 209). It is thereby fully temporalized as well, since "the atomization of the extensive continuum is also its temporalization" (72).[14] Only when a process of feeling has

---

13. For this account of time as "transition," I draw heavily on the discussion by Keith Robinson (2006, 74–77).

As for the idea that repetition produces newness, or difference, I am of course drawing it from Gilles Deleuze; repetition as difference is a central motif of his thought. However, Deleuze's sense of repetition as the affirmation of difference is developed mostly through his analysis of Nietzsche's eternal return, and seems to owe very little to Whitehead.

14. This latter development is something that Bergson would not accept, since he insists on time as the form of inner intuition, and on the absolute priority of such time over mere space. Whitehead's parallel between temporalization and spatialization follows from his endeavor to come to terms, more adequately than Bergson did, with Einsteinian relativity, and the consequent conceptual unity of spacetime. Though Whitehead says that his own idea of feeling "has . . . some kinship" with Bergson's "use of the term 'intuition' " (1929/1978, 41), he also objects that Bergson's notion of intuition is incomplete, since it "seems to abstract from the subjective form of emotion and purpose" (33).

completed itself and perished can it be circumscribed as a datum to be felt, "a definite fact with a date" (230).[15]

Under these conditions, every feeling is a " 'vector feeling,' that is to say, feeling from a beyond which is determinate and pointing to a beyond which is to be determined" (Whitehead 1929/1978, 163). In the material world, as it is described by modern (relativistic and quantum) physics, "all fundamental physical quantities are vector and not scalar" (177); "scalar quantities are constructs derivative from vector quantities" (212). The precedence of vectors over scalars, or of relational terms over atomistic ones, means that no point of spacetime can be isolated from the overall "physical electromagnetic field" (98), with its interplay of forces and its quantum interactions. This immanent connectedness, rather than any imposition from above of the Categories of the understanding, is the real basis for physical causality. In Whitehead's theory of feelings, correspondingly, "the crude aboriginal character of direct perception is inheritance. What is inherited is feeling-tone with evidence of its origin: in other words, vector feeling-tone" (119). Whitehead uses the language of vectors to speak about feelings, because he makes no essential distinction between physical causality (the way that one entity transmits energy or movement to another entity) on the one hand, and perception (the way

---

15. This is also the point at which, in Massumi's (2002) terms, impersonal "affect" has been captured and contained as a personal, psychological "emotion."

The whole question of Whitehead's theory of space and time requires a far lengthier, and more careful, exposition than I am able to give it here. In the present context, I only wish to emphasize how Whitehead, like Bergson, is the heir of what Deleuze calls Kant's revolutionary "reversal of the movement-time relationship," so that, instead of time being "subordinate to movement . . . it is now movement which is subordinate to time" (Deleuze 1984, vii). As a result, "time can no longer be defined by succession," and "space cannot be defined by coexistence" (viii). To the contrary, succession and coexistence can themselves only be understood as effects of the more fundamental, creative processes of temporalization and spatialization. Under Kant's new conceptualization, "time moves into the subject" as a force of affecting and being-affected (ix). This is how the Transcendental Aesthetic provides a basis for Whitehead's doctrine of feeling. When Whitehead attributes temporalization and spatialization to a prior movement of "feeling," he is expanding on, and radicalizing, Kant's own claim that sensible intuition is non- or precognitive.

that one entity feels, and responds to, another entity) on the other. To say that entity A is the cause of entity B as effect is also to say that entity B prehends entity A. Even mechanistic (and quantum-mechanistic) interactions are feelings, according to Whitehead; and even the most "simple physical feeling" is at once both "an act of perception" and "an act of causation" (236). The "emotional feeling" with which we receive sensa like color is not fundamentally different in kind from the manner in which subatomic particles relate to one another; it is only much broader in scope (163). Feeling, as such, is the primordial form of all relation and all communication.

To summarize, feeling can be conceived as vector transmission, as reference, and as repetition. These three determinations are closely intertwined. Every feeling involves a reference to another feeling. But reference moves along the line of the vector. Feeling as reference is a transmission through space, a direction of movement as well as a magnitude. This transmission is also a production of time. In the vector, time has a direction: the arrow of time is always moving from the already determined to the not-yet-determined and the to-be-determined. The feeling entity is "conditioned" by, or is an "effect" of, all the other entities that it feels (Whitehead 1929/1978, 236); and this entity, in turn, becomes a condition, or a cause, for whatever subsequent entities feel it in their own ways. Every entity thus "conforms to the data" that it receives from the past, "in that it feels the data" (85). But in the act of feeling its data, every entity also selects among, shapes, and alters these data, until it reaches a final determination. In so doing, it offers itself to be felt by other entities in its own turn, so that it is "referent beyond itself" (72). The "objectification" of the entity, once it has been completely determined, allows for its repetition. And this repetition is the key to the future as well as to the past; for every new process of becoming "involves *repetition* transformed into *novel immediacy*" (137).

An act of feeling is an encounter—a contingent event, an opening to the outside—rather than an intrinsic, predetermined relationship. And feeling changes whatever it encounters, even in the very act of "conforming" to it. That is why feeling is irreducible to cognition. It isn't anything that we already know. The problem with cognitive theories of mind, and with hermeneutical modes of interpretation, is that they reduce the unknown to the already known, the already determined. These theories assume that my not-knowing is only a contingency for myself, that ignorance is a particular state that I am in; they imagine that the object I am seeking to know is in itself already perfectly determinate, if only I *could* come to know it. They thereby elide "experience as a constructive functioning," and restrict their attention to that which has already been experienced and constructed. They only get half the picture; they trace the vector backward into the past, but not forward into the future. They grasp the actual, but miss the potential, the yet-to-be. They appreciate "conformity of feeling," but ignore deviation and novelty. They analyze whatever has already been felt, selected, and determined; but they miss the very process of selection and determination, which is feeling itself.

All this might sound like the sheerest romantic blather, the sort of naive protest of Life against Intellect, and Feeling against Thought, that decades of modernist critical theory, and postmodernist deconstruction, have taught us to distrust. But I want to insist that it is, rather, a rigorous expression of Whitehead's "critique of pure feeling," and of his conversion of Kant from transcendental idealism to transcendental empiricism. The process of this conversion is twofold. First, Whitehead recasts Kant's Transcendental Aesthetic so that the intuition of space and time is "not productive of the ordered world, but derivative from it" (Whitehead 1929/1978, 72). And second, Whitehead extends the scope of the Transcendental Aesthetic so that it also includes all those operations—like relations of causality—that Kant assigned to the Transcendental Logic. This means that, far from exalting anything like a sentimental cult of spontaneous feeling, or a Romantic theory of the creative imagination, Whitehead eliminates Kant's notion of spontaneity altogether. For Kant, "our *spontaneity* of cognition," or understanding, "is our ability to *think* the object of sensible intuition" (Kant 1996, 106–107), which is something entirely separate from the intuition itself. Whitehead rejects this dualism; he insists (against both Hume and Kant, but in accordance with certain suggestions that he finds in Locke) that the mere reception of sense impressions already implicates the fact that these impressions are "determine[d] to this or that particular existence" (1929/1978, 138). Whitehead thus refers all experience, thought included, to a process of being affected, a process located *within* what Kant calls the receptivity of sensible intuition.[16]

---

16. In this sense, "the receptivity of sensible intuition" includes, not just physical prehensions, or prehensions of actual entities (sensible data), but also what Whitehead calls "conceptual

Action, then, cannot be opposed to passive reception, in the way that traditional metaphysics opposes form to matter, or mind to body, or essence to accident. It is rather that activity, no less than passivity, is a dimension of receptivity itself. Every experience, every feeling, is at one and the same time an "inheritance" from the past and a fresh creation. And both of these dimensions are contained within an open affectivity. "The separation of the emotional experience from the presentational intuition," a separation that Kant presupposes, and that is necessary for cognition, is in fact quite rare, since it is only "a high abstraction of thought" (Whitehead 1929/1978, 162–163). More generally, there is a continuum from primordial, entirely "conformal feelings," to later, or higher, stages of "supplementary feeling." In conformal feeling, "the *how* of feeling reproduces what is felt," so that it "merely transforms the objective content into subjective feelings." Supplemental feelings, to the contrary, actively involve "the subjective appropriation of the objective data" (164–165). That is to say, supplemental feelings may alter the data, or wish to alter the data, or deny the data, or compare and contrast the given data with other (remembered or imagined) data, or self-reflexively respond to the first, conformal responses to the data—and so on, almost *ad infinitum*.[17]

---

prehensions," or prehensions of "eternal objects" (concepts and mere potentialities—see Whitehead 1929/1978, 23). In every act of sensation, perception, or prehension, "in some sense one actual existent repeats itself in another actual existent, so that in the analysis of the latter existent a component 'determined to' the former existent is discoverable" (139). This renders Kant's Transcendental Logic superfluous; everything that Kant wants it to accomplish has already been performed on the basis of the operations of the Transcendental Analytic.

17. Negation (denying the data) has its place within the many forms of supplemental feeling. Whitehead even gives negation an especially important place, arguing that "the general case of conscious perception is the negative perception," that more generally "consciousness is the feeling of negation," and that it is through negation that consciousness "finally rises to the peak of free imagination" (1929/1978, 161). In this way, Whitehead recognizes and acknowledges the role of Hegelian negativity. Nonetheless, negation remains a kind of feeling, and a rarefied and uncommon one at that. For Whitehead, the Hegelian tradition indulges in exaggeration and "overstatement," the vice of all philosophy (7–8), when it puts negation at the heart of being and treats the logic of negation as a cognitive principle, rather than attending to its emotional roots and emotional force.

But all of these are still forms of receptivity, still ways of feeling the data. There is no point at which we pass from receptivity to spontaneity, from relational response to pure originality, or from emotion to "clear and distinct" cognition. Even the most complex and reflexive modes of thought are still instances of supplemental feeling. As such, they continue to "involve essential compatibility" with the initial conformal feelings from which they arose, so that "the process exhibits an inevitable continuity of functioning" (165).

If feeling, rather than cognition, is the basis of all experience, and if "apart from the experiences of subjects there is nothing, nothing, nothing, bare nothingness" (Whitehead 1929/1978, 167), then the only way of organizing and ordering this experience must be an immanent one, from within subjective feeling itself. We know that, in fact, experience is not as chaotic as it would have to be if Hume's skeptical speculations were correct. Our experience always displays an immanent order; if anything, in fact, it has *too much* order. No Rimbaudian "dérèglement de tous les sens" is ever enough to disrupt it. Most traditional metaphysics is concerned with grounding the order of experience in "clear and distinct" cognition: as if, were it not for philosophy's strong guiding hand, everything would immediately break down. But Whitehead knows that such fears are baseless. Protecting rational order is not the problem. The real difficulty is how to *account for* the order, or the "essential compatibility," that continues to organize and regulate experience, no matter what we do to shake it up, and even in the absence of cognition. In other words, Whitehead is concerned with what today we would call "emergent order" or "self-organization." In rejecting Kant's Transcendental Logic as the source of this order, Whitehead is left only with his revised version of the Transcendental Aesthetic. Nothing else can provide an immanent principle, or criterion, for order within the boundaries of mere feeling.

This means that Whitehead's immanent criterion for order can only be an aesthetic one. Truth and understanding are not adequate to the task: feeling is more basic than cognition, and "it is more important that a proposition be interesting than that it be true" (Whitehead 1929/1978, 259; 1933/1967, 244). Indeed, "in itself, and apart from other factors, there seems to be no special importance about the truth-relation" (Whitehead 1933/1967, 265). These "other factors" that make truth "interesting" are, precisely, noncognitive feelings. Judgments of truth—or, as Whitehead prefers to call them, "propositions" or "theories"—are only important when they are felt, and to the extent that they are felt. In asserting this, Whitehead is very much a Jamesian pragmatist. The pragmatic test for truth is the interest that it sustains; "the primary function of theories is as a lure for feeling, thereby providing immediacy of enjoyment and purpose" (1929/1978, 184). Truth is finally a matter not of empirical verification, but of "enjoyment and purpose," or (to use Whitehead's more frequent term) "satisfaction." That is why "Beauty is a wider, and more fundamental, notion than Truth" (1933/1967, 265).[18]

In linking feeling to beauty, rather than subordinating it to truth, Whitehead unites the two senses of the word "aesthetic" that we find in Kant (and in the philosophical tradition more generally). On the one hand, the Transcendental Aesthetic has to do with sensation and the forms of sensibility; on the other hand, the Critique of Aesthetic Judgment in the *Third Critique* has to do with experiences of the beautiful and the sublime. Though Kant himself doesn't comment on the disparity between these two senses, other thinkers have found it problematic. As Deleuze puts it, "aesthetics suffers from a wrenching duality. On one hand, it designates the theory of sensibility as the form of possible experience; on the other hand, it designates the theory of art as the reflection of real experience. For these two meanings to be tied together, the conditions of experience in general must become conditions of real experience" (Deleuze 1990, 260). For Deleuze, such a transformation is accomplished in certain modernist art practices. In Joyce's *Finnegans Wake* and

---

18. It is important to point out, once again, that this means "not a relativity of truth, but, on the contrary, a truth of the relative." James's and Whitehead's pragmatism is not a slipshod relativism, but rather a claim about the *situatedness* of truth. A truth that is not "important," or not strongly felt, does not thereby cease to be true; and a false proposition doesn't become true, merely by virtue of being invested with intense feeling or great aesthetic appeal. An unimportant truth is just that: unimportant. But it may *become* important, if it is invested with feeling. And when a false proposition operates effectively as a "lure," so that it is invested with great feeling, one result may be the arousal of an "appetition" that works toward changing the world in order to *make* the proposition true. This is the very basis of change and creative advance: the "realization of what is not and may be" (Whitehead 1929/1978, 32).

Gombrowicz's *Cosmos*, among other works, "the conditions of real experience and the structures of the work of art are reunited" (261).[19]

But Whitehead unites the two senses of aesthetics without privileging modernist aesthetic experimentation in particular. This is because, for Whitehead as for Kant, the question of beauty pertains not just to the creation and reception of works of art, but to sensible experience more generally. The connection, unremarked by Kant, between the Transcendental Aesthetic and the Critique of Aesthetic Judgment is that acts of sensible intuition and judgments of beauty alike involve feelings that are receptive and not spontaneous, and for which there can be no adequate concepts. In both cases, there is a certain act of creative construction on the part of the subject; yet this construction is responsive to the given data, and cannot be described as arbitrarily imposed, or as merely subjective. Neither the attribution of time and space to phenomena, nor the attribution of beauty to phenomenal objects, can be justified on cognitive grounds. Yet both these attributions make universalizing claims that have to be taken seriously.

Whitehead emphasizes these continuities between the two senses of aesthetics. He notes that the creation of "subjective form," as an element in any act of sensible intuition, is already a proto-artistic process, involving as it does the selection, patterning, and intensification of sensory data. There is always already a "definite aesthetic attitude imposed by sense-perception" itself (Whitehead 1933/1967, 216). Even the most utilitarian, result- and action-oriented modes of perception nonetheless remain largely receptive,

---

19. Elsewhere, Deleuze states the same point slightly differently. Aesthetics is "divided into two irreducible domains: that of the theory of the sensible which captures only the real's conformity with possible experience; and that of the theory of the beautiful, which deals with the reality of the real insofar as it is thought. Everything changes once we determine the conditions of real experience, which are not larger than the conditioned and which differ in kind from the categories: the two senses of the aesthetic become one, to the point where the being of the sensible reveals itself in the work of art, while at the same time the work of art appears as experimentation" (Deleuze 1994, 68). Here, the emphasis is less on specific modernist art practices than on the broader way in which philosophical constructivism—particularly the post-Kantian thought of Nietzsche and of Bergson—converts Kant's transcendental conditions of possibility into generative conditions of actualization.

and thereby involve a certain "affective tone" and a certain degree of aesthetic contemplation—and, Whitehead adds, "thus art is possible" (ibid.). In the process of feeling, "any part of experience can be beautiful," and "any system of things which in any wide sense is beautiful is to that extent justified in its existence" (265). Though it falls to Whitehead to make these immanent connections explicit, they are already there, implicitly, in Kant's own accounts of sensible reception and aesthetic judgment. It is only Kant's privileging of cognition over affect that leads to the "wrenching duality" deplored by Deleuze.

If "the basis of experience is emotional," then the culmination of experience—what Whitehead likes to call its "satisfaction"[20]—can only be aesthetic. This is the reason for Whitehead's outrageously hyperbolic claim that "the teleology of the Universe is directed to the production of Beauty" (Whitehead 1933/1967, 265). Whitehead defines Beauty as "the mutual adaptation of the several factors in an occasion of experience"; it is the "Harmony" of "patterned contrasts" in the subjective form of any such occasion. The purpose of such "patterned contrasts" is to increase, as much as possible, the experience's "intensity of feeling" (252). Such a building-up of intensity through contrast is the basic principle of Whitehead's aesthetics, applying to all entities in the universe. At the low end of the scale, even the most rudimentary "pulses of emotion" (like the vibrations of subatomic particles) exhibit a "primitive provision of width for contrast" (Whitehead 1929/1978, 163). And at the highest end, even God is basically an aesthete. "God is indifferent alike to preservation and to novelty," Whitehead says. "God's purpose in the creative advance is the evocation of intensities" (105). Whitehead's

---

20. Whitehead uses "satisfaction" as a technical term. He defines it as the "final unity" of any actual occasion or experience, "the culmination of the concrescence into a completely determinate matter of fact" (Whitehead 1929/1978, 212). "Satisfaction" evidently does not mean that an experience has turned out happily, or favorably, or unfrustratingly, but just that the process of experiencing has terminated, and now only subsists as a "stubborn fact," or a "datum," for other experiences to prehend in their own turns. In the present context, the crucial point is that the same movement that transforms an affective encounter into an objectively cognizable state of affairs also, and simultaneously, offers up that state of affairs as an object for aesthetic contemplation.

overall principle of "creative advance," his "Category of the Ultimate" underlying all being (21), has nothing to do with Victorian notions of moral and political improvement, nor with the capitalist ideal of endless accumulation. Creative advance is rather an intensive, qualitative, and aesthetic drive for "depth of satisfaction" (93, 110). Emotions are intensified, and experiences made richer, when incompatibilities, instead of being excluded (negatively prehended), are transformed into contrasts that can be positively integrated within a greater "complexity of order" (100). But this process is not a tranquil or banally positive one, and Whitehead certainly does not regard "order" as an intrinsic good. The "patterned contrasts" must not be too tastefully arranged. Creative advance is stifled by any sort of static perfection. It demands, rather, the impetus for renewal that comes from "the emotional experience of aesthetic destruction" (Whitehead 1933/1967, 256–257). Whitehead always reminds us that "it is the business of the future to be dangerous" (1925/1967, 207); his aesthetics of feeling is both an expression of this danger, and the best means we have for coming to grips with it.

4
Interstitial Life

Both Whitehead and Deleuze place creativity, novelty, innovation, and the new at the center of metaphysical speculation. These concepts (or at least these words) are so familiar to us today—familiar, perhaps, to the point of nausea—that it is difficult to grasp how radical a rupture they mark in the history of Western thought. In fact, the valorization of change and novelty, which we so take for granted today, is itself a novelty of relatively recent origin. Philosophy from Plato to Heidegger is largely oriented toward *anamnesis* (reminiscence) and *aletheia* (unforgetting), toward origins and foundations, toward the past rather than the future. Whitehead breaks with this tradition when he designates the "production of novelty" as an "ultimate notion," or "ultimate metaphysical principle" (1929/1978, 21). This means that the new is one of those fundamental concepts that "are incapable of analysis in terms of factors more far-reaching than themselves" (Whitehead 1938/1968, 1). Deleuze similarly insists that the new is a value in itself: "the new, with its power of beginning and beginning again, remains forever new." There is "a difference . . . both formal and in kind" between the genuinely new and that which is customary and established (Deleuze 1994, 136). Deleuze and Guattari therefore say that "the object of philosophy is to create concepts that are always new" (Deleuze and Guattari 1994, 5). Philosophical concepts are not for all time; they are not given in advance, and they "are not waiting for us ready-made, like heavenly bodies." Instead, they must always be "invented, fabricated, or rather created" afresh; "philosophers must distrust . . . those concepts they did not create themselves" (5–6). For both Whitehead and Deleuze, novelty is the highest criterion for thought; even truth depends on novelty and creativity, rather than the reverse. As for creativity itself, it appears "that Whitehead actually coined the term—*our* term, still the preferred currency of exchange among literature, science, and the arts . . . a term that quickly became so popular, so omnipresent, that its invention within living memory, and by Alfred North Whitehead of all people, quickly became occluded" (Meyer 2005, 2–3).

What is the meaning, and what is the import, of our belief in creativity today? How does the new enter into the world? And how does the valuation of the new enter into thought? Deleuze explicitly invokes Nietzsche's call for a "revaluation of all values," and for the continual "creation of new values" (Deleuze 1994, 136). And Whitehead and Deleuze alike are inspired by Bergson's insistence that "life . . . is invention, is unceasing creation" (Bergson 2005, 27). But the real turning point comes a century before Bergson and Nietzsche, in Kant's "Copernican revolution" in philosophy. Kant himself does not explicitly value the new, but he makes such a valuation (or revaluation) thinkable for the first time. He does this by shifting the focus of philosophy from questions of essence ("what is it?") to questions of manner ("how is it possible?").[1] Kant rejects the quest for an absolute determination of being: this is an unfulfillable, and indeed a meaningless, task. Instead, he seeks to define the necessary conditions—or what today we would call the structural presuppositions—for the existence of whatever there is, in all its variety and mutability. That is to say, Kant warns us that we cannot think beyond the conditions, or limits of thought, that he establishes. But he also tells us that, once these conditions are given, the contents of appearance cannot be further prescribed. The *ways* in which things appear are limited, but appearances themselves are not. They cannot be known in advance, but must be encountered in the course of experience. This means that experience is always able to surprise us. Our categories are never definitive or all-inclusive. Kant's argument against metaphysical dogmatism, which both Whitehead and Deleuze endorse, entails that being always remains open. "The whole is neither given nor giveable . . . because it is the Open, and because its nature is to change constantly, or to give rise to something new, in short, to endure" (Deleuze 1986, 9). "Creative advance into novelty" (Whitehead 1929/1978, 222) is always possible, always about to happen.

---

1. Whitehead disparagingly remarks that, in philosophy since the eighteenth century, "the question, What *do* we know?, has been transformed into the question, What *can* we know? This latter question has been dogmatically solved by the presupposition that all knowledge

This also means that the *diversity* of the given (or of what Kant calls "sensible intuition") is irreducible. Diversity is always preserved as such in Kant's critical philosophy, even though it is *also* gathered into One under the rubric of what Kant calls the "transcendental unity of apperception." When Kant says that "the *I think* must be *capable* of accompanying all my presentations" (1996, 177), he is arguing against both Descartes and Hume. Hume mocks the Cartesian *cogito*, remarking that "when I enter most intimately into what I call *myself*, I always stumble on some particular perception or other," but never find an underlying "self" in addition to these particular perceptions (Hume 1978, 252). Kant follows Hume in rejecting the Cartesian ego as a substantial entity; but he insists, against Hume, that unity must be retained as a form, or as an organizing principle. If our perceptions were really as chaotic and unrelated to one another as Hume claims, then we would not be able to have anything like *experience* at all. It is only when every element of a multiplicity of perceptions is accompanied by an *I think*—or, more precisely, only when every element of this multiplicity is at least *capable* of being so accompanied—that it is even possible to think these perceptions *as* a multiplicity, or as what Kant calls the "manifold" of intuition.

---

starts from the consciousness of spatio-temporal patterns of such sense percepta" (1938/1968, 74). This is evidently a direct criticism of Kant and of nearly all post-Kantian philosophy. Whitehead deplores the way that Kant shifts the focus of philosophy from ontological questions to epistemological ones. But his greatest objection is to what he sees as the "dogmatic" way that Kant resolves the question of what we can know, by retaining his predecessors' restriction of experience to the realm of "presentational immediacy."

I want to suggest, however, that Kant's epochal shift of focus—from "do" to "can"—should *also* be read as a widening and enabling move. Since it does not preempt the empirical but meets it halfway, it opens a place for potentiality, and thereby for a Bergsonian open future, one that is not already predetermined by the past. To ask "how is it possible?" is to focus on *manner* instead of on *essence*. Kant implicitly does what Leibniz before him and Whitehead after him do explicitly: he invents a *mannerism* in philosophy, a way of thinking "that is opposed to the essentialism first of Aristotle and then of Descartes" (Deleuze 1993, 53). Both Whitehead and Deleuze may be seen as reviving Leibniz's mannerist project, in a world where Kantian critique has disallowed what Whitehead calls the "audacious fudge" of Leibniz's theodicy (Whitehead 1929/1978, 47).

Whitehead radicalizes Kant's argument about the manifold. Just as Kant insists on the formal unification of the sensible manifold in the transcendental unity of apperception, so Whitehead—with his "Categoreal Obligations" of Subjective Unity, Subjective Harmony, Subjective Intensity, and Freedom and Determination—insists on the formal unification of diverse data, and multiple prehensions, in every entity's concrescence or final satisfaction (1929/1978, 26–27). During a process of becoming, the prehended data are "unintegrated," or not yet integrated; but they are at least "compatible for integration" (26: Category of Subjective Unity). The integration finally happens when the process is done. Multiple prehensions are combined or coordinated by their "adaptation" to a particular "subjective aim"—even though this "aim" does not preexist, but itself only emerges in the course of the "adaptation." The process is circular and autotelic. It is not guided by any external criteria. Rather, we may say that the "subjective aim" that defines an entity's manner of being is, first of all, a principle of selection, and an act of self-selection. Each actual occasion selects among the data that it encounters, and thereby creates itself, establishing its own immanent criteria for a "preestablished harmony" of experience (27: Category of Subjective Harmony). These criteria are aesthetic, rather than logical; what is *aimed at* in the "subjective aim" is not mere compatibility, or noncontradiction, but a positive "intensity of feeling" (27: Category of Subjective Intensity). In this way, "the concrescence of each individual actual entity is internally determined and is externally free" (27: Category of Freedom and Determination). It is self-generated and self-unified; but it is also open to contingency.

Whitehead differs from Kant in seeing subjective unity as an ongoing process, rather than as a fixed form, and in describing this process as a matter of feeling, rather than as one of thinking. Also, Whitehead posits unity as an "obligation," a demand that always needs to be fulfilled, rather than as an already existing condition. For Kant, the formal unity of the subject is given once and for all; for Whitehead, this unity has to be produced afresh at every moment—since the subject itself must be produced afresh at every moment. This means that subjective unity is not the framework of experience (as it is for Kant), but rather a necessary *consequence* of experience. And that is what opens the door to novelty. Every achievement of unity is something that has never existed before: something different, something radically new. "An actual occasion is a novel entity diverse from any entity in the 'many' which it unifies.... The ultimate metaphysical principle is the advance from disjunction to conjunction, creating a novel entity other than the entities given in disjunction.... The many become one, and are increased by one" (Whitehead 1929/1978, 21). There is no permanent unity, but only a continual transition to unity. Whitehead thus *temporalizes* Kant's transcendental unity of apperception. The genesis of subjective unity in time is the continual production of novelty.

Whitehead—like Nietzsche and Bergson before him—denounces the way that, in traditional European philosophy, "changeless order is conceived as the final perfection, with the result that the historic universe is degraded to a status of partial reality, issuing into the notion of mere appearance" (Whitehead 1938/1968, 80). Kant would seem to be included within the scope of this criticism, insofar as he divides "things in themselves" from things as they appear to us. But although Kant does not quite abandon the old dualism of reality and appearance, at the very least he radically revalues it. For in the *Critique of Pure Reason*, the changeless real is dismissed as unattainable and unknowable, and therefore not a proper object of metaphysical speculation. In removing the noumenal realm from any possibility of cognition, Kant in effect endorses a version of Whitehead's "ontological principle," which asserts that "there is nothing that floats into the world from nowhere. Everything in the actual world is referable to some actual entity" (Whitehead 1929/1978, 244). In Kantian terms, this means that phenomena can only be referred to other phenomena—and not to noumena as (supposed) underlying causes. Everything that affects us, everything that *matters* to us, falls within the realm of mutable appearances.[2] In this way, even if he does not fully realize it, Kant makes it possible to think change, becoming,

---

2. What *matters*, or what makes a difference, is the important thing here. "Our enjoyment of actuality is a realization of worth, good or bad. It is a value experience. Its basic expression is—Have a care, here is something that matters! Yes—that is the best phrase—the primary glimmering of consciousness reveals something that matters" (Whitehead 1938/1968, 116). This may be compared to Gregory Bateson's famous definition of *information* as "a difference which makes a difference" (2000, 459).

and the emergence of the new, rather than subordinating them to "changeless order" or "static forms."[3]

Kant undermines the privilege of "changeless order" by introducing a new notion of time, one that reverses philosophical tradition. Before Kant, time was regarded as merely an external measurement of the relations among objects that did not fundamentally depend upon it. But with Kant, as Deleuze puts it, instead of time being the measure of movement, and thereby being "subordinate to movement . . . it is now movement which is subordinate to time" (Deleuze 1984, vii). It is only when time is not a mere measurement, but an inner principle of existence, that becoming is liberated from static being, and the new can be privileged over the eternal. It is only when time is no longer a mere quantitative measurement that it can take on the intensive form of what Bergson calls *duration*. Bergson tends to be highly critical of Kant; but Deleuze points out that, in fact, "Bergson is much closer to Kant than he himself thinks: Kant defined time as the form of interiority, in the sense that we are internal to time" (Deleuze 1989, 82). That is to say, when Kant defines time as the inner form of sensible intuition, he is not really saying that time is within us, or that time is something that we impose upon the world. He is saying, rather, that we are within time, and that our subjectivity can only be articulated in and through time. Once interiority has been temporalized, it cannot retain the static form of the Cartesian *cogito*.

---

3. Nietzsche, in his chapter "How the 'Real World' Finally Became a Fable: History of an Error," from *Twilight of the Idols* (1968, 20), distinguishes between the "Königsbergian" (Kantian) moment, with "the real world unattainable, unprovable, unpromisable, but the mere thought of it a consolation, an obligation, an imperative," and the subsequent "cock-crow of positivism" in which, because the "real world" is "unknowable," it is also no longer a source of "consolation, redemption, obligation." I am choosing instead to conflate these moments, both because it helps to show how Nietzsche, Whitehead, and Deleuze alike are drawing upon Kant to a greater extent than any of them is usually willing to admit, and because—as I discuss below—Kant's theory of morality, with its sense of "obligation," and its account of a double causality, has more force to it (even in Nietzschean terms) than Nietzsche is willing to acknowledge.

Kant thus unhinges time, or pulls it out of joint (Deleuze 1984, vii). For a time that actively articulates movement, rather than merely measuring it, cannot be divided into "durationless instants" (Whitehead 1938/1968, 146) or "instantaneous immobile sections" (Deleuze 1986, 3). It is no longer possible, after Kant, to maintain the Newtonian fiction of "the full reality of nature *at an instant*, in abstraction from any temporal duration and characterized as to its interrelations soley by the instantaneous distribution of matter in space" (Whitehead 1938/1968, 145). With his Copernican revolution, therefore, Kant starts down the path that culminates in the post-Newtonian physics of the twentieth century, for which, as Whitehead puts it, "process, activity, and change are the matter of fact. At an instant there is nothing. . . . Thus since there are no instants, conceived as simple primary entities, there is no nature at an instant. Thus all the interrelations of matters of fact must involve transition in their essence" (1938/1968, 146).

Of course, Kant's radical reconceptualization of time is compromised to the extent that he still privileges human subjectivity. His account of temporality only concerns the human or rational "I": the self that encounters, but keeps itself apart from, the phenomenal world. As Whitehead points out, Kant's "subjectivist position" is that "the temporal world [i]s merely experienced," and not actively entered into (Whitehead 1929/1978, 190). In fact, Whitehead himself "entirely accepts the subjectivist bias of modern [i.e. post-Kantian] philosophy" (166). Such an approach is the basis for his "rational scheme of cosmology in which a final reality is identified with acts of experience" (143). The problem with Kant, however, is that, "according to his form of the subjectivist doctrine, in the *Critique of Pure Reason*, no element in the temporal world [can] itself be an experient"—only the transcendental subject can be one (190). This means that Kant fails to push his Copernican revolution far enough. He resists the radical consequences of his own notions of temporality and experience. For if the phenomenal world is entirely temporal, and entirely a world of experience, then we should no longer say that it is "*merely* experienced" by a subject that remains outside it. Rather, the phenomenal world consists in the subjective experiences of all the entities that make it up. If "transition" is indeed universal, then duration, or primordial temporality, is the inner dimension of all entities in the universe—and not just of human subjects.

Whitehead, like Kant, rejects "the Newtonian 'absolute' theory of space-time" (Whitehead 1929/1978, 70), according to which time would be "self-subsistent . . . something that without there being an actual object would yet be actual" (Kant 1996, 87). Time is not given in advance; it needs to be effectively produced, or constructed, in the course of subjective experience. Whitehead radicalizes Kant's doctrine of time, however, by saying that such a special relationsip between subjectivity and time cannot apply to human or rational subjects alone. Rather, time is subjective only in the sense, and to the extent, that *every entity is a subject*. Whitehead thereby replaces Kant's "excess of subjectivity" (15) with what he calls the *reformed subjectivist principle*: "the way in which one actual entity is qualified by other actual entities is the 'experience' of the actual world enjoyed by that actual entity, as subject. . . . [T]he whole universe consists of elements disclosed in the analysis of the experiences of subjects" (166). Time is produced in and through experience; and experience, in turn, is implicitly temporal. But this circularity does not only apply to *us*. Taken in this expanded sense, Kant's Copernican revolution no longer puts human subjectivity at the center of everything. Rather—in better accord with the actual achievement of Copernicus—it decenters that subject. For subjectivity, in the first place, is not an exclusively human privilege. In the second place, it is a manner or formal principle, rather than anything substantial. And finally, subjectivity is decentered because it is itself subject to the very phenomenon that it produces: the inner passage of time.[4]

---

4. Kant's "Copernican revolution" is usually read as an assertion of what Quentin Meillassoux calls "correlationism": the theory that "affirms the indissoluble primacy of the relation between thought and its correlate over the metaphysical hypostatization or representalist reification of either term of the relation" (Brassier 2007, 18). Kant's thought would thus be anthropocentric; it would leave us with what Graham Harman calls "a single lonely rift between people and everything else." Even "the distinction between phenomena and noumena" is then "something endured by humans alone" (Harman 2007, 172). Meillassoux, Brassier, and Harman urge us to reject "this equation of being and thought," which "leaves us stranded in a human–world coupling" that is sterile and untenable (Harman 2007, 173).

My point is not to dispute this fairly evident reading of Kant. I merely wish to suggest that there are also other directions, other potentialities, to be found in Kant's *Critiques*. Kant's emphasis on conditions rather than essences can be separated from his anthropomorphism and

Kantian temporality, therefore, divides the self from itself. As Deleuze summarizes it, we must distinguish the I (*je*) "as an act which continually carries out a synthesis of time," from the Ego (*moi*) as a "constantly changing" entity within time. These two dimensions of the subject are "separated by the line of time which relates them to each other, but under the condition of a fundamental difference" (Deleuze 1984, viii). In the First Critique, subjectivity therefore has a double aspect. On the one hand, there is the "I" as an active process of determination; on the other hand, there is the "Ego" as something that is determined, from moment to moment, by this process. On one side, time is generated in the activity of the subject; on the other side, subjectivity is generated in and through the passage of time. The gap between these two sides is what makes novelty possible; or, to put the point more strongly, this gap *necessitates* creativity, by making it impossible for things to remain the same.

The doubling of the *je* and the *moi* is recapitulated, in the *Critique of Practical Reason*, in the form of a doubling between the subject as a rational being, whose will takes on the determining form of universal law, and the empirical subject, whose will is determined extrinsically and contingently.[5]

---

his "excess of subjectivity." Indeed, this is precisely what Whitehead does. Where Husserl and other phenomenologists continue to take correlationism for granted (Brassier 2007, 19; Harman 2007, 173), Whitehead rejects correlationism and anthropocentrism precisely by extending Kant's analyses of conditions of possibility, and of the generative role of time, to all entities in the universe, rather than confining them to the privileged realm of human beings, or of rational minds.

We might say much the same for Bergson. As Deleuze puts it, where Husserl seeks to overcome the "duality . . . of consciousness and thing" by asserting that "all consciousness is consciousness *of* something"—a move that leaves correlationism intact—Bergson more radically asserts that "all consciousness *is* something"—thus placing thought entirely within the phenomenal world, or within William James's single stream of experience, and thereby averting correlationist dualism altogether (Bergson 1986, 56).

5. I do not mean to conflate the "I" of the First Critique, the transcendental principle of temporal synthesis, with the "I" of the Second Critique, the noumenal self, or rational, legislating subject. These are, of course, entirely different entities. Rather, I am noting the *structural parallelism* between the two Critiques, in the way that they both posit a subject split between

The "*autonomy* of the will" is opposed to the "*heteronomy* of the power of choice" (Kant 2002, 48).[6] This opposition leads directly to the determination of moral laws as "principles that contain the determining basis of the will not by their matter but merely by their form" (40). If the moral law had any positive content, if it were anything more than "the pure form of universality," then it would be contingent rather than categorical, determined by its object rather than actively determining. Deleuze therefore says that "the law as empty form in the *Critique of Practical Reason* corresponds to time as pure form in the *Critique of Pure Reason*" (1984, x). In both Critiques, the determinate, empirical subject is separated from, and yet subjected to, a higher principle (a pure or empty form) that determines it. Kant attributes spontaneity or autonomy to this principle, thereby characterizing it as a (nonempirical) subject. But in both Critiques this principle corresponds to what, today, we would more likely regard as an impersonal, asubjective process of synthesis and subjectification.

This replacement of the form of the subject with the process of subjectification is a crucial move in post-Kantian thought. Deleuze often denounces the way that Kant "traces the so-called transcendental structures from the empirical acts of a psychological consciousness" (Deleuze 1994, 135). Such a "tracing of the transcendental from the empirical" (143) traps thought in a vicious circularity. The active force that is supposed to condition all possible experience is itself passively modeled on, and therefore in its own turn conditioned by, that experience. Subjectivity is preformed or prefigured, be-

---

active (productive, conditioning) and passive (receptive, conditioned) roles—even if these are not the "same" subject.

6. Kant's association of "choice" with the heteronomy of a will that has been extrinsically determined, and in opposition to an act of freedom, especially needs to be recalled today, given the current hegemony of neoliberal economics and "rational choice" political science. For these approaches, everything is, and ought to be, determined, by individuals making choices among various possibilities in a world of scarcity or limited resources. From a Kantian point of view, this sort of market-driven "choice" is absolutely incompatible with any genuine notion of freedom or autonomy. To put it a bit crudely, but not inaccurately, you can have consumerism and the "free market," or you can have democracy and self-determination, but you can't have both.

cause it is generated by something that has the form of the subject already. The problem with the Kantian transcendental subject is that it "retains the form of the person, of personal consciousness, and of subjective identity" (Deleuze 1990, 98). If this circularity were actually the case, nothing new could ever emerge. This is why Deleuze accuses Kant of misapprehending the "prodigious realm of the transcendental," even though this realm is Kant's own discovery (Deleuze 1994, 135). Kant describes the transcendental as something like a set of templates, preexisting conditions of possibility to which everything empirical must conform.

Deleuze "corrects" Kant, or converts him, by redefining the transcendental as the virtual, rather than as the merely possible. This means that the process of subjectification, or the force that impels this process, does not itself have the form of a subject. Rather, the virtual is what Deleuze calls "an impersonal and pre-individual transcendental field, which does not resemble the corresponding empirical fields. . . . This field can not be determined as that of a consciousness" (Deleuze 1990, 102). Deleuze, following Gilbert Simondon (2005), describes the transcendental as a field of potential energies in metastable equilibrium. These potentials can energize or "inform" a subject, but they do not determine its nature ahead of time. There is no resemblance, and hence no preformation. The subject cannot be given in advance; it must always emerge anew, in an unforeseeable way, as it is precipitated out of the metastable transcendental field. What's basic, for Simondon and Deleuze, is not the individual, but the always ongoing, and never complete or definitive, process of individuation.[7]

---

7. In chemistry and physics, "metastability" refers to a physical state that is stable, but just barely. Even a small disturbance will be enough to destabilize it. For instance, a supersaturated solution is metastable. Left to itself, it can persist indefinitely; but any perturbation will cause the dissolved substance to precipitate out of the solution. More generally, a metastable state is a state of tension, or "contradiction," full of potential energy that, given the right sort of push, will be discharged, causing a transformation. For Simondon, this is how the process of individuation takes place: the unleashing of potential energy, in a "preindividual" metastable state, leads to a process of emergence, as the formerly preindividual substance is divided into a more-or-less structured individual, on the one hand, and the milieu that supports it, out of which it emerges, and from which it distinguishes itself, on the other. But this process is never completed once and for all. Every individual is still metastable, rather than entirely stable, which is to say that it still

Evidently, there is no such theory of individuation in Kant. He accepts the figure of the subject as an already given form. Nonetheless, there are hints of a productive potentiality—going beyond mere conditions of possibility—in Kant's repeated doubling of this subject. For such doubling points to a *double causality* as well. In the Second Critique, the gap between the rational subject and the empirical subject corresponds to the distinction between "causality as freedom" and "causality as natural mechanism" (Kant 2002, 9). This distinction takes the form of an Antinomy: "The determination of the causality of beings . . . can never be unconditioned, and yet for every series of conditions there must necessarily be something unconditioned, and hence there must be a causality that determines itself entirely on its own" (69). The solution to the Antinomy is that physical, efficient causality always obtains in the phenomenal world, but "a freely acting cause" can be conceived as operating *at the same time*, to the extent that the phenomenal being who wills and acts is "also regarded as a noumenon" (67).

Kant poses a similar Antinomy in the "Critique of Teleological Judgment," the second half of the Third Critique. On the one hand, we *must* assume that the complex organization of living beings is "produced through the mere mechanism of nature"; indeed, no other explanation is possible. And yet, on the other hand, mechanistic determinism "cannot provide our cognitive

---

contains undischarged potential energy, still contains a degree of the preindividual, which is available for new transformations.

For a fuller treatment of Simondon's theory of individuation, and its relation both to the impasses of Kant's transcendental argument and to what I am calling Deleuze's correction or conversion of Kant, see Alberto Toscano's superb discussions in his book *The Theatre of Production* (2006). Toscano also finds a significant place for Whitehead, in the course of tracing the genealogy that runs from Kant's difficulties with the phenomena of living organisms and self-organizing systems to Deleuze's ontology of difference. However, I think that Toscano is too quick to dismiss the "teleology" present in Whitehead's notion of "subjective aim," and the "Platonic 'formalism' " of his theory of eternal objects (76–77), as well as his invocation of God (81–83). My own accounts of eternal objects in chapter 2, of decision and double causality in the present chapter, and of God in chapter 5, endeavor to show that all these elements of Whitehead's ontology remain vital and useful, rather than being the regressions to an outdated metaphysics that Toscano seemingly takes them to be.

power with a basis on which we could explain the production of organized beings." When we try to establish such a basis, we are *compelled* "to think a causality distinct from mechanism—viz., the causality of an (intelligent) world cause that acts according to purposes" (Kant 1987, 269). For "we cannot even think [living things] as organized beings without also thinking that they were produced intentionally" (281). We are unable to avoid the idea of purposive design, even though "we make no claim that this idea has reality" (269).[8]

In both the Second and the Third Critiques, then, Kant insists that linear, mechanistic causality is universally valid for all phenomena. But at the same time, he also proposes a second kind of causality, one that is purposive and freely willed. This second causality does not negate the first, and does not offer any exceptions to it. Rather, "freedom" and "purpose" exist *alongside* "natural mechanism": they are what Derrida would call *supplements* to it. According to the Second Critique, "nothing corresponding to [the morally good] can be found in any sensible intuition" (Kant 2002, 90); this is precisely why the moral law, or "causality as freedom," can only be a pure, empty form. The *content* of an action is *always* "pathological" or empirically determined, "dependen[t] on the natural law of following some impulse or inclination" (49). The second sort of causality, a free determination that operates according to moral law rather than natural law, may coexist with this "pathological" determination, but cannot suspend it. This is why Kant incessantly

---

8. Kant, of course, was writing long before Darwin. It is sometimes argued that Darwin's discovery of a naturalistic basis for the organized complexity of life—something that Kant considered impossible in principle (Kant 1987, 282–283)—entirely obviates the arguments of the "Critique of Teleological Reason." Yet the dichotomy Kant describes still exists in contemporary biology, even though its location has been displaced. Evolutionary biologists today are only able to explain an organism by speaking *as if* its features (eyes, or reproductive behaviors, or whatever) were purposive, even though they *know* that this purposiveness was never intended by any agency, but arose through the workings of natural selection. Kant is still correct in asserting that biologists must accept "the maxim that nothing in such a creature is *gratuitous*. . . . Indeed, they can no more give up that teleological principle than they can this universal physical principle" (256). Hardcore adaptationists are especially insistent that no features of an organism are gratuitous; their opponents (e.g., Gould, Goodwin, Kauffman) invoke teleology through their interest in emergent properties.

qualifies his affirmations of freedom, reminding us that "there is no intuition and hence no schema that can be laid at its basis for the sake of an application *in concreto*" (91), and that it is an "empty" concept theoretically speaking, which can be justified "for the sake not of the theoretical but merely of the practical use of reason" (75).

In the Third Critique, purposive (teleological) causality has a similarly ghostly, supplemental status. Kant says that "we do not actually *observe* purposes in nature as intentional ones, but merely add this concept [to nature's products] in our *thought*, as a guide for judgment in reflecting on these products" (Kant 1987, 282). Purpose, like freedom, is "a universal *regulative* principle" for coping with the universe (287); but we cannot apply it constitutively. The idea of "natural purpose" is only "a principle of reason for the power of judgment, not for the understanding" (289). That is to say, when we regard a given being as something that is alive, as an *organism*, we are rightly judging it to be an effectively purposive unity; but we do not thereby actually understand what impels it, or how it came to be. The understanding has to do with a one-way, "descending series" of "efficient causes," or "real causes." But judgment in terms of purposes invokes a nonlinear (both ascending and descending) series of "final causes," or "ideal causes" (251–252). The idea of purpose, or of final cause, involves a circular relation between parts and whole. The whole precedes the parts, in the sense that "the possibility of [a thing's] parts (as concerns both their existence and their form) must depend on their relation to the whole." But the parts also precede and produce the whole, insofar as they mutually determine, and adapt to, one another: "the parts of the thing combine into the unity of a whole because they are reciprocally cause and effect of their form" (252). An organism must therefore be regarded as "both an *organized* and a *self-organizing* being." It is both the passive effect of preceding, external causes, *and* something that is actively, immanently self-caused and self-generating. Only in this way can "the connection of *efficient causes* . . . at the same time be judged to be a *causation through final causes*" (253).

What Kant calls efficient causality is still the norm of reductionist science today. At the same time, Kant's account of final causes, or of teleological circularity and self-organization, lies at the root of most versions of dialectics, hermeneutics, and systems theory. What's most crucial to Kant's account, however, is the necessary coexistence of these two sorts of explanation, together with the irreducible distance between them. Efficient and final causality cannot be reconciled; nor is it possible to reduce one to the other, or to explain one away in terms of the other. Edward O. Wilson's "consilience" (Wilson 1999) is as dubious an ideal as any grand Hegelian scheme of unification. And indeed, atomistic reductionism and holistic systems theory alike propose schemas that are infinite in capacity and extent, but nonetheless fundamentally *closed*. No true novelty can emerge from the linear chain of cause and effect, when "all tangible phenomena, from the birth of stars to the workings of social institutions, are based on material processes that are ultimately reducible, however long and tortuous the sequences, to the laws of physics" (Wilson 1999, 291). But novelty is also excluded by what Niklas Luhmann calls the "operational closure" of any "self-referential system." For such a system can only be influenced from the outside to the extent that the external perturbation is coded as "information" in the system's own predefined terms. Luhmann rightly says that "such systems, which procure causality for themselves, can no longer be 'causally explained'" according to the mechanisms of linear, efficient causality (Luhmann 1996, 41). But these systems' autopoietic final causality also works to reproduce sameness and avert fundamental change. Can we imagine a form of self-organization that is not also one of self-preservation and self-reproduction? Kant opens up this question when he posits the Antinomy of the two kinds of causality.

Deleuze takes up this problem in *The Logic of Sense*, where he proposes his own version of "double causality" (Deleuze 1990, 94–99). Rather than referring directly to Kant, Deleuze reverts to what he describes as the ancient Stoics' "cleavage of the causal relation" (6). On the one hand, there is real, or physical, causality: causes relate to other causes in the depths of matter. This is the materialist realm of "bodies penetrating other bodies . . . of passions-bodies and of the infernal mixtures which they organize or submit to" (131). On the other hand, there is the idealized, or transcendental, "quasi-causality" of effects relating solely to other effects, on the surfaces of bodies or of things (6). This quasi-causality is "incorporeal . . . ideational or 'fictive,'" rather than actual and effective; it works, not to constrain things to a predetermined destiny, but to "assur[e] the full autonomy of the effect" (94–95). And this autonomy, this splitting of the causal relation, "preserve[s]" or "grounds freedom," liberating events from the destiny that weighs down upon them (6). An act is free, even though it is also causally determined, to the extent that the actor is able "to be the mime of what effectively occurs, to double the actualization with a counter-actualization, the identification with a distance" (161). That is to say, Deleuze's counter-actualizing "dancer," like the Kantian moral agent—and, as I will discuss shortly, like the Whiteheadian living occasion—makes a *decision* that supplements causal efficacy and remains irreducible to it, without actually violating it. This is what it means to preserve "the truth of the event," in its inexhaustible potentiality, from the catastrophe of "its inevitable actualization" (161).[9]

It is, however, Whitehead's treatment of the Antinomy of double causality that most directly addresses the problem of the new. Whitehead, no less than Kant, distinguishes between, and seeks to reconcile, efficient and final causes. These two modes of causality can be correlated, to a certain extent, with the two modes of perception recognized by Whitehead: causal efficacy and presentational immediacy. They can also be aligned with what Whitehead calls the "physical" and "mental" poles of any entity (Whitehead 1929/1978, 239). Efficient causality refers to the naturalistic chain of causes and effects, or the way that an entity inherits conditions and orientations from "the immortal past" (210). On this level, the causal dependency of a given entity upon its predecessors—its status as an *effect*—cannot be distinguished from that entity's prehension (its reception, or nonconscious perception) of those predecessors. "The problems of efficient causation and of knowledge receive a common explanation" (190). An entity *feels* its precursors, and is thereby both *affected* and *caused* by them. "All our physical relationships are made up of such simple physical feelings . . . the subjective

---

9. Strictly speaking, Deleuze differentiates Stoic double causality from what I am describing as a double causality of the Kantian sort. For with the Stoics (and in another way with the Epicureans) "one begins by splitting the causal relation, instead of distinguishing types of causality as Aristotle had done and as Kant would do" (Deleuze 1990, 6). I am arguing, however, for a more generous reading of Kant—one that is warranted by the overall pattern of Deleuze's borrowings from, and criticisms of, Kant. For one thing, Deleuze's adaptation of the Stoics can only be understood in terms of his overall post-Kantian framework; for another, Kant's very distinction between efficient and final causality is not merely a matter of categorization, but involves an Antinomy: the coexistence of two entirely different and irreconcilable logics. For, as Deleuze himself puts it, "this opposition between simple formal logic and transcendental logic cuts through the entire theory of sense" (1990, 96).

form of a physical feeling is re-enaction of the subjective form of the feeling felt. Thus the cause passes on its feeling to be reproduced by the new subject as its own, and yet as inseparable from the cause . . . the cause is objectively in the constitution of the effect" (237). Efficient causality is a passage, a transmission (210), an influence or a contagion. This objective inheritance constitutes the physical pole of the affected entity, its embodiment in a material universe.

However, as this process of causality-as-repetition unfolds, "the re-enaction is not perfect" (Whitehead 1929/1978, 237). There's always a glitch in the course of the "vector transmission" of energy and affect from past to present, or from cause to effect. There are at least two reasons for this. In the first place, nothing can ever purely and simply recur, because of the "cumulative character of time," its "irreversibility" (237). Every event, once it has taken place, adds itself to the past that weighs upon all subsequent events. No matter how precisely event B mimics event A, B will be different from A simply due to the "stubborn fact" that A has already taken place. The pastness of A—or what Whitehead calls its "objectification," or "objective immortality"—is a constitutive feature of B's world, a crucial part of the context in which B occurs. Thus, by the very fact that B repeats A, B's circumstances must be different from A's. "Time is cumulative as well as reproductive, and the cumulation of the many is not their reproduction as many" (238). The effect is subtly different from the cause whose impulsion it inherits, precisely to the extent that the effect prehends (or recognizes) the cause as an additional factor in the universe. Whitehead thus extends Leibniz's Principle of Indiscernibles. Not only can no two occasions ever be identical, but also "no two occasions can have identical actual worlds" (210).

In the second place, the causal reproduction of the past in the present is imperfect, because no inheritance, and no feeling, is entirely neutral. The "subjective form," as an element in the process of reception, differentially evaluates the data it receives, and thereby selects among these data.[10] Every prehension,

---

10. Or, more precisely, it selects not among the data themselves, which are simply given and "cannot be evaded" (Whitehead 1929/1978, 43), but among the "eternal objects" implicit in these data. By virtue of "a selection of relevant eternal objects . . . what is a datum from

every causal connection, involves a "valuation" on the part of the receiving entity: a valuation that does not just take the transmitted data as given, but "values [them] up or down" (Whitehead 1929/1978, 241). As a result, "the actual world [is] selectively appropriated" (233), according to the "qualities of joy and distaste, of adversion and of aversion, which attach integrally" to every experience (234). This affective response, with its selective and gradated "conceptual prehension" of the qualities (eternal objects) implicit in the data, constitutes the mental pole of the affected entity, its potential for change or novelty.

Whitehead insists that every entity is "essentially dipolar, with its physical and mental poles; and even the physical world cannot be properly understood without reference to its other side, which is the complex of mental operations" (1929/1978, 239). Every entity's simple physical feelings are supplemented by its conceptual feelings. Of course, these "mental operations," or conceptual feelings, "do not necessarily involve consciousness"; indeed, most of the time, consciousness is entirely absent. But in every occasion of experience, both physical and mental poles are present. This means that everything happens according to a double causality. A final (or teleological) cause is always at work, alongside the efficient (mechanistic) cause. If "transition [from the past] is the vehicle of the efficient cause," then concrescence, or the actual becoming of the entity—its orientation toward the future—"moves toward its final cause" (210). As with Kant, so too for Whitehead: the final cause does not suspend or interrupt the action of the efficient cause, but supervenes upon it, accompanies it, demands to be recognized alongside it. And once again, Whitehead radicalizes Kant by extending the scope of his "subjectivist"

---

without is transformed into a complete determination as a fact within" (154). The principle of this selection is the need for compatibility among the forms selected, as required by the Categories of Subjective Unity and Subjective Harmony. This means that Whitehead's criterion for selection is, like Kant's, an entirely *formal* one. The Categorical Imperative in the Second Critique has to do, not with the content of any action, but only with the question of whether the action can be generalized to the form of a universal law. Similarly, in the Third Critique, aesthetic judgment does not depend upon the actual feelings aroused by any object, but only upon the formal possibility for the universal communicability of those feelings. Whitehead's demand for compatibility or harmony is similarly a purely formal condition, without any particular predetermined contents.

arguments: they now apply, not just to human or rational beings, but to all entities in the universe.

For Whitehead, the final cause is the "decision" (1929/1978, 43) by means of which an actual entity becomes what it is. "However far the sphere of efficient causation be pushed in the determination of components of a concrescence . . . beyond the determination of these components there always remains the final reaction of the self-creative unity of the universe" (47). This "final reaction" is the way that "the many become one, and are increased by one" (21) in every new existence. The point is that " 'decided' conditions are never such as to banish freedom. They only qualify it. There is always a contingency left open for immediate decision" (284). This contingency, this opening, is the point of every entity's self-determining activity: its creative self-actualization or "self-production" (224). And this is how novelty enters the universe. The decision is always a singular one, unique to the entity whose "subjective aim" it is. It cannot be categorized or classified: for that would mean returning the decision to the already decided, to the efficient causes at the point of whose conjunction it arose.[11]

---

11. I think that Whitehead is already pointing here to a logic of singularity and universality, such as the one developed more explicitly by Deleuze. For Deleuze, singularities are acategorical: they cannot be categorized in any terms broader than their own. That is to say, they cannot be fitted into a hierarchy of species and genera, of the particular and the general; just as they cannot be derived as instances of any larger, more overarching and predetermining structure. But in their very uniqueness, singularities are thereby also universal. The singular directly touches the universal without the mediation of any intervening terms. The extreme concreteness of a singularity is also the mark of an extreme abstraction. The *thisness*, or what Deleuze and Guattari call the *haecceity* (1987, 260ff.), of an event is "universalized" in itself, as it is in all its details, rather than being subordinated to some vaguer or more general category.

An example might be helpful here. When Proust—an extremely important author for Deleuze—writes about jealousy, in his great novel, he is being at once universal and singular. Universal, because he isn't merely describing the narrator's feelings about Albertine. The book's analyses extend far beyond the psychology of particular characters in a particular situation. They make connections that reflect upon other characters and situations in the novel, and upon the reader's experiences outside the text, as well. The novel describes, enacts, or creates an abstract, universal portrait of jealousy: what I am tempted to call the transcendental

To be sure, much of the time, this decision or final cause is "negligible" in scope, and can safely be ignored (Whitehead 1929/1978, 115, 245). In many inorganic physical processes, the space of "contingency left open for immediate decision" is vanishingly small. Novelty is nearly nonexistent, and linear, efficient causality can explain (almost) everything. It is only in cases of higher-order emergence—processes that were mostly ignored by the physics of Whitehead's own time, but that are intensively studied today by chaos and complexity theory—that anything genuinely new is produced. "Deterministic chaos" is, like all empirical phenomena, entirely determined in principle (or, as Kant would say, "theoretically") by linear cause and effect. But since its development is sensitive to differences in initial conditions too slight to be measured, it is not actually determinable ahead of time pragmatically (or, as Kant

---

form of this emotion. At the same time, Proust's description remains highly contingent and limited: that is to say, singular. It is embedded in a thick constellation of concrete details and textures, having to do with the particularities of the book's characters, of their gender and social class and historical moment in France, and all the other aspects of their social setting. It is this sense of concrete embeddedness that most fully differentiates Proust's text from an essay in psychology. In short, Proust universalizes his description of the narrator's jealousy over Albertine, by abstracting it away from the merely anecdotal. But what he universalizes in this manner remains entirely singular and concrete. He doesn't generalize by leaving out details and anomalies; rather, it is only his exhaustive examination of all the anomalies and minutiae of the situation that makes the universalization possible. Proust plumbs the utmost depths of jealousy, all the more so because he examines it in and for itself, in its special circumstances, rather than placing it in relation to other emotions, or classifying it as an instance of some more widespread class of behaviors or feelings. Proust universalizes the singular, while rejecting any sort of generalization.

Whitehead never offers an explicit theory of singularity, in the way that Deleuze does. But I think that a similar logic is at work in his discussion of the decision made by every actual entity. This decision is always singular, because it is unique to the entity that makes it, and that circularly determines what it is by having made it. No general principles or rules can guide this decision, or circumscribe it. And yet the singular decision is also a universal one, because it is affected by everything that precedes it, and in turn affects everything that follows it. Every concrescence is a "conjunctive unity," gathering together the "disjunctive 'many' " (Whitehead 1929/1978, 21). It is a determination of the entire universe, reducing its

would say, "practically"). In these cases, linear, mechanistic causality is inadequate for the purposes of our understanding, and an explanation in terms of purpose, "subjective aim," or "decision" becomes necessary.[12]

The role of subjective "decision" becomes especially important—so that it can no longer be dismissed as "negligible"—when we get to those emergent processes of self-organization known as living things. It is precisely in the case of living entities that the recourse to efficient causes is most inadequate, and that "we require explanation by 'final cause' " instead (Whitehead 1929/1978, 104). Indeed, Whitehead defines "life" itself (to the extent that a concept with such fuzzy boundaries can be defined at all) as "the origination of conceptual novelty—novelty of appetition" (102). By "appetition," Whitehead means "a principle of unrest . . . an appetite towards a difference . . . something with a definite novelty" (32).[13] Most broadly, "appetition" has to do with the fact that "all physical experience is accompanied by an appetite for, or against, its

---

potentiality and multiplicity to the actuality of one "stubborn fact." This actuality has never existed before: it is an absolute novelty. As such, it reverts to being "one" rather than "everything": "it is a novel entity, disjunctively among the many entities which it synthesizes" (21). This is why Whitehead can describe the decision, or final cause, of an entity, both as the unique activity—"the absolute, individual self-enjoyment" (1938/1968, 150)—of that entity itself, and as "the final reaction of the self-creative unity of the universe" as a whole.

12. Though I have just said that an explanation in turns of final cause is required "for the purposes of our understanding," this should not be taken as merely the contingent result of our empirical ignorance or uncertainty. The difficulty is ontological, rather than epistemological. It is not just that our particular powers of observation are limited and that the quantity of information we happen to possess is finite. For any possible observer will be in the same situation. There *cannot be* a Laplacean God, or a supercomputer, that knows everything and that can trace all the lines of efficient causality for all the particles in the universe. Such a position of omnipotence is simply not possible. In Whitehead's terms, to posit such a position is to violate both the "ontological principle" (that everything actual must come from somewhere) and the "reformed subjectivist principle" (that everything actual must be disclosed in the experience of some actual subject). Even the actual entity Whitehead calls "God" is not omnipotent. He is also subject to these restrictions, and he cannot transcend them.

13. It is important to note that Whitehead uses "appetition" as a technical term. He warns us against the "danger which lurks in technical terms" of taking them according to their common meanings in ordinary language. In the case of "appetition," this can lead to the improper

continuance: an example is the appetition of self-preservation" (32). But experience becomes more complex when the appetition pushes beyond itself, and does not merely work toward the preservation and continuation of whatever already exists. This is precisely the case with living beings. When an entity displays "appetite toward a difference"—Whitehead gives the simple example of "thirst"—the initial physical experience is supplemented and expanded by a "novel conceptual prehension," an envisioning (or "envisagement"—34) of something that is not already given, not (yet) actual. Even "at a low level," such a process "shows the germ of a free imagination" (32).

This means that it is insufficient to interpret something like an animal's thirst, and its consequent behavior of searching for water, as merely a mechanism for maintaining (or returning to) a state of homeostatic equilibrium. "Appetition toward a difference" seeks transformation, not preservation. Life cannot be adequately defined in terms of concepts like Spinoza's *conatus*, or Maturana and Varela's *autopoiesis*. Rather, an entity is alive precisely to the extent that it envisions difference and thereby strives for something other than the mere continuation of what it already is. " 'Life' means novelty. . . . A single occasion is alive when the subjective aim which determines its process of concrescence has introduced a novelty of definiteness not to be found in the inherited data of its primary phase" (Whitehead 1929/1978, 104). Appetition is the "conceptual prehension," and then the making-definite, of something that has no prior existence in the "inherited data" (i.e., something that, prior to the appetition, was merely potential). But if life is appetition, then it cannot be understood as a matter of continuity or endurance (for things like stones endure much longer, and more successfully, than living things do), nor even in terms of response to stimulus (for "the mere response to stimulus is characteristic of all societies whether inorganic or alive"—104). Rather, life must be understood as a matter of "*originality* of response to stimulus" (emphasis added). Life is "a bid

---

anthropomorphization of a process that applies to all entities. The word also potentially "suggests a degrading notion of this basic activity in its more intense operations." Terms that are technically synonymous have different ranges of connotation in ordinary speech. This means that we must be particularly careful and attentive when using any of them (Whitehead 1929/1978, 32–33).

for freedom," and a process that "disturbs the inherited 'responsive' adjustment of subjective forms" (104). It happens "when there is intense experience without the shackle of reiteration from the past" (105). In sum, Whitehead maintains "the doctrine that an organism is 'alive' when in some measure its reactions are inexplicable by *any* tradition of pure physical inheritance" (104).

Of course, contemporary biology is not prone to speak of final causes, or to define life in the way that Whitehead does. According to the mainstream neo-Darwinian synthesis, "pure physical inheritance," when combined with occasional random mutation and the force of natural selection, is sufficient to account for biological variation. On this view, innovation and change are not primary processes, but adaptive reactions to environmental pressures. Life is essentially conservative: not oriented toward difference and novelty as Whitehead would have it, but organized for the purposes of self-preservation and self-reproduction. It is not a bid for freedom, but an inescapable compulsion. The image of a "life force" that we have today is not anything like Bergson's *élan vital*; it is rather a virus, a mindlessly, relentlessly self-replicating bit of DNA or RNA. Even the alternatives to the neo-Darwinian synthesis that are sometimes proposed today—like Maturana and Varela's theory of autopoiesis (1991), Stuart Kauffman's exploration of complexity and self-organizing systems (2000), Lynn Margulis's work on symbiosis (Margulis and Sagan 2002), James Lovelock's Gaia theory (2000), and Susan Oyama's developmental systems theory (2000)—share mainstream biology's overriding concern with the ways that organisms maintain homeostatic equilibrium in relation to their environment and strive to perpetuate themselves through reproduction. It would seem that organic beings only innovate when they are absolutely compelled to, and as it were in spite of themselves.

Nevertheless, when biologists actually look at the concrete behavior of living organisms, they encounter a somewhat different picture. For they continually discover the important role of "decision" in this behavior. And not only in the case of mammals and other "higher" animals. Even "bacteria are sensitive, communicative and decisive organisms . . . bacterial behaviour is highly flexible and involves complicated decision-making" (Devitt 2007). Slime molds can negotiate mazes and choose one path over another (Nakagaki, Yamada, and Toth 2000). Plants do not have brains or central nervous systems, but "decisions are made continually as plants grow," concerning such matters as the placement of roots, shoots, and leaves, and orientation with regard to sunlight (Trewavas 2005, 414). In the animal kingdom, even fruit flies exhibit "spontaneous behavior" that is nondeterministic, unpredictable, "nonlinear and unstable." This behavioral variability cannot be attributed to "residual deviations due to extrinsic random noise." Rather, it has an "intrinsic" origin: "spontaneity ('voluntariness') [is] a biological trait even in flies" (Maye et al. 2007). In sum, it would seem that *all* living organisms make decisions that are not causally programmed or predetermined. We must posit that "cognition is part of basic biological function, like respiration" (Devitt 2007, quoting Pamela Lyon). Indeed, there is good evidence that, in multicellular organisms, not only does the entire organism spontaneously generate novelty, but "each cell has a certain intelligence to make decisions on its own" (Albrecht-Buehler 1998).

Thus, biologists have come to see cognition, or "information processing," at work everywhere in the living world: "all organisms, including bacteria, the most primitive (fundamental) ones, must be able to sense the environment and perform internal information processing for thriving on latent information embedded in the complexity of their environment" (Ben Jacob, Shapira, and Tauber 2006, 496). Organisms would then make decisions—which are "free," in the sense that they are not preprogrammed, mechanistically forced, or determined in advance—in accordance with this cognitive processing. This fits quite well with Whitehead's account of "conceptual prehension" as the "valuation" (1929/1978, 240) of possibilities for change (33), the envisioning of "conditioned alternatives" that are then "reduced to coherence" (224). But it is getting things backward to see this whole process as the *result* of cognition or information processing. For "conceptual prehension" basically means "appetition" (33). It deals in abstract potentialities, and not just concrete actualities; but it is emotional, and desiring, before it is cognitive. Following Whitehead, we should say that it is the very act of *decision* (conceptual prehension, valuation in accordance with subjective aim, selection) that makes cognition possible—rather than cognition providing the grounds for decision. And this applies all the way from bacteria to human beings, for whom, as Whitehead puts it, "the final decision . . . constituting the ultimate modification of subjective aim, is the foundation of our experience of responsibility, of approbation or of disapprobation, of self-approval or of self-reproach, of freedom, of emphasis" (47). We don't make decisions because we are free and responsible; rather, we are free and responsible because—and precisely to the extent that—we make decisions.

Life itself is characterized by indeterminacy, nonclosure, and what Whitehead calls "spontaneity of conceptual reaction" (1929/1978, 105). It necessarily involves "a certain absoluteness of self-enjoyment," together with "self-creation," defined as "the transformation of the potential into the actual" (Whitehead 1938/1968, 150–151). All this does not imply any sort of mysticism or vitalism, however; it can be accounted for in wholly Darwinian terms. In fruit fly brains no less than in human ones, "the nonlinear processes underlying spontaneous behavior initiation have evolved to generate behavioral indeterminacy" (Maye et al. 2007, 6). That is to say, strict determinism no longer apples to living things, or rather it applies to them only to a limited extent, because "freedom," or the ability to generate indeterminacy, has itself been developed and elaborated in the course of evolution. As Morse Peckham speculated long ago, "randomness has a survival value. . . . The brain's potentiality for the production of random responses is evolutionarily selected for survival. As evolutionary development increases and more complex organisms come into existence, a result of that randomness, the brain's potentiality for randomness accumulates and increases with each emerging species" (1979, 165). The power of making an unguided and unforeseeable decision has proven to be evolutionarily adaptive. It has therefore been forwarded by natural selection. Some simple life processes can be regulated through preprogrammed behavior; but "more complex interactions require behavioral indeterminism" in order to be effective (Maye et al. 2007, 8). Organisms that remain inflexible tend to perish; the flexible ones survive by transforming themselves instead of merely perpetuating themselves. In this way, the "appetition of self-preservation" itself creates a counter-appetition for transformation and difference. Life has evolved so as to crave and to generate novelty.[14]

---

14. The implicit Whiteheadian reading of Darwin that I am proposing here can be compared with Nietzsche's explicit critique of Darwin. Under the heading *Anti-Darwin*, Nietzsche writes: "As regards the celebrated 'struggle for life,' it seems to me, in the meantime, to be more asserted than proved. It occurs, but only as an exception; the general aspect of life is *not* a state of want or hunger; it is a state of opulence, luxuriance, and even absurd prodigality,—where there is struggle, it is a struggle for *power*.—We must not confound Malthus with nature" (Nietzsche 1968, 46).

Such is Whitehead's version of double causality. We might summarize it by expanding Marx's famous maxim to apply to all organisms, and not just human beings: all organisms "make their own history, but they do not make it just as they please: they do not make it under circumstances chosen by themselves, but under circumstances directly encountered, given and transmitted from the past" (Marx 1968, 97). Whitehead reminds us again and again that we never simply transcend efficient causality. Every experience "is concerned with the givenness of the actual world, considered as the stubborn fact which at once limits and provides opportunity for the actual occasion.... We are governed by stubborn fact" (1929/1978, 129). We are impelled by the accumulation of the past, and by the deterministic processes arising out of that past. But at the same time, these deterministic processes themselves open up an ever-widening zone of indetermination. In this way, "efficient causation expresses the transition from actual entity to actual entity; and final causation expresses the internal

---

Whitehead concurs with Nietzsche in asserting that survival (or mere self-preservation) is secondary in relation to "power"—though the term Whitehead uses is "self-creation" (1929/1978, 85). This is arguably a major facet of what Nietzsche means by "power." Note that Whitehead explicitly defines "power" as a matter of "how each individual actual entity contributes to the datum *from which* its successors arise and *to which* they must conform" (56). This definition is drawn from Locke, rather than Nietzsche; but I think that it is largely compatible with the Spinozian–Nietzschean sense of "power" as a capacity to affect and to be affected.

Whitehead also maintains that struggle or competition in general (whether for power, or for mere survival), is secondary in relation to the *aesthetic* concerns of generosity, opulence, and prodigality, or what he calls "the evocation of intensities" (105). Again, this is arguably in accord with Nietzsche's position, since Nietzsche says only that power is more important than mere survival "where there is struggle"; overall, exuberance and prodigality remain more important.

Neither Nietzsche nor Whitehead denies the "causal efficacy" of natural selection; but they both argue for a supplemental, self-determining intensity of life that arises in the very course of this selection. Both Nietzsche and Whitehead point toward the phenomena of "biological exuberance" (Bagemihl 1999), involving the continuing production and proliferation of traits and variations that are not necessarily favored by, or explicable in terms of, natural selection alone.

process whereby the actual entity becomes itself. There is the becoming of the datum, which is to be found in the past of the world; and there is the becoming of the immediate self from the datum. . . . An actual entity is at once the product of the efficient past, and is also, in Spinoza's phrase, *causa sui*" (150).

Whitehead thus repeats Kant's assertion that a final cause ("causality as freedom") subsists alongside (or supplements) the efficient cause ("causality as natural mechanism"). But Whitehead attempts to naturalize Kant's distinction, to make it entirely immanent and phenomenal, without thereby effacing it. This is a tricky move, and one that "the popular positivistic philosophy" (Whitehead 1938/1968, 148) will not accept. For once the subject has been absorbed back into the phenomenal realm, there is no longer any Archimedean point for the exercise of freedom. How can a subject that is entirely determined by material causes also be said to freely determine itself? Whitehead's answer is to replace Kant's noumenal subject with a "subject-superject" that is both a producer and a bearer of novelty, and that expires in the very movement by which it comes into being. Creativity, or the Category of the Ultimate (Whitehead 1929/1978, 21), replaces the categorical imperative as the inner principle of freedom.[15] It remains the case, under this principle, that "whatever is determinable is determined" according to efficient causality; but at the same time "there is always a remainder for the decision of the subject-superject" (27–28). But rather than being noumenal or eternal, this decision or final cause is immanent to the phenomenal world. The entity that makes this decision, and that is determined by it, is evanescent or "perpetually perishing." It fades away before it can be caught within the chains of deterministic causality. Or more precisely, its so being caught *is* precisely the event of its "satisfaction" and passing-away. Thus "actual entities 'perpetually perish' subjectively, but are immortal objectively. Actuality in perishing acquires objectivity, while it loses

---

15. Whitehead says that "creativity is without a character of its own. . . . It cannot be characterized, because all characters are more special than itself." It is "always found under conditions, and described as conditioned"; but it does not intrisically possess any of these conditions (1929/1978, 31). In this way, creativity is neutral, and entirely formal, just like Kant's categorical imperative. Whitehead also equates creativity with appetition (32); in this way, too, it is parallel to Kant's determination of the categorical imperative as the highest form of the faculty of desire.

subjective immediacy. It loses the final causation which is its internal principle of unrest, and it acquires efficient causation whereby it is a ground of obligation characterizing the creativity" (29). Freedom, or the "internal principle of unrest," is superseded by causal necessity, or the external conformity of the present to the past. The initiative that created something new in the moment of decision subsists afterward as an "obligation" of "stubborn fact," conditioning and limiting the next exercise of freedom.

Whitehead's conversion, or phenomenalization, of Kant cannot be described as a form of vitalism. For the ghost, or the trace, that the noumenal leaves in the phenomenal world is more an absence than a presence, more a vacuum than a force. If life is a locus of appetition and decision, this can only be because "life is a characteristic of 'empty space.'... Life lurks in the interstices of each living cell, and in the interstices of the brain" (Whitehead 1929/1978, 105–106). Life involves a kind of subtraction, a rupturing or emptying-out of the chains of physical causality. As a result of this delinking, "the transmission of physical influence, through the empty space within [the animal body], has not been entirely in conformity with the physical laws holding for inorganic societies" (106). These empty spaces or interstices are the realm of the potential, of a futurity that already haunts the present—or of what Deleuze will call the virtual. For, just as the past remains active within the present by means of the "vector transmission" of efficient causality, so the future is already latent within the present, thanks to the "multiplicity of pure potentiality" (164) that can be taken up by the living actual occasion. "The past is a nexus of actualities" (214); it is still actual, still a force in the present, because it is reproduced as a "datum," physically prehended by each new actual occasion. On the other hand, the future is *available*, without having yet been actually determined: it takes the form of eternal objects, or "pure potentials," that may be conceptually prehended (or not) by each new actual occasion. Whitehead says, therefore, that "the future is merely real, without being actual" (214). Strikingly, this is the same formula that Deleuze (borrowing from Proust) uses to describe the virtual (Deleuze 1994, 208). Where Deleuze describes novelty or invention as the actualization of the virtual, Whitehead says that "reality becomes actual" (1929/1978, 214) in the present, or in the decision of each living occasion. The process of actualization is the hinge, or the interstice, not only between past and future, but also between the two forms of causality.

5
God, or The Body without Organs

God is the most perplexing figure in Whitehead's metaphysics. Who is he, what does he want, and what is he doing in *Process and Reality*? Whitehead's thought is entirely about process and transformation; it values becoming over being, relation over substance, and continual novelty over the perpetuation of the same. It rejects the "bifurcation of nature" (Whitehead 1920/2004, 30–31), or the separation of reality from appearance (1929/1978, 72). It holds that there is nothing besides "the experiences of subjects" (167); and it grants to all subjects—including inhuman and nonsentient ones—and to all their experiences—conscious or not—the same ontological status. Such a thought has no room for a specially "eminent" entity: one that would be absolute, unchanging, transcendent, and supersensible, as God is usually taken to be. Given Whitehead's rejection of traditional metaphysics and theology, why does God remain such a "stubborn fact" throughout *Process and Reality*? What role does this God play in Whitehead's cosmological system?[1]

---

1. For the purposes of this chapter, I deliberately ignore the extensive literature on "process theology." Instead, I approach Whitehead's notion of God from an insistently nontheological perspective. That is to say, I seek to situate Whitehead in relation to the radical critique of transcendence that runs through Spinoza, Nietzsche, and Deleuze: a critique that is also, in a certain manner, one of the major stakes in Kant's transcendental argument, and in William James's "radical empiricism." From this point of view, it is tempting to follow Donald Sherburne's effort to excise God altogether from Whitehead's vision, the better to affirm a "neo-Whiteheadian naturalism" (Sherburne 1986, 83). But I think that God is too insistently present throughout the text of *Process and Reality* for this to be a viable option. I seek instead to develop a nonreligious, or atheological, understanding of Whitehead's God.

Evidently, the God described by Whitehead bears little resemblance to the God of Christianity, or any other organized religion. Indeed, Whitehead is repulsed by the "Greek, Hebrew, and Christian" picture of "a static God condescending to the world" from transcendent heights (Whitehead 1929/1978, 347). He deplores the way that "the vicious separation of the flux from the permanence leads to the concept of an entirely static God, with eminent reality, in relation to an entirely fluent world, with deficient reality" (346). He rejects what he wryly calls the "unfortunate habit . . . of paying [God] metaphysical compliments" (1925/1967, 179). He protests against the traditional adulation of God as a figure of might: the "worship of glory arising from power is not only dangerous; it arises from a barbaric conception of God" (1926/1996, 55). And he denounces "the doctrine of an aboriginal, eminently real, transcendent creator, at whose fiat the world came into being, and whose imposed will it obeys," as a pernicious "fallacy which has infused tragedy" into the history of the world (1929/1978, 342). For he judges that, despite the ethical content of Jesus' own teachings, through most of European history "the Gospel of love was turned into a Gospel of fear. The Christian world was composed of terrified populations" (1926/1996, 75).[2]

Whitehead rejects the more refined philosophical notions of God as much as he does the "barbaric," popular or traditional ones. For instance, despite his own affinity with Leibniz, Whitehead dismisses "the Leibnizian theory of the 'best of possible worlds' " as "an audacious fudge produced in order to save the face of a Creator constructed by contemporary, and antecedent,

---

2. The exemption of Jesus' ethical teachings from an otherwise thoroughgoing rejection of Christianity is a frequent theme in modern antireligious thought. Even Nietzsche often takes this position. Whitehead has little interest in Nietzsche; in fact, he claims in conversation never to have read *The Antichrist* (Price 2001, 131). Nonetheless, Whitehead, like Nietzsche, puts the blame for all that is bad in historical Christianity upon St. Paul. In conversation, Whitehead describes Paul as the man who "did more than anybody else to distort and subvert Christ's teaching" (303); and he says that Paul's "idea of God, to my mind, is the idea of the devil" (186). In his published works, he explicitly prefers John to Paul (Whitehead 1926/1996, 76). All this is worth recalling at a time when such thinkers as Badiou (2003) and Žižek (2003) have cited Paul as an exemplary revolutionary figure. Whitehead evidently rejects the explicitly antipluralist universalism that Badiou and Žižek champion and attribute to Paul.

theologians" (1929/1978, 47). Leibniz's God selects among "an infinite number of possible universes," choosing the one that is the best. He bases his choice on these worlds' different degrees of perfection: "each possible world [has] the right to claim existence in proportion to the perfection which it involves" (Leibniz 1973, 187). Perfection, however, has already been defined by Leibniz as a "magnitude of positive reality" (185). So God chooses the world that is already, in itself, the most real. But Whitehead does not accept the Leibnizian notion of different degrees of reality. There is no ontological preeminence. The world, as "merely 'given' . . . does not disclose any peculiar character of 'perfection' " (Whitehead 1929/1978, 47). For "no reason, internal to history, can be assigned why that flux of forms, rather than another flux, should have been illustrated" (46). The world is not predetermined, but radically contingent, because it is open to the immanent "decision" of each actual entity. God cannot have the power to decide *for* all these entities. Hence no "possible universe" can be judged *a priori* to be more perfect, or more intrinsically real, than any other. This is really just another way of saying that, for Whitehead as for Deleuze, "Being is univocal" (Deleuze 1994, 35). In addition, Whitehead notes that, if God is held to be omnipotent, and is given the credit for everything good that happens, "then the evil in the world is in conformity with the nature of God" as well (Whitehead 1926/1996, 95).

Whitehead's rejection of the Leibnizian God is entirely in accord with Kant's demonstration, in the Transcendental Dialectic of the First Critique, of the fallacies of speculative theology. Kant distinguishes three philosophical endeavors to prove the existence of God: the ontological, cosmological, and physiotheological proofs (Kant 1996, 577). But Kant rejects all of these alleged proofs, because in all of them, "a *regulative* principle is transformed into a *constitutive* one" (599). That is to say, these ostensible proofs take relations and determinations that are valid for entities within the world, and illegitimately apply them in order to explain the "*thoroughgoing determination*" of the world itself as a whole and in the first place (563). They then go on to hypostasize this principle of determination in the form of a supreme "*being of all beings*" (569). All such attempts to prove the existence of God thus make the mistake of applying empirical principles to establish something that is supersensible and nonempirical. This can never work, because "if the empirically valid law of causality is to lead to the original being, then this being would likewise have to belong to the chain of objects of experience; but in that case this being would itself, like all appearances, be conditioned in turn" (613).

Whitehead's own discussions of theology largely follow Kant's logic. Thus Whitehead dismisses the "ontological proof" of God's existence, because "any proof which commences with the consideration of the character of the actual world cannot rise above the actuality of this world. . . . In other words, it may discover an immanent God, but not a God wholly transcendent" (Whitehead 1926/1996, 71). And he rejects the "cosmological argument," on the grounds that "our notion of causation concerns the relations of states of things within the actual world, and can only be illegitimately extended to a transcendent derivation" (1929/1978, 93).[3] Any attempt to ground immanence in

---

3. Whitehead does not explicitly mention Kant's third argument, the physiotheological one, or the claim that a "*determinate experience*" (Kant 1996, 600) can provide proof of God's existence. This is the line of argument more commonly known as *natural theology*, or the *argument from design*. It maintains that the "manifoldness, order, purposiveness, and beauty" of the empirical world are such as to point to, and indeed necessitate, the existence of a Creator or Designer (602). Kant rejects this argument because "no experience at all can ever be congruent with," or adequate to, the Idea of a transcendent Being. Kant's argument is a formalization of Hume's demonstration, in *Dialogues Concerning Natural Religion* (1998), of the indeterminacy of the argument from design: if we do not limit induction to the empirical world, then nearly any transcendent conception, no matter how bizarre, can be equally well inferred from our observations of empirical order. Whitehead explicitly places himself within this line of argument; he states that his own speculation on the nature of God "is merely an attempt to add another speaker to that masterpiece, Hume's *Dialogues Concerning Natural Religion*" (Whitehead 1929/1978, 343).

Moreover, Whitehead implicitly follows Kant's rejection of the physiotheological proof in the very way that he structures his own argument. In his discussion of *Religion in the Making* (1926/1996), Whitehead proceeds from the "fact" of humankind's "religious experience" (86); he is concerned with the social, psychological, and affective basis of religion, rather than with its possible objective truth. From this perspective, the argument from design is itself an emotional response. It arises, as religion itself does, from our sense of wonder at the universe, and from humankind's long habit of "artificially stimulating emotion" through ritual (22). But the emotions that are both the cause and the effect of religious practices cannot in themselves count as proof for any conception of God. If anything, religion's "authority is endangered by the intensity of the emotions which it generates. Such emotions are evidence of some vivid experience; but they are a very poor guarantee for its correct interpretation" (83).

transcendence, or explain "stubborn fact" (the empirically given) by reference to an Absolute, would violate Whitehead's "ontological principle," which states that "there is nothing which floats into the world from nowhere" (244), that "every explanatory fact refers to the decision and to the efficacy of an actual thing" (46), and that, therefore, "the reasons for things are always to be found in the composite nature of definite actual entities" (19).

The one philosophical account of God that would seem to be exempt from this Kantian critique, and that does not violate the ontological principle, is Spinoza's. For Spinoza does indeed propose an entirely immanent God, who does not transcend the given world, but is coextensive with it (*Deus sive natura*). Nonetheless, and even though his own philosophy "is closely allied to Spinoza's scheme of thought," Whitehead rejects the Spinozistic God, just he does the Leibnizian one (Whitehead 1929/1978, 7). For Spinoza still privileges God excessively. Even in Spinoza's monistic, immanent account of substance, "the ultimate is illegitimately allowed a final, 'eminent' reality, beyond that ascribed to any of its accidents" (7). Spinoza distinguishes between substance and its attributes, on the one hand, and the multiple "individualized modes," or affections of this substance, on the other. This in itself is unexceptionable; "in all philosophic theory there is an ultimate which is actual in virtue of its accidents." But Whitehead warns us that this ultimate "is only then capable of characterization through its accidental embodiments, and apart from these embodiments is devoid of actuality" (7). That is to say, the ultimate—or what Whitehead also calls "creativity" (21)—is altogether virtual or potential. It has no actuality of its own, but exists merely through its actualizations or embodiments. It cannot be conceived as an "actual entity" at all, "for its character lacks determinateness." Correlatively, the "temporal world" as a whole cannot be regarded "as a definite actual creature," because all actual entities are complete in themselves, whereas the world as a whole "is an essential incompleteness" (Whitehead 1926/1996, 92).

According to Whitehead's reading, Spinoza ignores all this to the extent that he grants a higher, more "eminent" order of reality to substance itself, or to what he calls God, than he does to the merely finite accidents of substance. Spinoza's God may be immanent, or coextensive with the world, but this only compounds the difficulty. For Spinoza's monism thereby treats the world as a totality, entirely apprehensible through God, or through the "third kind of knowledge." The "eminence" of the ultimate as creator (*natura naturans*) is replicated in the form of a total knowledge through first causes of the world as creature (*natura naturata*). And there is still a "gap" between this ideal knowledge and the actual existence of a "multiplicity of modes," each with its own particular actions and passions (Whitehead 1929/1978, 7). Spinoza eliminates empirical contingency; and with it, he disallows all novelty, all hope for a future different from the past. Spinoza's error, therefore, is precisely to *substantialize* the ultimate, to treat the totality of all accidents (or, more precisely, the total set of conditions for the "thoroughgoing determination" of all conceivable "accidental embodiments") as if it were somehow actual in itself. In this way, Spinoza remains within the bounds of speculative theology, and his notion of God remains susceptible to Kantian critique.

I have dwelt at such length on Whitehead's criticisms of Spinoza and Leibniz precisely because, in spite of everything, their notions of God are closer than anyone else's to his own. Whitehead especially values these two thinkers, because they stand apart from the otherwise ubiquitous dualism of post-Cartesian thought (Whitehead 1925/1967, 143). But nevertheless, on a broader time scale, Spinoza and Leibniz do not escape the compromises made by their peers. Like nearly all thinkers of the last two thousand years, they allow "ethical and religious interests . . . to influence metaphysical conclusions" (173). Leibniz's mathematizing God, and Spinoza's immanent and impersonal one, are preferable to the deity of Christianity, or to the notion of "a personal God in any sense transcendent or creative" (Whitehead 1926/1996, 87). But Leibniz and Spinoza still share traditional ethical and religious biases. Whitehead insists that "dispassionate criticism of religious belief is beyond all things necessary" (83). But Leibniz's "pious dependence upon God" to shore up his metaphysics (Whitehead 1929/1978, 190) prevents him from making any such criticism; and even Spinoza—radical as he is in his deconstruction of religious revelation and authority in the *Tractatus Theologico-Politicus*—does not sufficiently provide it.

Whitehead is not usually thought of as a "critical" thinker in the Kantian mold. But his "criticism of religious belief" is precisely a Kantian, transcendental one, rather than a Spinozian, immanent one. This "criticism," in turn, is what motivates his own construction of the figure of God. For Whitehead does not announce the "death of God," just as he does not announce the "end of metaphysics." He bypasses Nietzsche, no less than Heidegger. Rather than rejecting metaphysical speculation, Whitehead seeks for a way to do metaphysics otherwise. And rather than eliminating God, he seeks to accomplish "the secularization of God's functions in the world" (1929/1978, 207). This is one of the most startling proposals in all of *Process and Reality*. The secularization of God, Whitehead writes, "is at least as urgent a requisite of thought as is the secularization of other elements in experience" (207).

In saying this, Whitehead positions himself within the general Enlightenment project of emancipation—but with a twist. For secularization is not the same thing as outright elimination. It works in a way that is quieter and less confrontational. Religion is not abolished, nor even really deposed; but it does lose a certain degree of *importance*. "The concept of God is certainly one essential element in religious feeling. But the converse is not true: the concept of religious feeling is not an essential element in the concept of God's function in the universe" (Whitehead 1929/1978, 207). Religion, for Whitehead, is not without value; it may even be pragmatically indispensable, to the extent that it conveys a "longing of the spirit" for some sort of "justification" of its own existence, and of existence generally (Whitehead 1926/1996, 85). But religion, like science, still occupies only a subordinate position in Whitehead's overall scheme of values. "Religion requires a metaphysical backing" (83), which means that theology, like ethics, is subordinate to metaphysics and cosmology. Whitehead seeks to establish a God without religion, in the same way that he seeks to articulate a metaphysics without essentialism, and to respect the findings of physical science without endorsing science's reductionist positivism or its tendentious separation of facts from values.

What might the "secularization" of God actually entail? There is only one model for such an undertaking. In *Science and the Modern World*, Whitehead credits Aristotle with being "the last European metaphysician of first-rate importance" to contemplate God disinterestedly and in a truly philosophical manner. Aristotle alone, in his conception of the Prime Mover, approaches the question of God in an "entirely dispassionate" way, with "no motive, except to follow his metaphysical train of thought withersoever it led him." Aristotle posits the figure of an ultimate being, not for extrinsic (ethical, religious, or theological) reasons, but only because "the general character of things requires that there be such an entity" (Whitehead 1925/1967, 173–174). Aristotle is thus the last prereligious thinker of God; Whitehead proposes to be the first postreligious, or secular, one. "Apart from any reference to existing religions as they are, or as they ought to be," he writes, "we must investigate dispassionately what the metaphysical principles, here developed, require on these points, as to the nature of God." Whitehead therefore offers, not definitive formulations, but "suggestions as to how the problem [of God] is transformed in the light of [his own theoretical] system" (1929/1978, 343).

In pursuing this task, Whitehead needs to divest himself of all preexisting theology, which of course is something that Aristotle never had to do. But Whitehead parallels Aristotle in that his own approach to divinity is equally a matter of "follow[ing] his metaphysical train of thought withersoever it [leads] him." Whitehead posits God, neither out of piety and devotion, nor as a defense against nihilism and chaos, but simply because his own logic requires it. As Isabelle Stengers often reminds us, when Whitehead does metaphysics and cosmology, he continues to think like a mathematician. That is to say, he poses a specific problem, and works under the "obligation" to construct a solution that establishes coherence, while respecting all the constraints and conditions imposed by the problem (Stengers 2002b, 17, *passim*). In this sense, Whitehead's God, like Aristotle's, is a construction, necessary for the coherence and adequacy of his understanding of the world.

Aristotle posited his Prime Mover because he was "enmeshed in the details of an erroneous physics and an erroneous cosmology" (Whitehead 1925/1967, 174). He "required" an originary source of motion, because he wrongly supposed that things would not continue to move on their own. Today, we know from the principle of inertia that things do not need a Mover in order to continue moving. But in the modern age of relativity and quantum mechanics, "an analogous metaphysical problem arises which can be solved only in an analogous fashion. In the place of Aristotle's God as Prime Mover, we require God as the Principle of Concretion" (174).[4] That is to say, we need God in order to explain "the puzzling fact that there is an actual course of

---

4. The verb "to require" has particularly strong implications for Whitehead. It denotes a vital, imperious necessity that is grounded neither in formal logic nor in actual matter of fact. It is a kind of transcendental imperative, although in Kantian language it is a "hypothetical" and not a "categorical" one. Stengers describes Whitehead's sense of what "we require" as a demand, a "cry of the . . . soul," leading to an "experience of transformative disclosure." For instance, we "require," not a proof that reductionism is wrong, but rather the positive capacity

events which is itself a limited fact, in that metaphysically speaking it might have been otherwise" (172). We need God in order to move from the potential to the actual—given that there is no particular rationale for why one set of potentials should be actualized, rather than another. We need God, perhaps, in order to make the wave function collapse, so that quantum indeterminacy can give way to a determinate physical outcome.

Leibniz invoked God in order to explain why the actual world was the best of all possible worlds; Whitehead, to the contrary, invokes God precisely in order to explain why the actual world cannot be conceived as an optimal one. Far from being the guarantor of rationality and order, "God is the ultimate limitation, and His existence is the ultimate irrationality" (Whitehead 1925/1967, 178). In short, Whitehead devises his own notion of God in order to resolve the problem of how—in the absence of any prior determining justification—a concrete and limited "actuality" can coherently exist "in essential relation to an unfathomable possibility" (Whitehead 1925/1967, 174). All this is worked out quite suddenly, in the course of just a few pages, in the eleventh chapter of *Science and the Modern World*.[5] The situation in *Process and Reality* is far more complicated, as we shall see. But in that later book, Whitehead still defines what he calls "the primordial nature of God" in terms of "the principle of concretion—the principle whereby there is initiated a definite outcome from a situation otherwise riddled with ambiguity" (Whitehead 1929/1978, 345).

---

actually to think and act nonreductively (Stengers 2005, 42–43). Whitehead's "requirement" is the demand to fulfill a metaphysical "obligation"; this is why it can only be met by means of a "construction," in the mathematical sense of the term. Whitehead's God is precisely such a construction.

5. According to Lewis Ford, Whitehead's chapter 11, with its discussion of God, is a late addition to the manuscript of *Science and the Modern World* (Ford 1984, 96–125). Presumably Whitehead had not speculated about God, or even postulated his existence as a hypothesis, prior to his final revisions of this manuscript in 1925. In what follows, I am concerned with the role that Whitehead's notion of God plays in his overall "theoretic system" (1929/1978, 343), rather than with the genesis and development of this notion. But Ford provides essential background knowledge for any understanding of Whitehead's construction.

Whitehead needs to posit his notion of God in order to ensure the overall coherence of his metaphysical system. *Coherence* is the crucial issue here. The notion of coherence is so important to Whitehead that he defines it on the first page of *Process and Reality*: " 'Coherence,' as here employed, means that the fundamental ideas, in terms of which the scheme is developed, presuppose each other so that in isolation they are meaningless. This requirement does not mean that they are definable in terms of each other; it means that what is indefinable in one such notion cannot be abstracted from its relevance to the other notions" (1929/1978, 3). That is to say, coherent terms cannot be reduced to one another, or to anything more basic; but they also cannot be separated from one another. Coherence, then, is more than just a logical entailment. It it something quite different from, and greater than, mere " 'logical' consistency, or lack of contradiction"—though this latter is also, of course, required in metaphysical speculation (3). For coherence implies, not just noncontradiction in principle, but also a kind of contextual solidarity. The principle of coherence stipulates that "no entity can be conceived in complete abstraction from the system of the universe" (3). In order to exist, a given entity presupposes, and requires, the existence of certain other entities, even though (or rather, precisely because) it cannot be logically derived from those other entities, or otherwise explained in their terms. Coherence means, finally, that "all actual entities are in the solidarity of one world" (67).

In other words, coherence is not logical, but ecological. It is exemplified by the way that a living organism requires an environment or milieu—which is itself composed, in large part, of other living organisms similarly requiring their own environments or milieus. In this way, and despite the difference in vocabulary, Whitehead's *coherence* is close to what Deleuze and Guattari call *consistency*. For "consistency concretely ties together heterogeneous, disparate elements as such" (Deleuze and Guattari 1987, 507): it means that things are irrevocably connected to one another, despite not having any sort of underlying element in common. In Deleuze and Guattari's famous example, the orchid and the wasp are coupled, the flower feeding the insect, and the insect fertilizing the flower. In themselves, these two beings "have absolutely nothing to do with each other" (10), and yet neither can survive without the other. Whitehead's notion of coherence and Deleuze and Guattari's notion of consistency are both principles yoking together elements that nonetheless remain singular and disjunct from one another. Both notions posit a world in which everything is connected to everything else. However, these connections are not principles of internal definition or determination. Rather, they remain what Manuel De Landa calls "relations of exteriority" (2006, 10ff). Such relations are "*contingently obligatory*," rather than "logically necessary"; they arise in the course of a history that could have been otherwise (11).[6]

On the highest level of generality, then, Whiteheadian "coherence" has to do with the way that things—or, more precisely, events—are entirely interdependent, yet also mutually independent. The world is both a disjunctive multiplicity of discrete entities, and a continuous web of interconnections. Neither of these dimensions can be ignored; "the individuality of entities is just as important as their community" (Whitehead 1926/1996, 88). Every

---

6. De Landa follows Deleuze in insisting that, although an entity is always involved in relations with other entities, "a relation may change without the terms changing" (De Landa 2006, 11, citing Deleuze and Parnet 2002, 55). An entity is never fully defined by its relations; for it is always possible to detach an entity from one particular set of relations, and insert it instead in a different set of relations, with different other entities. Every entity has certain "properties" that are not defined by the set of relations it finds itself in at a given moment; the entity can take these properties with it when it moves from one context (or one set of relations) to another. At the same time, an entity is never devoid of (some sort of) relations: the world is a plenum, indeed it is overfull, and solipsism or atomistic isolation is impossible.

Put differently, no entity can be entirely isolated, because it is always involved in multiple relations of one sort or another, and these relations *affect* the entity, cause it to change. But this is not to say that the entity is *determined* by these relations. For the entity has an existence apart from these particular relations, and apart from the other "terms" of the relation, precisely insofar as it is something that is able to affect, and to be affected by, other entities. The entity is a function not just of its present relations, but of a whole history of relations in which it has affected other entities and been affected by them.

De Landa thus distinguishes between the *properties* of an entity (which are what it takes with it to another context) and the *capacities* of that same entity (its potential to affect, and to be affected by, other entities). "These capacities do depend on a component's properties but cannot be reduced to them since they involve reference to the properties of other interacting

entity is related, positively or negatively, to all the other entities in its universe. And yet, within this network of relations, "the ultimate metaphysical truth is atomism" (1929/1978, 35). Whitehead's philosophy is "an atomic theory of actuality" (27). In the actual world, "each ultimate unit of fact is a cell-complex, not analysable into components with equivalent completeness of actuality" (219). From the quantum level on up, each "actual occasion," or process of becoming, both embodies interconnection, and asserts its own independence from all the past occasions from which it is derived and to which it is connected. It both inherits everything that comes before it and breaks away from everything that it inherits. Each "novel entity is at once the togetherness of the 'many' which it finds, and also it is one among the disjunctive 'many' which it leaves; it is a novel entity, disjunctively among the many entities which it synthesizes. The many become one, and are increased by one. In their natures, entities are disjunctively 'many' in process of passage into conjunctive unity" (21). Conjunction and disjunction, unification and diversification, must always go together, in the "process of passage" which is "the ultimate metaphysical truth."

This means that each of Whitehead's "actual occasions" marks the point of a *synthesis*, taking this word in the strict Kantian sense: "by *synthesis*, in the most general sense of the term, I mean the act of putting various presentations

---

entities" (2006, 11). An entity's capacities are as real as its properties; but we cannot deduce the capacities from the properties; nor can we know (entirely) what these capacities are, aside from how they come into play in particular interactions with other particular entities.

Whitehead's notion of coherence is largely consistent with De Landa's account of relations of exteriority. The difference is that De Landa has no account of process, or of how the shift from one set of relations to another actually occurs. His ontology is excessively, and needlessly, static. Whitehead avoids this problem because he identifies entities with processes, which all at once become and thereby perish. De Landa's entities correspond, not to Whitehead's "actual entities," but rather to what Whitehead calls societies. Societies are aggregations of actual entities; these aggregations possess spatial extent and temporal duration, which is what allows them to affect and be affected by other societies. What De Landa calls the innate "properties" of an entity (as distinct from its capacities) would be defined by Whitehead rather as the aggregate of the free (not predetermined) "decisions" made by all the actual entities that constitute the society in question.

with one another and of comprising their manifoldness in one cognition" (Kant 1996, 130). Whitehead, of course, rejects Kant's overall subjectivist and cognitivist orientation. But the crucial point here is that, for Kant, the cognitive faculty does not itself produce the synthesis. "Rather, synthesis of a manifold . . . is what first gives rise to a cognition. . . . Hence, if we want to make a judgment about the first origin of our cognition, then we must first direct our attention to synthesis" (130). That is to say, synthesis precedes cognition, and it alone renders cognitive judgment possible. In itself, the act of synthesis is primordial, prelogical, and precognitive. Synthesis is an action "produced by the imagination, which is a blind but indispensable function of the soul without which we would have no cognition whatsoever, but of which we are conscious only very rarely" (130). Kant's whole philosophy is organized around the question of synthetic judgment; but here, the constructive act of synthesis is separated from, and placed before, any judgment whatsoever. Kant's notion of synthesis is thus one of the ways that, as Whitehead says, he "first, fully and explicitly, introduced into philosophy the conception of an act of experience as a constructive functioning" (Whitehead 1929/1978, 156).

It is very much in this Kantian and Whiteheadian spirit that Deleuze, first in *The Logic of Sense* (1990, 174) and then more expansively (with Guattari) in *Anti-Oedipus* (1983, *passim*), proposes three basic syntheses of experience: the connective, the disjunctive, and the conjunctive. These syntheses are all modes of production; and what they produce is the Real itself. Or, better, these syntheses do not produce reality, so much as they are, themselves, the ultimate, "molecular" components of reality. "Everything is production: *production of productions*, of actions and passions [connective synthesis]; *productions of recording processes*, of distributions and of co-ordinates that serve as points of reference [disjunctive synthesis]; *productions of consumptions*, of sensual pleasures, of anxieties, and of pain [conjunctive synthesis]" (Deleuze and Guattari 1983, 4). A productive synthesis corresponds to what Whitehead calls a *concrescence*: the "production of novel togetherness" (Whitehead 1929/1978, 21), or the coming-together of multiple prehensions into "one determinate integral satisfaction" (26). The syntheses are processes that aggregate other processes, or perspectives on things that are themselves also perspectives (since "there are no points of view on things, but . . . things, beings, are themselves points of view"—Deleuze 1990, 173). They are productions whose "raw materials" are other productions, and whose "products" are themselves taken up as materials in further processes of production.[7] Every synthesis ends in what Whitehead would call its "satisfaction," which leads in turn to the "objective immortality" of having completed the process, and thereby having become an object, or a product. This is how the world is always being "given" to us (and not only to us), as something already there, already accomplished. But this accomplishment is never final. For immediately, "the pure 'thisness' of the object produced is carried over into a new act of producing. . . . The rule of continually producing production, of grafting production onto the product, is a characteristic of desiring-machines or of primary production" (Deleuze and Guattari 1983, 7).

When they evoke this first, connective synthesis of primary production, Deleuze and Guattari seduce us with an enticing picture. How nice it would be, they tell us, if we could live in a wholly immanent, happily pluralistic world. Such a world would be a "plane of immanence" of pure process and

---

7. A synthesis is therefore not quite the same thing as a Spinozian *conatus*, or striving to persist in being. Deleuze and Guattari warn us that a synthesis, or a process of production, "must not be viewed as a goal or an end in itself; nor must it be confused with an infinite perpetuation of itself" (1983, 5). It is oriented toward becoming, rather than continuation.

More generally, there is a subtle, and never fully explored, tension in Deleuze's work (both with and without Guattari) between two different ways—closely related but nonetheless distinct—of conceiving the process of auto-creation. On the one hand, there is Spinoza's *conatus*, best defined as "a tendency to maintain and maximize the ability to be affected" (Deleuze 1988, 99, citing Spinoza's *Ethics* IV, 38). *Conatus* is quite close to Varela's concept of autopoiesis, the process by which a relational system maintains itself through dynamic interaction with its environment, re-creating the very processes that produce it. On the other hand, there is Gilbert Simondon's notion of individuation, the process by which an entity continually reconstitutes itself by actualizing potentials that preexist in a metastable environment. Individuation has strong affinities with Whitehead's concrescence, the way that an entity constitutes itself as something radically new, by selecting among, and recombining, aspects of already existing entities. All four of these terms (*conatus*, autopoiesis, individuation, concrescence) imply a certain sort of auto-creation, in which virtualities are actualized. But in *conatus* and autopoiesis, the emphasis is on a continuity that is created and preserved in and through continual change and interaction with the environment, whereas in individuation and concrescence, the emphasis is on the production of novelty, the entity's continual redefinition, or becoming-other than what it was.

pure desire. There would be nothing but flows, nothing but rhizomes, nothing but connections and cuts. Everything would flow, and every flow would intersect with many other flows. Everything would be connected to everything else; "any point of a rhizome can be connected to anything other, and must be" (Deleuze and Guattari 1987, 7). In such a world, desire would not know deferral, and production would be indistinguishable from play. "Desire constantly couples continuous flows and partial objects that are by nature fragmentary and fragmented. Desire causes the current to flow, itself flows in turn, and breaks the flows. . . . Amniotic fluid spilling out of the sac and kidney stones; flowing hair; a flow of spittle, a flow of sperm, shit, or urine" (Deleuze and Guattari 1983, 5). In such a world, everything would proliferate and transmogrify, continually renewing itself in the process: "at the limit-point of all the transverse or transfinite connections, the partial object and the continuous flux, the interruption and the connection, fuse into one: everywhere there are breaks-flows out of which desire wells up" (36–37). Deleuze and Guattari thus depict a world of gratified desire: a world in which everything is process, and nothing is ever static or self-contained. Life is then a continual wonder of strange encounters and wild metamorphoses.

But Deleuze and Guattari also warn us that things are never really that simple. The rhizomatic, connected world of pure desire is not the world we live in. Things don't actually happen in so direct and unmediated a way. Indeed, if the world really were this way—that is, if it were always and only this way—then nothing would ever *happen* at all. If the world were entirely composed of flows and cuts, connections and intersections, then everything would remain in a state of mere potential. Nothing could ever be accomplished or actualized, and nothing could be distinguished from anything else. If the world were entirely composed of singularities, then there would be no "series of ordinary points" over which those singularities could be extended or expressed (Deleuze 1990, 109ff.). In such a world, there would be no continuities and no consequences. Everything would contain an immense "potential for every becoming" (Whitehead 1929/1978, 22), but nothing would ever actually *become*.[8]

---

8. It is precisely on these grounds that Ernst Bloch (1986, 201) criticizes Bergson, the common predecessor of Whitehead and Deleuze. Bloch warns us that relentless novelty can itself

In other words, once "we conceive actuality as in essential relation to an unfathomable possibility," then some sort of "Principle of Concretion" is needed, in order for anything to be actualized at all (Whitehead 1925/1967, 174). The connective synthesis is not in itself enough to define the actual becoming of a world. This is why, alongside the connective synthesis of flows and cuts, there must also be a *disjunctive synthesis* of routes and permutations. The economy of production (Deleuze and Guattari 1983, 5–6) is supplemented by an economy of circulation and distribution (12). This supplemental economy corresponds to a torsion in the field of desiring production. The connective synthesis is still more or less straightforward, in the sense that its logic remains linear, or at most "multilinear" (Deleuze and Guattari 1987, 295ff.). But the disjunctive synthesis of recording is far more convoluted and indirect. Its twists and turns are those of Nietzsche's "abyssal thought" of the Eternal Return (Deleuze 1990, 264), or of the "most terrible labyrinth of which Borges spoke" (176). For the disjunctive synthesis does not just split and connect terms in series. Rather, it "endlessly ramif[ies]" (59) the entire series of terms. It presents a "system of possible permutations between differences that always amount to the same as they shift and slide about" (Deleuze and Guattari 1983, 12). The disjunctive synthesis establishes a positive relation among a multiplicity of radically incompatible alternatives. It affirms all these alternatives together, indiscriminately, and defines itself in terms of the distances that separate them from one another. It is "an operation according to which two things or two determinations are affirmed *through* their difference," on the basis of "a positive distance of different elements" (Deleuze 1990, 172).

The disjunctive synthesis is deeper and more basic than logical contradiction, which it at once precedes, generates, and exceeds. It is not the case

---

become wearyingly repetitious and static. Incessant innovation, without real consequence, simply results in boredom: the continual passage of "senselessly changing fashions," the "rigidity of a surprise that is always the same." A "constantly required change of direction, required for its own sake," ends up taking us nowhere in particular, but only through the endless "zig-zag" of a random walk. The trouble with a process metaphysics, Bloch says, is that "the process remains empty and repeatedly produces nothing but process." It never arrives at any finished product; and therefore it never arrives at the Novum, the genuinely new.

that two items are affirmed disjunctively, because they logically contradict one another. It is rather that they can only contradict one another logically, as a result of their having first been put into contact by the workings of the disjunctive synthesis. Two items can only be in contradiction if they have already actively clashed with one another pragmatically. As Deleuze puts it, "contradiction results always from a process of a different nature. Events are not like concepts; it is their alleged contradiction (manifest in the concept) which results from their incompatibility, and not the converse" (Deleuze 1990, 170). Whitehead makes a similar point, enunciating what he calls the "principle of compatibility and contrariety" (Whitehead 1929/1978, 148). Two items are "contraries to each other" when they "cannot coexist in the constitution of one actual entity." They have proven themselves to be incompatible, at least in this particular concrescence. But such an incompatibility is not a matter of logic. For " 'feelings' are the entities which are primarily 'compatible' or 'incompatible.' All other usages of these terms are derivative" (148). Another concrescence, productive of another actual entity, might well exhibit vastly different feelings; the "subjective form" with which it prehended its data would be different. It might then be able to positively prehend both items, thereby rendering them compatible. It would thus "convert its exclusions into contrasts" (223). Whitehead's conversion of exclusions into contrasts, like Deleuze's disjunctive synthesis, cannot be defined in terms of negativity and contradiction.[9]

In making these arguments, Whitehead and Deleuze both draw on Leibniz's notions of *compossibility* and *incompossibility*. These notions, Deleuze says, "must be defined in an original manner"; they do not presuppose "the identical and the contradictory," but are themselves the primordial grounds

---

9. This is why Deleuze (explicitly) and Whitehead (implicitly) both reject the Hegelian notion of contradiction as the motor of change, or of history. Deleuze is always concerned to define philosophical thought as a power of affirmation, rather than one of negation. But he is always quick to add that the negative still has its place, as long as we see "negations *as powers of affirming*," instead of invoking negativity "as a motor, a power, and a quality" in its own right (Deleuze 1983, 179). Every new necessarily provides its own negations; but negativity is not in any sense the inner principle of the new.

for our judgments of identity and contradiction (Deleuze 1990, 173). Events, which in themselves are pure singularities, and hence fundamentally neutral and impassive, enter into relations of compossibility and incompossibility with one another before questions of logic can even arise. It is only when two events turn out to be pragmatically incompatible—that is to say, when they cannot occur in the same timeline or occupy places in the same "possible world," because the actualization of one would block the actualization of the other—that we can then say, derivatively, that the states of affairs corresponding to these two events are logically contradictory. The disjunctive "communication of events" (169–176) exceeds any logic of identity and contradiction, even as it alone provides the necessary conditions for judgment according to such a logic.

The disjunctive synthesis takes the grammatical form of an indefinitely extended "either . . . or . . . or . . ." (Deleuze and Guattari 1983, 12).[10] Things may happen this way, or they may happen that way, or they may happen yet another way, without any definitive preference. This is a Leibnizian situation, a movement among incompossibles; but for Deleuze and Guattari, as for Whitehead, there is no Leibnizian God to choose, among the incompossible series of events, the one that is most perfect or most fully real. Instead, all the series are affirmed in turn, as each gives way to another, over and over again. As Deleuze summarizes the difference: "For Leibniz . . . bifurcations and divergences of series are genuine borders between incompossible worlds. . . . For Whitehead (and for many modern philosophers), on the contrary,

---

10. In *The Logic of Sense*, Deleuze expresses the disjunctive synthesis with the phrase *ou bien . . . ou bien*, translated as "either . . . or" (1990, 174). In *Anti-Oedipus*, Deleuze and Guattari express it rather with the phrase *soit . . . soit*, translated as "either . . . or . . . or." This *soit* is then explicitly opposed to the *ou bien* (translated "either/or"): *soit* expresses an active, affirmative (inclusive and nonrestrictive) use of the disjunctive synthesis, whereas *ou bien*, implying as it does "decisive choices between immutable terms (the alternative: either this or that)," expresses its limitative and reactive (exclusive and restrictive) use (Deleuze and Guattari 1983, 12; cf. 75ff.). The distinction between *ou bien* and *soit* is hard to convey in English. But the question of the difference between affirmative and limitative uses of the disjunctive synthesis is an important one, to which I return below.

bifurcations, divergences, incompossibilities, and discord belong to the same motley world" (1993, 81). Such a world, with its process of disjunctively affirming incompossibles, is exemplified in late modernist fictions like Beckett's *Malone* (Deleuze and Guattari 1983, 12), Borges's "Garden of Forking Paths" (Deleuze 1990, 114; Deleuze 1989, 49), and Gombrowicz's *Cosmos* (Deleuze 1993, 154, n. 15) and *Pornographia* (Deleuze 1990, 289–290). It is also exemplified in the cinema of the "time-image" (Deleuze 1989), in which time repeatedly forks (49), and incompatible images and sounds are linked through the disjunctions of "irrational cuts" (181, 248, and *passim*). In all these works, "incompossible worlds, despite their incompossibility, have something in common," for they "appear as instances of solution for one and the same problem" (Deleuze 1990, 114).

Deleuze's allusion here to problems and solutions recalls the way that, in *Difference and Repetition*, he equates problems with Kantian transcendental or regulative Ideas, seeing them as "focal points or horizons" that "embrace" multiple, incompatible solutions (Deleuze 1994, 168–169). Today we might say, in the language of complexity theory, that these incompossible worlds correspond to alternative paths through the same phase space. Or we might think of how the "many worlds" interpretation of quantum mechanics has figured in recent science fiction novels and comics. In Warren Ellis's *Night on Earth* (2003), for instance, the superheroes of the Planetary group are "rotated through the multiverse" from one actualization of Gotham City to another. As a result, they meet multiple iterations of Batman, from Bob Kane's avenger to Adam West's campy put-on to Frank Miller's borderline psychopath. Only one Batman can be encountered at a time, as his various iterations are incompatible with one another and belong to incompossible worlds. But the disjunctive synthesis consists precisely in the restless movement from one Gotham City and Batman to another. No Gotham City and Batman can be privileged above the rest—not even Bob Kane's "original" conception, which is just as much a particular, circumstantial actualization as are all the others. Rather, the "positive distance" between the various iterations is what generates all of them, or "distributes the divergent series . . . and causes them to resonate through their distance and in their distance" (Deleuze 1990, 174). Each Batman is a particular "solution for one and the same problem," which is to say a particular actualization of the same constellation of potentialities, the same virtual configuration.

The logic of the disjunctive synthesis is also the logic of the simulacrum. According to Deleuze's reading, Plato is always concerned "to select lineages: to distinguish pretenders; to distinguish the pure from the impure, the authentic from the inauthentic" (Deleuze 1990, 254). The crucial Platonic distinction is neither between the original and the copy, nor between the Ideas of the rational world and their images in the sensible world. It is rather a distinction within the sensible world itself, "between two sorts of images. *Copies* are secondary possessors. They are well-founded pretenders, guaranteed by resemblance; *simulacra* are like false pretenders, built upon a dissimilarity, implying an essential perversion or a deviation" (256). Copies refer back to an original (the Idea), and can be judged hierarchically on the basis of their fidelity to this original. On the other hand, "the simulacrum is built upon a disparity or upon a difference. It internalizes a dissimilarity. This is why we can no longer define it in relation to a model imposed on the copies, a model of the Same from which the copies' resemblance derives" (258). The simulacrum cannot be referred back to the originary Idea at all; it can only be understood as part of a "signal-sign system," one that is "constituted by placing disparate elements or heterogeneous series in communication" (261).

In this sense, Batman is a simulacrum. There is no Platonic Idea of Batman, no model that all the iterations of Batman would conform to more or less, and in relation to which they could all be hierarchically ranked according to the degree of their resemblance. There is also no best of all possible Batmans, no iteration that can be judged more perfect than all the rest. Rather, the disparity between the different iterations of Batman, their distance from one another, is itself the only common measure between them. Each Batman arises independently, as a unique "solution" to a common disparity or problem (let us say, to the young Bruce Wayne's primordial trauma of witnessing the murder of his parents). And between these solutions, "there is no longer any possible selection" (Deleuze 1990, 262). In the absence of any Platonic criterion, or any Leibnizian God, there is only the disjunctive synthesis that affirms each iteration, one at a time, in its divergence from all the rest. This means that any particular iteration of Batman is entirely contingent, although the synthesis itself, with its affirmation of all these mutiple iterations, responds to a necessity.

In Whitehead's terms, the multiple iterations of the disjunctive synthesis correspond to the ungrounded "decisions" that each actual entity must make, in the course of becoming itself. Every entity's decision is "internally determined and . . . externally free" (1929/1978, 27). This is because there is no preexisting norm or standard to guide it, and no antecedent principle of selection. In every occasion, "whatever is determinable is determined"; but beyond all determinability, there remains a "final modification of emotion, appreciation, and purpose" made by the entity as a whole, and thereby reflexively determining it *as* a whole (27–28). The disjunctive synthesis is thus an expression of radical contingency: "It is true that any flux must exhibit the character of internal determination. So much follows from the ontological principle. But every instance of internal determination assumes *that* flux up to *that* point. There is no reason why there could be no alternative flux exhibiting that principle of internal determination" (46–47). The "logic" of this history, the reason things happened the way they did, can only emerge retrospectively.

Deleuze derives his account of the disjunctive synthesis from an analysis of the "disjunctive syllogism" by means of which Kant presents the Idea of God (Deleuze 1990, 294–297). As I have already mentioned, Kant's critique of speculative theology, in the section of the First Critique on "The Ideal of Pure Reason" (Kant 1996, 560–616), defines God, not as the origin or creator of the world (its first cause), but rather as the principle of the "thoroughgoing determination" of reality (563, 567). This means that everything that exists must be derived from God by a process of selection and limitation. The "thoroughgoing determination of any thing rests on the limitation of this *total* of reality," Kant says, "inasmuch as some of this reality is attributed to the thing but the rest is excluded" (567–568). God encompasses all possible predicates; but any finite individual thing includes only some of these predicates. Or as Deleuze puts it: "God is defined by the sum total of all possibility, insofar as this sum constitutes an 'originary' material or the whole of reality. The reality of each thing 'is derived' from it: it rests in effect on the limitation of this totality. . . . [T]he sum total of the possible is an originary material from which the exclusive and complete determination of the concept of each thing is derived through disjunction" (Deleuze 1990, 295–296). Any individual thing must be either *this* or *that*; God's role is to be the *community*, the being-together, of all these alternatives. Through what Deleuze describes as Kant's "irony," God is "deprived of his traditional claims—to have created subjects or made a world" and presented instead, much more humbly, as merely "the principle or master of the disjunctive syllogism" (294–295).[11]

This means that Kant's God, like Leibniz's God, is basically a principle of selection: which is to say, of exclusion and limitation. "In Kant, therefore, we see that God is revealed as the master of the disjunctive syllogism only inasmuch as the disjunction is tied to exclusions in the reality which is derived from it, and thus to a *negative and limitative use*" (Deleuze 1990, 296). Deleuze opposes to this an affirmative and inclusive use of the disjunctive syllogism, which he finds in Klossowski's figure of the Baphomet (the Antichrist or anti-God). Under God, "a certain number of predicates are excluded from a thing in virtue of the identity of the corresponding concept." With the Baphomet, to the contrary, "each thing is opened up to the infinity of predicates through which it passes" (296). On the one side, each entity is locked into a fixed identity, because it is restricted to specific predicates; on the other side, each entity loses its identity, as it is opened up to the multiplicity of possible predicates

---

11. As Deleuze more fully explains, Kant "poses [a link] between Ideas and syllogisms. . . . This extraordinary theory of the syllogism . . . consists in discovering the ontological implications of the latter" (1990, 294–295). The three Ideas of Reason that Kant analyzes in the Transcendental Dialectic are Self, World, and God. Each of these is aligned with one of Kant's three categories of relation, and with one of the three kinds of syllogism. The Idea of the Self is correlated with the category of substance and the categorical syllogism, since this Idea "relates a phenomenon determined as a predicate to a subject determined as substance" (295). The idea of the World is correlated with the category of causality and the hypothetical syllogism, for this is how one entity is linked to another through the chains of cause and effect. These links determine the genesis and becoming of the world as a whole. Finally, the idea of God is correlated with the category of community and the disjunctive syllogism. That is to say, it is through God—defined as the being whose task is "to enact disjunctions, or at least to found them" (295)—that all the entities of the world can be said to *reciprocally determine* one another, so that they cohere together as a system (cf. Kant 1996, 136: "*community* is the causality of a substance reciprocally determining [and being determined by] another substance"). Deleuze and Guattari's revision or correction of Kant in *Anti-Oedipus* consists in referring each of these clusters of Idea, category, and relation back to a corresponding synthesis; The Idea of Self is correlated with the conjunctive synthesis; the Idea of the World with the connective synthesis; and the Idea of God with the disjunctive synthesis.

through which it passes. The limitative order of the world, as guaranteed by God, is opposed to the affirmative order of the Baphomet, "a 'chaosmos,' and no longer a world" (176), which is characterized by "singularity, or even multiple singularities" rather than by fixed identities (297). The entities of the Baphomet's chaosmos do not have identity, because they are caught up in continual metamorphoses. But they can be described, nevertheless, as *singularities*, because—even as they pass through all possible predicates—they do not have these predicates *all at once*. Batman has no fixed identity, but each iteration of Batman is a singular one.[12]

However, it may well be that Deleuze draws too hasty a distinction between negative and affirmative uses of the disjunctive synthesis. In *Anti-Oedipus*, Deleuze and Guattari state that "for the exclusive and restrictive use of the disjunctive synthesis, [the schizophrenic] substitutes an affirmative use. . . . That is why the schizophrenic God has so little to do with the God of religion, even though they are related to the same syllogism" (1983, 76–77). As any deconstructionist will gleefully point out, this amounts to making an exclusive use of the disjunctive synthesis, in the very act of defending its affirmative,

---

12. The fact that the disjunctive syllogism, or synthesis, passes through its multiple predicates *one at a time*, discarding each one as it affirms another, is what separates it from the movement of the Hegelian dialectic. Hegel famously writes that the "arising and passing away" of Appearance is the one thing that "does not itself arise and pass away," and that "the True is thus the Bacchanalian revel in which no member is not drunk" (Hegel 1977, 27). This formulation does not thus far contradict the Baphomet's affirmative use of the disjunctive syllogism. But Hegel adds that "the revel is just as much transparent and simple repose," and that "in the *whole* of the movement, seen as a state of repose, what distinguishes itself therein, and gives itself particular existence, is something that *recollects* itself [das sich *erinnert*], whose existence is self-knowledge, and whose self-knowledge is just as immediately existence" (27–28). In Klossowski's and Deleuze's accounts of the disjunctive syllogism, to the contrary, there can be no such repose. Recollection (*Erinnerung*) is impossible. There is no gathering-together of the dispersed limbs of Dionysus. The movement of the disjunctive syllogism is not one of recollection, but rather one of continual *forgetting*—as Klossowski especially emphasizes in his discussion of Nietzsche's eternal return (1998), upon which Deleuze quite heavily draws. Disjunctive syntheses therefore cannot be equated with Hegelian "syntheses of contradictory elements" (Deleuze and Guattari 1983, 76).

inclusive use. But Deleuze himself is fully aware of this criticism, and does not seem particularly bothered by it. As he notes, "we have seen, however, how often negative or exclusive disjunctions still subsist in Klossowski's work," especially "between God's order and the order of the Antichrist. But it is precisely inside God's order, and only there, that disjunctions have the negative value of exclusion. And it is on the other hand, inside the order of the Antichrist, that the disjunction (difference, divergence, decentering) becomes as such an affirmative and affirmed power" (Deleuze 1990, 296–297). This suggests a Nietzschean reversal of perspectives (cf. 173), a continual movment back and forth between the order of God on the one hand, and the order of the Antichrist on the other. In one direction, the disjunctive synthesis tends toward exclusion; in the other direction, toward multiplicity and affirmation. But neither of these movements is ever completed. No identity is ever so firmly in place as to resist all modification; and affirmative metamorphosis, by its very nature, is always incomplete and partial. This is why Deleuze and Guattari can proclaim, incorporating both ways of using the synthesis: "To anyone who asks: 'Do you believe in God?' we should reply in strictly Kantian or Schreberian terms: 'Of course, but only as the master of the disjunctive syllogism, or as its a priori principle (God defined as the *Omnitudo realitatis*, from which all secondary realities are derived by a process of division)'" (1983, 13).

Indeed, Kant himself moves beyond a merely limitative use of the disjunctive syllogism. For he insists that "the derivation of all other possibility" from the original nature of God "cannot, strictly speaking, be regarded as a *limitation* of this being's supreme reality and, as it were, a *division* of this reality. . . . Rather, the supreme reality would underlie the possibility of all things as a *basis* [*Grund*], and not as a *sum*. And the manifoldness of those things would rest not on the limitation of the original being itself, but on that of its complete consequence" (1996, 569). This means that "limitation" is just a defective manner of speaking—even if, given our lack of access to any transcendent reality, it turns out to be an unavoidable one. God, as the master of the disjunctive syllogism, must actively distribute the disjunctions that constitute reality, deriving them as positive consequences of his own being—rather than acting as a principle of limitation. In this way, Kant's God is not opposed to Klossowski's Baphomet, so much as the two are inextricably conjoined. We might even say that Kant passes over to the side of the Baphomet, to the extent that he warns us against the "natural illusion" of trying to "hypostasize this idea of the sum of all reality" (571). Empirically, all we can understand is "the *passage* of each thing through all of its possible predicates" (Deleuze 1990, 296); we can reach the "determinability" of all things in this way, but we cannot ever know the presumed principle of their complete determination.

In all this, Kant affirms the "a priori principle" of disjunction—even at the expense of the figure of God himself. In his discussion of the "Transcendental Ideal" of the "thoroughgoing determination" of reality, Kant points out that the mere presentation of such an ideal "does not presuppose the existence of such a being as conforms to this ideal" (Kant 1996, 568). Kant's argument treats God only as a *personification* of the disjunctive syllogism (cf. 572, note 83). This is a very different matter from attributing the power of operating the disjunction to a God whose existence would already have been established on other grounds. Indeed, it is precisely Kant's characterization of God in terms of the disjunctive syllogism that allows him to refute the traditional arguments for God's existence. When God is defined as the principle of the disjunctive syllogism and thereby invested with all possible predicates, the ironic result is to divest him of the so-called predicate of existence. For "no matter through which and through how many predicates I think a thing . . . not the least is added to this thing by my going on to say that this thing *is*" (584). Even all the possible predicates in the universe gathered together cannot add up to any necessary existence. The idea of God as master of disjunctions allows us to represent the world disjunctively, as a "distributive unity"; but such a unity is a limited one, and it "does not allow us to conclude that his Idea represents a collective or singular unity of a being in itself which would be represented by the Idea" (Deleuze 1990, 296, referring to Kant 1996, 571–572). In other words, to say that existence is not a predicate is to say that the philosophical idea of God—as the priniciple of the disjunctive synthesis, or of the "thoroughgoing determination" of reality—is not a constitutive idea, but only a regulative (or problematic) one. And this is why Kant insists that God's existence cannot be proven cognitively, but only affirmed practically (as happens in the Second Critique).

In *Anti-Oedipus*, Deleuze and Guattari replace Kant's God with what they call the body without organs (BwO). Following the opposition between God and the Antichrist already established in *The Logic of Sense*, they say that "the body without organs is not God, quite the contrary" (1983, 13). I've been trying to suggest, however, that this opposition is a bit too easy and abrupt. The conditions as Deleuze and Guattari actually describe them are much more tangled. The body without organs, just like Kant's God, oscillates between the two poles of the disjunctive synthesis. At times, it is exclusive and restrictive, like Leibniz's God with its exclusion of incompossibles; at other times, it is inclusive and nonrestrictive, in the manner of Schreber's God or Klossowski's Baphomet. This follows from the way that the body without organs is introduced as "a third term" (7), interrupting the binary logic of the connective synthesis of flows and cuts. The body without organs is a recording surface, a site of inscription for this disjunctive synthesis. "Everything stops dead for a moment, everything freezes in place—and then the whole process will begin all over again" (7). The body without organs is not itself a dynamic process. It is rather "an enormous undifferentiated object . . . the unproductive, the sterile, the unengendered, the unconsumable" (8). It does not itself flow, does not connect and cut; but every flow passes over it, and every cut is recorded upon it. For every "process of production" requires "an element of antiproduction" (8), a point where the process stops altogether: in short, a dose of mortality. "From a certain point of view it would be better if nothing worked, if nothing functioned" (7). Deleuze and Guattari go so far as to identify the body without organs with the Freudian and Lacanian *death drive*: "for desire desires death also, because the full body of death is its motor, just as it desires life, because the organs of life are the *working machine*" (8). And this death, this antiproduction, is precisely a figure of God.[13]

---

13. Angela Carter works through a similar dynamic in her novel *The Infernal Desire Machines of Doctor Hoffman* (1986). We are told that the novel's eponymous mad scientist (perhaps named after the discoverer of LSD) "was waging a massive campaign against human reason itself" by using his "desire machines" to flood the city with waves of "actualized desire." In Doctor Hoffman's profusion of surrealistic "mirages" made flesh, "life itself had become nothing but a complex labyrinth and everything that could possibly exist, did so." With all possibilities, desires, and fantasies equally present, "nothing . . . was identical with itself any more." The result is "a complexity so rich it can hardly be expressed in language." However, the narrator, who ironically calls himself Desiderio, is "bored" by the wonders and complexities that Doctor Hoffman generates with his desire machines. He wearies of relentless novelty, and develops, instead, "an admiration for stasis" (12). "I myself had only the one desire," he says. "And that was, for everything to stop" (11).

The notion of the body without organs is, of course, taken from the late writings of Antonin Artaud. Deleuze first introduces the body without organs in *The Logic of Sense*, where it is associated with a "universal depth," resulting from a catastrophic "collapse of the surface" (Deleuze 1990, 87). In *Anti-Oedipus*, however, Deleuze and Guattari associate the body without organs with a different concept developed in *The Logic of Sense*: the concept of *quasi-causality*. Deleuze and Guattari posit an "apparent conflict" (1983, 9)—a Kantian Antinomy—between the active material causality of desiring production, and the quasi-causal "antiproduction" of the body without organs. Just as quasi-causality, in *The Logic of Sense*, qualifies and alleviates the "poisonous mixtures" and "abominable necromancies" of material causality (Deleuze 1990, 131), so in *Anti-Oedipus* the body without organs repels the "larvae and loathsome worms" of desiring production (Deleuze and Guattari 1983, 9). And just as the Stoic doctrine of events, in *The Logic of Sense*, involves an exploration and elaboration of the surface, and the separation of this surface from the schizophrenic depths, so in *Anti-Oedipus* the body without organs "plays the role of a recording surface . . . an enchanted recording or inscribing surface that arrogates to itself all the productive forces and all the organs of production" that were previously rumbling in the depths (1983, 11–12).[14]

---

14. Even the figure of Oedipus plays an analogous role in both texts, despite the later book's attacks on the logic of Oedipalization that was articulated in the earlier one. In *The Logic of Sense*, Oedipus is the "pacifying hero" who "dispelled the infernal power of depths and the celestial power of heights, and now claims only a third empire, the surface, nothing but the surface" (Deleuze 1990, 201). In *Anti-Oedipus*, this function is condemned rather than celebrated; but it remains the case "that Oedipus is a requirement or a consequence of social reproduction, insofar as this latter aims at domesticating a genealogical form and content that are in every way intractable" (Deleuze and Guattari 1983, 13). In both texts, Oedipal quasi-causality tames (but cannot altogether master) the schizophrenic intensities produced in the depths of materiality and of bodies.

Anti-Oedipus is usually read as repudiating the depth–surface opposition that structured *The Logic of Sense*. But the actual relation between the two books is more complicated than such a formulation would indicate. In *The Logic of Sense*, quasi-causality is described as an effect of the surface; to the contrary, Artaud's Body without Organs is presented as a pure experience of the depths (Deleuze 1990, 82–93, *passim*). In *Anti-Oedipus*, however, the imageless figures

Deleuze and Guattari seek to avoid both the idealized notion of a plenum with total continuity, in which nothing could happen because nothing would be missing, and the Hegelian logic of negativity and lack, in which absence and contradiction would be the motors of change. The body without organs is the solution to this Antinomy. For it is neither an integral whole nor an emptiness. Rather, as an "amorphous, undifferentiated fluid" (1983, 9), it is utterly ambiguous, partaking of both fullness and emptiness, but not reducible to either. "The body without organs is not the proof of an original nothingness, nor is it what remains of a lost totality" (8). It is best thought of as Being Degree Zero: that which stubbornly remains, resisting all negation, even when every positive quality has been taken away. The body without organs in itself produces nothing; but it must be "perpetually reinserted into the process of production" (8). Within the process, it *makes things happen* by imposing its pauses and blockages, disjunctions and alternatives. Desiring production always also involves antiproduction. Every cause is accompanied by its shadow: a quasi-cause that is ephemeral, "anonymous," and "nondifferentiated" (9), but altogether real for all that.

This is the point at which Deleuze and Guattari encounter Marx. There are two ways in which the logic of the body without organs can be identified with the logic of capital that Marx describes. In the first place, when the body without organs interrupts and deadens production, it also captures the fruits of production (the products), attributes these products to itself, and distributes them all across its surfaces. This is what Marx calls exploitation, or the extraction of surplus value. And in the second place, just as, for Marx, the surplus value extracted in the process of production cannot be realized without a concomitant movement of circulation, so, for Deleuze and Guattari, the

---

of quasi-causality on the surface, and of the Body without Organs in the depths, are equated with one another. This is why the Body without Organs is described as both a "recording surface" and a "full body." The "nondifferentiated" blankness of antiproduction is both a surface effect and a deep "counterflow of amorphous, undifferentiated fluid" (Deleuze and Guattari 1983, 9). Thus *Anti-Oedipus* retains both the distinction between surface and depth, and the distinction between material causality (production) and quasi-causality (antiproduction); only it redistributes these two distinctions, instead of aligning them with one another.

productions of the connective synthesis cannot be actualized without the concomitant circulations and inscriptions of the disjunctive synthesis, as recorded on the surface of the body without organs. This is how the body without organs is a "machine" of both repulsion and attraction. It takes the form both of a "recording surface," and of what Deleuze and Guattari call the *socius*: "a full body" of social production (1983, 10). Under the capitalist mode of production, this socius is the body of capital itself, "the body that Marx is referring to when he says that it is not the product of labor, but rather appears as its natural or divine presupposition" (10). Human labor is the actual, material cause of social reproduction today; but capital is the quasi-cause, sterile and seemingly unengendered or self-engendered, upon whose surfaces this reproduction is recorded, through whose mediations it is organized, and to whose depths we cannot avoid attributing it.[15]

Marx describes how capital arrogates the products of living labor to itself, so that it *appears as if* the surplus value extracted from that labor were a "natural" result of capital's own autonomous process of "self-valorization." But this "appears as if" is not a mere falsification; part of Marx's point is that the self-valorization of capital is, in its own right, a sort of *objective illusion*, or what Deleuze and Guattari call an "apparent objective movement" (1983, 10–11). In capitalism's image of itself, labor is placed alongside raw materials, machinery, rent, and so on as a mere input of production; profit is calculated as a function, and indeed a product, of the total capital advanced. The creative role of living labor is thereby occluded. But this image is not *just* a mystification (though it is also that). For it is less a false representation of the capitalist system than it is an actual aspect of capital's self-representation. And this "ideological" self-representation is itself necessary to Capital's own internal functioning. Entrepreneurs and enterprises *must* themselves adopt this image, this

---

15. "Human labor" must here be taken to include the productivity of what Virno (2004) and Hardt and Negri (2001) call "immaterial labor," "affective labor," and "general intellect." Though certain theorists (e.g., Lazzarato 2004) seem to think that such phenomena invalidate Marx's insights about the exploitation of "living labor," they actually conform all too fully to the ways in which productive causal processes are appropriated by, and assimilated to, the quasi-causality of capital.

method of calculation, in order for the capitalist mode of production to work at all. This is what it means to say that capital *per se* is the quasi-cause of social production—in contrast to living labor as its material cause. Marx says that "the movement of capital is . . . limitless," because "the circulation of money as capital is an end in itself . . . the valorization of value takes place only within this constantly renewed movement" (Marx 1992, 253). In Deleuze and Guattari's terms, capital as the body without organs incessantly "falls back on [*se rabat sur*] all production, constituting a surface over which the forces and agents of production are distributed, thereby appropriating for itself all surplus production and arrogating to itself both the whole and the parts of the process, which now seem to emanate from it as a quasi cause . . . the socius as a full body forms a surface where all production is recorded, whereupon the entire process appears to emanate from this recording surface" (1983, 10).[16]

Evidently, Whitehead says nothing about the dynamics of capitalism in *Process and Reality*. Nonetheless, Whitehead's God, just like the body without organs, is best understood—in the way first adumbrated by Kant—as the operator of the disjunctive synthesis, in both its limitative and inclusive uses. "We conceive actuality as in essential relation to an unfathomable possibility," Whitehead says (1925/1967, 174). God, like the body without organs, figures and embodies this "essential relation." He facilitates the passage—in both

---

16. Capital is not the material cause of what it produces; but, as that which organizes and conceptualizes the system of production, it emerges retrospectively as the quasi-cause. This is perhaps why we should be suspicious of the current mania for *self-organization* and *emergence*. There is nothing inherently liberating about such concepts. For every Deleuzian account of self-organization, like the brilliant one worked out by Brian Massumi (2002), there is also an account, by the likes of Friedrich Hayek (1991) or Kevin Kelly (1994), of the capitalist market as a wondrously self-organizing system. The theology of market self-organization is the postmodern version of Adam Smith's capitalist/Calvinist notion of the invisible hand; like its predecessor, this theology simply ignores all questions of exploitation. For Deleuze and Guattari, the problem is how to imagine a form of self-organization that is not exploitative, and that does not just reproduce and expand itself, pushing itself to its limit and then recomposing itself anew at every limit. This is also the problem of how genuine novelty, as imagined by Whitehead and by Deleuze, might be something other than incessant capitalist innovation, "capitalistic fashion-novelty."

directions—between limitless potentiality on the one hand, and the concrete existence, or "givenness" (Whitehead 1929/1978, 43), of actual occasions, on the other. Much like the body without organs, God is only a quasi-cause. He does not actually create the universe: for Whitehead, creation happens in the concrescent decisions of all actual occasions, just as, for Deleuze and Guattari, creation is the productive activity of all the desiring machines. But God can be regarded as a sort of adjoining cocreator. In *Science and the Modern World*, Whitehead suggests that God provides the "antecedent limitation among values" that is the condition of possibility for all creation (1925/1967, 178). And in *Process and Reality*, Whitehead says that God both stimulates each occasion's concrescent decisions (the "primordial nature of God"), and registers them (the "consequent nature of God"). In this way, Whitehead's God can well be regarded, like the body without organs, as a figure of *induction, circulation*, and *communication*.[17]

My aim here is not to identify Whitehead's God with the body without organs, but only to suggest that the two concepts are structurally parallel. They both respond to the same necessity: that of conceiving a nontotalizing and

---

17. I will touch only briefly here on the vexed question of the relation between what Whitehead calls the "primordial" and "consequent" natures of God. The primordial nature of God is purely conceptual, as it involves potentiality or virtuality: "viewed as primordial, he is the unlimited conceptual realization of the absolute wealth of potentiality. In this aspect, he is not *before* all creation, but *with* all creation" (Whitehead 1929/1978, 343). This is God as "the principle of concretion—the principle whereby there is initated a definite outcome from a situation riddled with ambiguity" (345). The consequent nature of God, on the other hand, is physical and actual. It "is derived from the objectification of the world in God . . . the concrescent creature is objectified in God as a novel element in God's objectification of that actual world" (345). That is to say, the consequent nature of God involves something like the inscription, or recording, of everything that has happened on all actual occasions. The primordial nature of God is an opening toward futurity, the condition of possibility for every becoming. The consequent nature of God is like Bergsonian memory, or "pure recollection": the "being in itself of the past" (Deleuze 1991, 60), or its preservation *as* past. Very roughly speaking, the primordial nature of God corresponds to the body without organs as virtual "full body," whereas the consequent nature of God corresponds to the body without organs as "recording surface."

open "whole" in which all potentiality may be expressed. A metaphysics of process and becoming cannot do without some principle of unification, lest it drift off into atomized incoherence. But it also cannot allow such a principle to fix it into any sort of finality or closure.[18] Deleuze and Guattari therefore proclaim that they "believe only in totalities that are peripheral. And if we discover such a totality alongside various separate parts, it is a whole *of* these particular parts but does not totalize them; it is a unity *of* all of these particular parts but does not unify them; rather, it is added to them as a new part fabricated separately" (1983, 42). The body without organs is a "whole" or "unity" that does not subsume, but subsists alongside, the flows and cuts whose permutations it records and attributes to itself. Whitehead's God is also such a peripheral "whole" or "unity." Indeed, "each temporal occasion embodies God, and is embodied in God" (Whitehead 1929/1978, 348). But this God only sits alongside the world, rather than actually containing and determining it.

This is evident especially in the way that Whitehead revises Kant. Whitehead's God, like Kant's, is concerned with "*possibility in its entirety*" (Kant 1996, 564). But where Kant's God encompasses, or grounds, all possible predicates, Whitehead's God merely "envisages" eternal objects (cf. Whitehead 1929/1978, 44). Eternal objects are not quite the same thing as predicates;[19]

---

18. This is what differentiates process thought from any form of the dialectic. For Bergson, Whitehead, and Deleuze, and contrary to Hegel (1977, 407), "the wounds of the Spirit" can never be made whole; and they always *do* leave scars behind. The past persists *as past*, in its entirety: an "objective immortality" that cannot be subsumed or sublated. But this persistence is itself the condition for a radically open future, one that cannot be prefigured or contained by any sort of dialectical movement.

19. Whitehead defines a "predicate" as a "complex eternal object" that is assigned to some "logical subject," which may be an actual entity or a society of such entities (1929/1978, 24). This means that predicates are elements of "propositions," or of limited hypotheses concerning matters of fact. "The predicates define a potentiality of relatedness for the subjects" of a proposition (188). The point is that predicates are only a subset of eternal objects. Every actual entity aside from God "entertains," or admits into feeling, particular predicates. But God envisages all eternal objects, indiscriminately. Predication in propositional thought is a kind of limitative use of the disjunctive synthesis; but God's envisagement of eternal objects is not thus limited.

Also, it is only with "the acceptance of the "substance-quality" concept as expressing the ultimate ontological principle" that potentialities are limited to the status of predicates (157).

and envisagement is a far more modest activity than "thoroughgoing determination." If God "envisages" potentialities, this carries the suggestion that he is merely approaching them from the outside. And indeed, Whitehead's God displays a basic *appetition*: "an urge towards the future based upon an appetite in the present" (32). God's desire consists in "yearning after concrete fact—no particular facts, but after *some* actuality" (33). This would be superfluous, and indeed ridiculous, in the case of a Being who was already the principle of a "thoroughgoing determination" of reality. But for Whitehead, it is only possible to conceive of God at all if we conceive of him as an empirical phenomenon, "an actual entity immanent in the actual world" (93). God is "primordial," in the sense that his "aversions and adversions" encompass "the complete conceptual valuation of all eternal objects"—in contrast to all other entities, which just prehend a limited selection of them. But this "primordial nature" must itself be recognized, not as an overarching transcendence, but simply as "an actual efficient fact" (32).

In other words, Whitehead accepts the challenge that Kant throws down to speculative theology: "if the empirically valid law of causality is to lead to the original being, then this being would likewise have to belong to the chain of objects of experience; but in that case this being would itself, like all appearances, be conditioned in turn" (Kant 1996, 613). Whitehead's God is a special sort of entity, but one that is still *conditioned*, still part of "the chain of objects of experience." He is transcendent, but only in the way that other entities also are: "the transcendence of God is not peculiar to him. Every actual entity, in virtue of its novelty, transcends its universe, God included" (Whitehead 1929/1978, 93–94). God is himself subject to what Whitehead calls the ontological principle: "that actual entities are the only *reasons*; so that to search for a *reason* is to search for one or more actual entities" (24). Whitehead's

---

Once we free ourselves of the "substance-quality" concept, we can conceive of eternal objects as more than predicates. Whitehead ultimately defines eternal objects as "Pure Potentials for the Specific Determination of Fact"; it is thanks to the "ingression" of these pure potentials into actual entities that "it belongs to the nature of a 'being' that it is a potential for every becoming" (22). This "principle of relativity" corresponds to an inclusive and nonrestrictive use of the disjunctive syllogism.

God, through his desires, provides a "reason" for all other actual entities; but these entities, in turn, also provide reasons for him. Any account of "sufficient reason" must include God; but such an account can never be limited just to God.

Where Kant's God directly corresponds to the overarching relational category of "community" (the reciprocal determination of all entities), Whitehead's God is only another member of this community. "The actual world must always mean the community of all actual entities, including the primordial actual entity called 'God' and the temporal actual entities" (1929/1978, 65). God does not determine the relation of community, but is caught up within this relation as one of its terms. Or, to put it in another way, God cannot himself be the principle of the reciprocal determination of entities in the world, because God and the World already reciprocally determine one another, in the larger movement of what Whitehead calls "creativity." This is why Whitehead can posit a series of strange and striking Antinomies in the relationship between God and World. These two terms "stand over against each other," mutually interpenetrating but never coinciding. For "God and the World are the contrasted opposites in terms of which Creativity achieves its supreme task of transforming disjoined multiplicity, with its diversities in opposition, into concrescent unity, with its diversities in contrast" (348).

When Whitehead first introduces the notion of God, in *Science and the Modern World*, he stresses the limitative use of the disjunctive synthesis. God's role is to impose "an antecedent limitation composed of conditions, particularizations, and standards of value.... Some particular *how* is necessary, and some particularization in the *what* of matter of fact is necessary" (1925/1967, 178). This emphasis on limitation is modified and complicated, but not altogether dropped, in *Process and Reality*. In that text, Whitehead reaffirms that "God is the principle of concretion; namely, he is that actual entity from which each temporal concrescence receives that initial aim from which its self-causation starts" (1929/1978, 244). Every entity makes its own "transcendent decision"; but "transcendent decision includes God's decision" (164) as one of its initial conditions. In this way, God stands for the constrictions of "stubborn fact which cannot be evaded" (43). He imposes "the limitation whereby there is a perspective relegation of eternal objects to the background.... He is the actual entity in virtue of which the *entire* multiplicity of eternal objects obtains its graded relevance to each stage of the concrescence" (164). God contemplates all potentialities without exception. But he also governs the passage from "general" or "absolute" potentiality, which he alone is able to envisage, to "'real' potentiality, which is conditioned by the data provided by the actual world," and which is "relative to some actual entity, taken as a standpoint whereby the actual world is defined" (65). God makes the eternal objects (potentialities) available to each actual entity; but he organizes these eternal objects according to their "graded relevance" to that particular entity.

In other words, God stands for the fatality whereby a single definitive route has been chosen through the labyrinthine branchings of Borges's Garden of Forking Paths, and the steps can no longer be retraced. This limitative use of the disjunctive synthesis is a consequence of the irreversibility of time. Once the selection has been made, it cannot be reverted to, or altered. The "inevitable ordering of things, conceptually realized in the nature of God," is without appeal, and without justification: "this function of God is analogous to the remorseless working of things in Greek and in Buddhist thought. The initial aim is the best for that *impasse*. But if the best be bad, then the ruthlessness of God can be personified as *Atè*, the goddess of mischief. The chaff is burnt" (244). The "inital aim," once it has been chosen, cannot be reversed or reverted back to. This is at the root of Whitehead's objection to Leibniz. It all comes down to the way that Leibniz seeks to justify this fatality, to insist that God makes a rational selection among possible worlds, and that this selection is ultimately for the best. To the contrary, Whitehead insists that if "God is the ultimate limitation," then "His existence is the ultimate irrationality. For no reason can be given for just that limitation which it stands in His nature to impose" (1925/1967, 178). God is not just inexorable; he is also arbitrary.[20]

But if God enforces the irreparability of the past, he also guarantees the openness of the future. And in this role, he stands for an inclusive and nonrestrictive use of the disjunctive synthesis. God "embod[ies] a basic completeness

---

20. This is yet another way in which Whitehead remains an heir to Kant's critical revolution, rather than reverting to precritical thought. Deleuze lists as one of Kant's great "poetic formulas" the way that "Kant reverses the relationship of the law and the Good." Where traditional metaphysics, from Plato onward, derives all moral laws from the ideal of the Good,

of appetition" (Whitehead 1929/1978, 316): that is to say, his "urge towards the future," or "yearning after fact," embraces all potentials (all eternal objects) absolutely indiscriminately. God's "primordial nature" involves "the unconditioned conceptual valuation of the entire multiplicity of eternal objects" (31). This means that Whitehead's God, no less than Schreber's or Klossowski's, envisages a passage through all possible combinations of predicates (or better, of qualities and affects) without regard for their incompatibilities with one another. In this sense, God encompasses "the general potentiality of the universe" (46), unconstrained by the limits of particular actualizations. If he governs the movement from general to real potentiality, he also holds out the prospect of the inverse movement, from the constraints of limited, real potentiality to a surplus of general, absolute potentiality. And this surplus is never exhausted; it "retains its proximate relevance to actual entities for which it is unrealized" (46). That is to say, "the vector prehensions of God's appetition" (316) enter into the experience of every actual occasion. God's envisagement of all eternal objects—including the ones that a given occasion would not otherwise encounter in its environment—is itself an objective datum for every new concrescence.

The presence of God's "conceptual feelings" as "data" for all actual occasions (Whitehead 1929/1978, 247) is the reason why there is never just mere repetition. In every concrescence, "physical inheritance is essentially accompanied by a conceptual reaction partly conformed to it, and partly introductory of a relevant novel contrast, but always introducing emphasis, valuation, and purpose" (108). God is the source of such a "conceptual reaction" involving "contrast"; he provides the alternatives that allow the entity to make its own

---

for Kant "it is the Good which depends on the Law, and not vice versa. . . . The Law as empty form in the *Critique of Practical Reason* corresponds to time as pure form in the *Critique of Pure Reason*" (Deleuze 1984, x). Whitehead replaces Kant's "empty form" of the Categorical Imperative with God's merely empirical arbitrariness; but he remains Kantian in his refusal to subject this arbitrary "decision" to any preexisting standard of rationality or Goodness, or to any higher form of justification. "What is metaphysically indeterminate has nevertheless to be categorically determinate. We have come to the limits of rationality" (Whitehead 1925/1967, 178).

"decision." This is why Whitehead proclaims, again and again, that "apart from God, there could be no relevant novelty" (164); that "God is the organ of novelty, aiming at intensification" (67); that, "apart from such orderings" of eternal objects as occur in the primordial nature of God, "novelty would be meaningless, and inconceivable" (40); and that "apart from the intervention of God, there could be nothing new in the world" (247).

God is a force for novelty, precisely because he does not determine the actual course of events. To the contrary, he ensures the indeterminacy of this course, its openness to difference in the future. God's own "decision" offers the raw material, as it were, for the decisions made by all other entities. Whitehead's God is therefore an antientropic force; without him, "the course of creation would be a dead level of ineffectiveness, with all balance and intensity progressively excluded by the cross currents of incompatibility" (Whitehead 1929/1978, 247). God renovates the universe by making incompossibles compatible. In case of contradiction or exclusion, he "converts the opposition into a contrast" (348), so that formerly irreconcilable terms become thinkable and realizable together. Whitehead's God may not quite embody the category of community (reciprocal determination) in the way that Kant's does; but at least he widens the scope of such community. God is the reason why mere linear causality (the "causal efficacy" of "physical inheritance") cannot completely determine (although, of course, it strongly constrains) the course of events. Even more, God is a stimulus for change: in Whitehead's most striking phrase, he is "the goad towards novelty" (88). God provides the "lure for feeling" (189, 344) that seduces an entity into its process of becoming, or that draws it into difference.

Whitehead's God is the Principle of Concretion, then, in a double sense. Through the limitative use of the disjunctive synthesis, God enforces the narrowing-down of potentials that is a necessary part of any movement of concrete actualization. He embodies the requirement that each actual entity must make a "decision," in order to exhibit a "determinate attitude towards every element in the universe" (1929/1978, 45). Deleuze would have to say that, for such a God, "disjunctions have the negative value of exclusion" (Deleuze 1990, 297). But at the same time, through the inclusive use of the disjunctive synthesis, Whitehead's God *also* distributes multiple (and even incompatible) potentials, widening the scope of the actual entity's "decision," and allowing it, or forcing it, to enact "the modification of its initial subjective aim" (Whitehead 1929/1978, 245). This is the God that, according to Deleuze's reading of Whitehead, "becomes Process, a process that at once affirms incompossibilities and passes through them" (Deleuze 1993, 81). In Whitehead's own terms, through God's intervention "the actual includes what (in one sense) is 'not-being' as a positive factor in its own achievement," so that "fact is confronted with alternatives" (Whitehead 1929/1978, 189, repeating 1925/1967, 176). The entity is now able to depart from mere "conformation to pattern," and instead express "novel conceptual feeling," by claiming and proclaiming "its own flash of autonomous individual experience" (1929/1978, 245). All in all, "the creative process is a process of exclusion to the same extent as it is a process of inclusion" (1926/1996, 113). Every entity's creative "decision" is an act both of narrowing down (as multiple potentials are congealed into a single actuality) and of opening up (as alternative possibilities are "entertained"); and God is the promoter, or the catalyst, of both of these facets of the process.[21]

On the technical level of Whitehead's metaphysics, this account of God is needed in order to resolve the difficulties raised by the Category of Conceptual Reversion. Whitehead initially formulates this Category as follows:

---

21. Tim Clark (2002), in his lucid and powerful discussion of Deleuze's encounter with Whitehead, argues against Deleuze's reading of Whitehead's God as a figure of affirmation and metamorphosis. For Clark, Whitehead's God never performs the disjunctive synthesis in a fully affirmative or Deleuzian manner. Rather, since for Whitehead "*restriction* and *limitation* are the conditions of value," Whitehead's God "is still required to enact, or at least to found, disjunctions that are not yet positively synthetic or wholly affirmative" (198). Whitehead never quite reaches the condition of a Deleuzian "chaosmos," because "within Whitehead's system the universe remains, in principle, only semi-open and therefore partially predictable" (202). Deleuze is misreading, therefore, when he attributes his own "total affirmation" of difference to Whitehead, who never fully escapes "the weight of ontotheological tradition bearing down upon him" (205).

I have learned a lot from Clark's discussion; in particular, I am indebted to him for reading Whitehead's notion of God in the light of Deleuze's discussion of the Kantian (and Klossowskian) disjunctive syllogism. And Clark is entirely right to see elements of limitation and exclusion at work in Whitehead's account of God. I differ from Clark in that I see a movement between the exclusive and inclusive uses of the disjunctive synthesis at work in

"There is secondary origination of conceptual feelings with data which are partially identical with, and partially diverse from, the eternal objects forming the data in the first phase of the mental pole. The diversity is a relevant diversity determined by the subjective aim" (1929/1978, 26). That is to say, an actual occasion is not limited to prehending only those eternal objects that are realized in the empirical data in front of it. Even if everything that it sees is blue, it is also able to imagine red. It is capable of forming feelings, and yearning after potentialities, that are "diverse from" those provided by "the data in the first phase" of experience.

This is a categorical requirement of Whitehead's system, or what Kant would call a necessary "transcendental presupposition": for otherwise novelty would be impossible. Without some notion of "conceptual reversion," an actual entity that prehended only blue-colored data would never be able to posit redness. But it is hard to see how the Category of Conceptual Reversion is consistent, or coherent, with Whitehead's basic ontological principle, which states that "every condition to which the process of becoming conforms in any particular instance has its reason *either* in the character of some actual entity in the actual world of that concrescence, *or* in the character of the subject which is in process of concrescence" (24). Where, then, does the imagination of redness come from? Since, by definition, the datum of a novel conceptual prehension is not present in any "actual entity in the actual world of that concrescence," it must arise out of "the character of the subject which is in process of concrescence," which is to say, out of the entity's "subjective aim."

But how does such a previously "unfelt eternal object" (249) ingress into, and alter, an entity's subjective aim in the first place? What enables "the positive conceptual prehension of relevant alternatives" (249)? Traditional idealist metaphysics resolves this problem by appealing to some Platonic principle of

---

both Whitehead's account of God and Deleuze's account of the body without organs—and, indeed, already in Kant's account of God. Though Deleuze tends to describe the opposition between the two uses of the synthesis polemically and absolutely, in practice he slides back and forth between them—because every actualization of the virtual unavoidably involves some sort of limitation, and because the analysis of forms of coding and capture, on the one hand, and of the mobilization of "lines of flight" on the other, necessarily makes reference to the tension between these two uses.

recollection: the Idea of red exists in itself, independently of my thinking it; and for that very reason it is accessible to my thought. Today's cognitive science, following Kant, retains this argument by subjectivizing it: the Idea of red may not exist in and of itself, but it is a necessary product of innate structures of the human mind. But Whitehead is loath to accept this line of reasoning—even though he compares what he calls "eternal objects" to the Platonic forms (44). For any appeal to already given forms would mean limiting the scope of novelty by reducing it to mere structural permutations or variations of a theme.

At first, Whitehead entertains the idea that eternal objects might have the power within themselves to refer to other, related eternal objects: "the determinate definiteness of each actuality is an expression of a selection from these forms. It grades them in a diversity of relevance. This ordering of relevance starts from those forms which are, in the fullest sense, exemplified, and passes through grades of relevance down to those forms which in some faint sense are proximately relevant by reason of contrast with actual fact" (43–44). But ultimately Whitehead rejects this argument, because "the question, how, and in what sense, one unrealized eternal object can be more, or less, proximate to an eternal object in realized ingression—that is to say, in comparison with any other unfelt eternal object—is left unanswered by this Category of Reversion" (249–250). The "grades of relevance" and proximity among eternal objects can only be determined to the extent that these objects can be ordered in a closed and well-defined set. But this is belied by the fact that "nature is never complete," that "it is always passing beyond itself" (289). Whitehead states that "there are no novel eternal objects" (22); but he also requires us to conceive the "whole" of eternal objects as something other than a closed set. (The notion of a whole that is not a closed set is formulated by Deleuze in relation to Bergson: Deleuze 1986, 10–11.) These considerations lead Whitehead to insist that the question of the ingression of previously unrealized eternal objects "can be answered only by reference to some actual entity." In accordance with the ontological principle, there must be some empirical source for the "missing" eternal objects. The "conceptual prehension" of alternative potentialities must have its roots in a prior "physical prehension." God is the actual entity who fulfills this condition—or, whose existence Whitehead infers from the requirement to fulfill this condition. God prehends all eternal objects indiscriminately, and thereby makes them available to any "temporal entity" whatsoever. Through this appeal to God, "the Category of [Conceptual] Reversion is then abolished, and Hume's principle of the derivation of conceptual experience from physical experience remains without any exception" (250).[22]

To summarize, Whitehead posits, discovers, or constructs the figure of God for reasons that lie deep in his metaphysics. Like Aristotle, Whitehead is forced to move in this direction because "the general character of things requires that there be such an entity" (1925/1967, 173–174). And in contrast to Leibniz, Whitehead seeks to posit the figure of God in such a way that it does not come off as merely "an audacious fudge" (1929/1978, 47) used to resolve metaphysical discomforts. When Whitehead figures God as a process, and as an empirical being rather than a transcendent one, this means that God cannot be cited as an excuse, or invoked as an ultimate fallback explanation. For the point is precisely that God accounts for nothing, and excuses nothing. "No reason can be given for the nature of God; because that nature is the ground of rationality" (1925/1967, 178). That is to say, the "ground" is itself groundless and nonrational; it is even "the ultimate irrationality" (178). Where Leibniz (and Hegel too, for that matter) invokes God in order to confirm the rationality of the real, Whitehead invokes God precisely in order to acknowledge the all-too-evident absence of any such higher rationality. Whitehead's God helps to make things happen (in his "primordial" nature); and he contemplates and preserves everything that *has* happened (in his "consequent" nature). But God cannot be used in order to *explain* or *justify* anything.

In all this, Whitehead reveals himself, once again, to be Kant's inheritor, to a far greater extent than has generally been recognized. In his quest to secularize the notion of God, Whitehead, like Kant, moves from a speculative stance to a "practical" one. Whitehead makes this point explicitly when he says

---

22. Whitehead's struggle with this problem, and his initial assertion, and subsequent rejection, of the Category of Conceptual Reversion, is traced in detail by Lewis S. Ford (1984, 211–241, *passim*). The crucial point is that Whitehead's recourse to God is in fact, odd as this might seem, a way of rejecting transcendent solutions and embracing instead an immanent one. God is the correlate of Whitehead's "transcendental empiricism," just as the body without organs is of Deleuze's.

that his own "line of thought" in regard to God "extends Kant's argument. [Kant] saw the necessity for God in the moral order. But with his metaphysics he rejected the argument from the cosmos. The metaphysical doctrine, here expounded, finds the foundations of the world in the aesthetic experience, rather than—as with Kant—in the cognitive and conceptive experience" (Whitehead 1926/1996, 104–105). Kant, of course, tells us that "it is morally necessary to assume the existence of God" (Kant 2002, 159). We cannot ever prove, or cognitively establish, that God exists; but our moral duty impels us to assume that he does, and to act as if he does.[23]

Whitehead posits God on the basis of "aesthetic experience," rather than morality. To the extent that we make "decisions"—and, for Whitehead, *decision* "constitutes the very meaning of actuality" (1929/1978, 43)—we are engaged in a process of selection. We "feel" (or positively prehend) certain data, and "eliminate from feeling" (or negatively prehend) certain others (23). But this process of selection is an aesthetic one. It is felt, rather than thought (or felt before it is thought); and it is freely chosen, rather than being obligatory. The process of selection rests upon aesthetic critera, rather than either cognitive or moral ones. These criteria are what Whitehead calls the Categorial Obligations of "Subjective Harmony" and "Subjective Intensity" (27). The "subjective aim" of every actual occasion is first, to harmonize all its data, by making them "compatible for integration" into "one complex fully determinate feeling" (22); and second, to maximize the intensity of this feeling. The goal of every decision is therefore Beauty, defined by Whitehead as "the mutual adaptation of the several factors in an occasion of experience"

---

23. Kant is careful to point out that "this moral necessity is *subjective*, i.e. a need, and not *objective*, i.e. itself a duty; for there can be no duty whatever to assume the existence of a thing (because doing so concerns only the theoretical use of reason)" (2002, 159). It is not even our *duty* to believe in God; it is only the case that we are pragmatically *forced* to believe in God—i.e., that we are unable not to believe in God—to the extent that we follow the commands of moral obligation. God cannot even be invoked as the basis of moral obligation; rather, moral obligation itself provides the sole basis for any belief in God. Whitehead follows Kant in the way that he posits God's existence adjunctively, rather than foundationally. But for Whitehead, it is aesthetics, rather than morality, that forces us to assume the existence of God.

(1933/1967, 252). As for the intensity with which this "adaptation" is felt, Whitehead simply notes that "an intense experience is an aesthetic fact" (1929/1978, 277).

These aesthetic decisions are singular in every case; they cannot be determined in advance, or made according to any rule. God is not the source of aesthetic selection for Whitehead, just as he is not the source of moral obligation for Kant. But the fact of aesthetic decision impels Whitehead to posit God, much as the fact of moral obligation forces Kant to assume that God exists. God is not the origin of creativity, then; but he emerges as a factor "which has to be taken account of in every creative phase" (1926/1996, 94). Whitehead's God may be regarded as a sort of baseline. He embodies the maximum of both harmony and intensity; and he provides a degree zero, in relation to which all particular harmonies and intensities can be measured. His "basic completeness of appetition" (1929/1978, 316) enters as a contrast into the particular appetitions (desires) of all actual occasions. God is the one being who never makes an aesthetic selection; for he positively prehends, or aesthetically appreciates, everything—rather than singling out certain things in preference to others. But such an act of universal appreciation must itself be a singular occurrence: "Unfettered conceptual valuation, 'infinite' in Spinoza's sense of that term, is only possible once in the universe; since that creative act is objectively immortal as an inescapable condition characterizing creative action" (247). Whitehead's God is not omnipotent, but he *is* "inescapable": no actual occasion can avoid encountering him as a datum.

All this makes Whitehead's God into a sort of ultimate aesthete: "The primordial appetitions which jointly constitute God's purpose are seeking intensity, and not preservation. . . . He, in his primordial nature, is unmoved by love for this particular, or that particular. . . . In the foundations of his being, God is indifferent alike to preservation and to novelty. He cares not whether an immediate occasion be old or new, so far as concerns derivation from its ancestry. His aim for it is depth of satisfaction as an intermediate step towards the fulfillment of his own being. . . . Thus God's purpose in the creative advance is the evocation of intensities" (1929/1978, 105). There is something quite cold here: something akin to Kantian aesthetic disinterest. Where Spinoza's God contemplates the world *sub specie aeternitatis*, understanding all phenomena in terms of their ultimate causes, Whitehead's God looks rather to effects and consequences, unfolding within time, insofar as these contribute to his own self-enjoyment.[24] Such is the difference between an Ethics and an Aesthetics.

I can't say that I particularly like Whitehead's God; but then, I don't suppose that Whitehead wants us to. For even as a figure of unlimited affirmation, God remains a singular being, rather than a totalizing or all-embracing one. Whitehead reminds us that "every actual entity, including God, is something individual for its own sake" (1929/1978, 88). This means that God too is acting for his own sake—rather than (as most religions and most philosophers have tended to suppose) for ours. In any case, the question of my own like or dislike of God is irrelevant. What matters is the indispensable function that God performs in Whitehead's universe. In practice, God is the "goad toward novelty," even though novelty *per se* leaves him indifferent. And he stimulates and cultivates intensities, even when such intensities are inimical to our persistence or survival.[25] In his very restlessness and relentlessness, God figures the way that difference can emerge in an ostensibly deterministic cosmos, and that newness can arise out of the recombination of already existing elements. These questions of emergent order, and of innovation through appropriation and citation, are ones that centrally engage us today. Whitehead's most abstruse and abstract metaphysical formulations remain strikingly relevant, not just (as Whitehead himself says) to the "insistent craving . . . of our immediate actions" (348), but also to the social, political, and ecological concerns of our postmodern world.

---

24. "Self-enjoyment" is a word, or concept, that Whitehead uses sparingly, but tellingly. In *Process and Reality*, he states that "an actual entity considered in reference to the privacy of things is a 'subject': namely, it is a moment of the genesis of self-enjoyment." This is contrasted with the way in which every actual entity must also be considered "in reference to the publicity of things [a]s a 'superject' "; in this latter respect, the entity is "objectively immortal"—which is to say it is a dead datum (1929/1978, 289). Later, in *Modes of Thought*, Whitehead writes more categorically that "the notion of life implies a certain absoluteness of self-enjoyment. . . . Life implies the absolute, individual self-enjoyment arising out of [a] process of appropriation" (1938/1968, 151). All entities, God included, must be defined in terms of this self-enjoyment.
25. As Whitehead dryly says, "God's purpose in the creative advance is the evocation of intensities. The evocation of societies is purely subsidiary to this absolute end" (1929/1978, 105). This aphorism becomes rather chilling when we realize that "the evocation of societies" means precisely the self-perpetuation of living organisms such as ourselves.

6
Consequences

Whitehead's "free and savage creation of concepts" (Stengers 2002b) goes well beyond anything that I have discussed in this book. I have scarcely considered, for instance, Whitehead's important theory of propositions (cf. especially Whitehead 1929/1978, 184–207) and the ways these serve as "lures for feeling" (25, 85ff., 184ff.), linking the potential to the actual. Nor have I gone into his extensive reflections on "hybrid prehensions," those perceptions and feelings that have both "physical" (material, causal) and "conceptual" (mental, potential, or hypothetical) aspects, and that are crucial, in turn, to his accounts of "symbolic reference" (168–183), language, and the emergence of consciousness. Moreover, I have not said nearly enough about the crucial distinction between "actual entities" or "actual occasions," the ultimate atomistic components of the universe in Whitehead's metaphysics, and the aggregations of these entities that Whitehead calls "societies," which include ourselves, and all the things that we come upon in the course of everyday experience. I have also not considered Whitehead's mathematics, or the question of how his thought relates to modern physics (relativity and quantum mechanics). All of these are matters for further research and elucidation.

My aim in *Without Criteria* has been a limited and specific one. I began this book counterfactually, with the "philosophical fantasy" of a situation in which Whitehead, rather than Heidegger, "had set the agenda for postmodern thought." I have therefore focused on those aspects of Whitehead's metaphysics that might especially *make a difference* in how we understand the world today. To this end, I have considered Whitehead's formulations regarding aesthetics and beauty, events and becoming, affect, causality, innovation and creativity, the nature of life and the conditions of biological science, and our "envisagement" of the ultimate. I have also traced the Enlightenment roots of Whitehead's thought: most notably, its engagement with Kant's critical project, and its participation in the modernist endeavor to *secularize* the elements of experience and thought. And I have linked crucial aspects of Whitehead's metaphysics to related movements in the philosophy of Gilles Deleuze. But in doing all this, I have barely opened the discussion that might ensue from taking Whitehead's ideas seriously.

Indeed, there can be no end to such discussions. For Whitehead's thought is capacious, open, and continually inventive; it does not reach (and, in principle, it can never reach) any sort of completion or self-reflexive closure. Whitehead continually reminds us that no metaphysical formulation is definitive. "In its turn every philosophy will suffer a deposition," he says, including his own (1929/1978, 7). It is a commonplace to say that "philosophy begins in wonder"; but Whitehead less commonly insists that, "at the end, when philosophic thought has done its best, the wonder remains" (1938/1968, 168). Wonder is not dissipated by philosophical speculation, because explaining things *adequately*, as Whitehead's philosophy strives to do,[1] means giving all phenomena and all experiences their due, and never explaining any of them away. "Philosophy destroys its usefulness when it indulges in brilliant feats of explaining away" (1929/1978, 17). Against all reductionism, Whitehead insists that "we may not pick and choose. For us the red glow of the sunset should be as much part of nature as are the molecules and electrical waves by which

---

1. Whitehead's technical use of the term *adequacy* is far removed from the common philosophical meaning of this term as a representational correspondence between ideas and things. Rather, Whitehead defines the "adequacy" of a "philosophic scheme" as meaning "that the texture of observed experience, as illustrating the philosophic scheme, is such that all related experience must exhibit the same texture" (1929/1978, 4). As Didier Debaise glosses this passage, "the scheme must be 'adequate' not to observed experience, which would return us to the idea of correspondence to a state of things or to an event, but rather to *related experiences*. The relationship is transversal: adequacy becomes *a relation among portions of experiences*" (Debaise 2006, 29–30; translation mine). There are continual relays, or resonances, between the experience of constructing the "philosophic scheme," and other, concurrent experiences; the aim of philosophy is to extend these relays and resonances as far as possible, so that everything experienced may be comprehended within them. "Adequacy" has to do with extension, rather than with correspondence. It is never given in advance, or once and for all; rather, it continually needs to be constructed, in the ongoing process of philosophical speculation.

men of science would explain the phenomenon" (1920/2004, 29). The phenomenologist only considers the red glow of the sunset; the physicist only considers the mechanics of electromagnetic radiation. But Whitehead insists on a metaphysics that embraces both. For "philosophy can exclude nothing" (1938/1968, 2).

This is not just a matter of philosophical method. Philosophical speculation has no finality, because the world within which (as well as about which) the philosopher speculates has no finality. Whitehead's thought has important *consequences*, but it does not offer us any firm conclusions. Everything within it is subject to revision. A thought that aims at adequacy cannot be ahistorical, and it cannot remain static. For "no actuality is a static fact. The historic character of the universe belongs to its essence" (Whitehead 1938/1968, 90). Indeed, adequacy is a goal that we will never fully reach. The best we can do is to make "an asymptotic approach" to it (1929/1978, 4), in the form of an "approximation" (13). Even at the end of his very last lecture, "Immortality," Whitehead is still warning us against "the absurd trust in the adequacy of our knowledge." For "the exactness" that rational discourse lays claim to "is a fake" (1951b, 699–700). There will always be new data to consider, and new contexts to take into account. "When anything is placed in another situation, it changes. . . . In fact, there is not a sentence, or a word, with a meaning which is independent of the circumstances under which it is uttered" (699).

This might seem to be just a commonplace of twentieth-century (and now twenty-first-century) thought. Surely the battle against essentialism, and against context-independent theories of meaning, was won long ago. Whitehead's diagnosis of the fallacies of "misplaced concreteness" (1929/1978, 7) and "simple location" (137), his rejection of "subject-predicate forms of thought" (7), and his insistence on the limitations of perception in the mode of "presentational immediacy" (61ff. and *passim*) run parallel to the critiques proffered in various ways by Heidegger and by Wittgenstein, and more recently by Derrida and by Rorty—not to mention already in the nineteenth century by Nietzsche, who mocked traditional philosophers' "hatred of the very idea of becoming," and worried that "we are not getting rid of God because we still believe in grammar" (Nietzsche 1968, 16, 19). All these thinkers reject essentialism, substantialism, positivism, and the notion of simple presence. They greatly differ, however, in terms of *style* and *manner*: which is to say, in their language, in the logical forms they use, and in the ways that they make their arguments. This means that they differ, above all, in terms of the *consequences* that can be drawn from their critiques. The arguments of these thinkers may run parallel in terms of logic, but *pragmatically* they are quite distinct.

For Whitehead, the insistence on ever-changing "circumstances" and contexts does not mean that philosophical discussion must end up in a hopeless aporia, as the deconstructionists maintain. Nor does it imply that philosophy is nothing more than a polite but ultimately inconsequential "conversation," and that the only "point of edifying philosophy is to keep the conversation going," as Richard Rorty suggests (1981, 377). Of course every metaphysical discourse is subject to what we now call deconstruction; for as Whitehead categorically states, "if we consider any scheme of philosophic categories as one complex assertion, and apply to it the logician's alternative, true or false, the answer must be that the scheme is false" (1929/1978, 8). This is unavoidable, since "metaphysical categories are not dogmatic statements of the obvious." Rather, at best, "they are tentative formulations of the ultimate generalities" (8). But the inevitable failure of these "tentative formulations" to pass logical muster tells us more about the limited pertinence of merely logical criteria than it does about the weakness of metaphysical speculation per se. Whitehead started his career as a logician; it is from his deep knowledge of the subject that he is able to "dismiss deductive logic as a major instrument for metaphysical discussion" and assert that "logic presupposes metaphysics," rather than the reverse (Whitehead 1938/1968, 107).

Whitehead insists that thought is stimulated, rather than paralyzed, when it is pushed to its limit, and when its "tentative formulations" break down under the pressure of changed circumstances, or simply in the face of additional evidence. Such is the point at which new concepts, and new categories, need to be invented. Philosophical speculation then becomes an urgent necessity, and not just a source of edifying conversation.[2] We live in a

---

2. In her article "Beyond Conversation" (2002a), Isabelle Stengers considers Whitehead's efforts toward "the fabrication of peace-making propositions" (245) through which oppositions can be transformed into contrasts. She insists that this project necessarily involves "the challenge

world, as Whitehead says, in which "the very meaning of life is in doubt" (1938/1968, 148). If this was already true in Whitehead's own time, it is even more urgently the case today, as we stand on the threshold of radically new technologies for manipulating life at the biochemical level. The meaning of life is radically in doubt, more than ever before; philosophy has the crucial task of constructing this meaning—or better, many such meanings.

Whitehead presents us with a highly systematized philosophy, and he seeks after "the most general systematization of civilized thought" (1929/1978, 17). But he also insists that, before any work of systematization can even begin, the "primary stage" of philosophy is a process of "*assemblage*" (1938/1968, 2). Philosophical speculation collects the most heterogeneous materials and puts them together in the most unexpected configurations. It is something like the practice of collage in modernist painting; or better—to use an analogy not from Whitehead's time, but from our own—it is like a DJ's practice of sampling and remixing. By extracting "patterned contrasts" (1929/1978, 115) from its assemblages, philosophy works toward "the entertainment of notions of large, adequate generality" (1938/1968, 3). For in the broadest sense, "metaphysics is nothing but the description of the generalities which apply to all the details of practice" (1929/1978, 13).

---

of not accepting the facile charms of academic conversation" (248). Rather, what is at stake is a philosophical construction or fabrication, "an ecological production of actual togetherness, where 'ecological' means that the aim is not toward a unity beyond differences, which would reduce those differences through a goodwill reference to abstract principles of togetherness, but toward a creation of concrete, interlocked, asymmetrical, and always partial graspings" (248–249). Rorty's "edifying conversation" is premised upon the notion that nothing, beyond such a "goodwill reference to abstract principles of togetherness," is really at stake in philosophical discussions. For Whitehead, however, philosophical disputes are intrinsically important, because they focus our attention on the often unnoticed background contexts and assumptions that frame our existence in the world. These contexts and assumptions need explicit consideration, because "there are no brute, self-contained matters of fact, capable of being understood apart from interpretation as an element in a system" (Whitehead 1929/1978, 14). This is why it is so crucial that, in the course of systematizing and generalizing, we must incorporate antagonistic perspectives without explaining any of them away, and also without reconciling them in a spurious sublation or higher unity.

These generalities are not given to us in advance; they need to be fabricated or discovered in the course of philosophical speculation. That is why assemblage is so important. Or, as Whitehead describes the process with a different metaphor, "the true method of discovery is like the flight of an aeroplane. It starts from the ground of particular observation; it makes a flight in the thin air of imaginative generalization; and it again lands for renewed observation rendered acute by rational interpretation" (1929/1978, 5). These repeated flights and landings allow for the addition of new elements into the assemblage, and for the continual expansion of meanings and contexts. Philosophical assemblage is itself a particular sort of practice: one that is of limited duration, and that is always partial and incomplete. Its value lies in the way that it helps us to renew other practices, those of the seemingly more precise "special sciences," by allowing us to "challenge the half-truths constituting the scientific first principles" (10), and to put them into broader perspective.

Deleuze and Guattari, no less than Whitehead, practice the art of philosophical assemblage.[3] And Whitehead's sense of philosophy as "providing generic notions which add lucidity to our apprehension of the facts of experience" (1929/1978, 10) is not far from Deleuze and Guattari's definition of philosophy as "the art of forming, inventing, and fabricating concepts" (1994, 2). In both cases, the aim is not a totalization, a definitive tracing of limits, or a final theory of everything. It is rather an expansion of possibilities, an invention of new methods and new perspectives, an active "entertainment" of things, feelings, ideas, and propositions that were previously unavailable

---

3. *Assemblage* is the usual English translation of Deleuze and Guattari's term *agencement* (1987, 503ff. and *passim*). An *agencement* is defined as a conjunction "of bodies, of actions and passions, an intermingling of bodies reacting to one another," and also "of acts and statements, of incorporeal transformations attributed to bodies" (88). Manuel De Landa generalizes these formulations into what he calls *assemblage theory*, emphasizing multiple, heterogeneous, and changeable "relations of exteriority" (De Landa 2006, 10ff. and *passim*). Whitehead's use of the term *assemblage* is far less systematic; indeed, he uses it precisely for that stage in philosophical speculation that precedes systematization. Nonetheless, my association of Whitehead's *assemblage* with Deleuze and Guattari's *agencement/assemblage* is justified in that both involve the construction of relations among heterogeneous terms that remain heterogeneous to one another even within these relations.

to us. The point of making generalizations, or of inventing concepts, is not to prove a thesis, but to expand and stimulate thought. Both Whitehead and Deleuze and Guattari seek to discover new facets of experience: to work out the notions and trace the relations that allow us to encounter aspects of the world, and things within the world, to which we have never paid attention before—or even which have never come into existence before. As Whitehead says, philosophy "make[s] it easier to conceive the infinite variety of specific instances which rest unrealized in the womb of nature" (1929/1978, 17). Regarded in this way, philosophy is turned toward the potential (or what Deleuze calls the virtual) and is concerned with the process of actualizing this potential. As Whitehead says, "a new idea introduces a new alternative" (11). It offers us a new way of approaching and understanding experience. In doing this, it is itself a new experience; and it also makes additional new experiences possible. Philosophy is, then, what Whitehead calls an "experimental adventure" (9), or an "adventure of ideas" (1933/1967). And even, or especially, in the grimmest of times, there is good reason to pursue this adventure.

If philosophy is an adventure, involving the creation of new concepts, this is because every aspect of life and thought already is (and always must be) creative. Whitehead insists that creation is not a rarity; nor is it something that happened only once, at the beginning of time. Rather, the process of creation is essential to the world as a whole; it is a generic feature of existence as such. Of course, there are always different degrees of creativity; a living organism is more creative, and generates considerably more novelty, than a stone. But even a stone is not a stolid, motionless entity. It is rather "a society of separate molecules in violent agitation" (1929/1978, 78). And these molecules, or the atoms and subatomic particles composing them, are themselves eventful, which is to say creative. For Whitehead, " 'creativity' is the universal of universals characterizing ultimate matter of fact" (21); it applies to every actual occasion, without exception. Indeed, each actual occasion is creative in its very nature. For each new occasion is "a novel entity diverse from any entity in the 'many' which it unifies," and out of which it emerges (21). The "creative advance into novelty" is thereby "the ultimate metaphysical ground" of everything (349).

It is worth reflecting on how strange and untimely Whitehead's attitude is. In the course of the past century, we have learned to distrust any sort of foundationalism, and hence any talk of universals, ultimates, or grounds. We find nothing more disreputable than unfettered metaphysical speculation. Positivist and antipositivist thinkers alike proclaim the end of Western metaphysics.[4] There would seem to be only three alternatives open to us today. Either we accept scientific reductionism, with its claim to derive everything from the hard facts of quantum physics and evolutionary biology; or we "annul *knowledge* in order to make room for *faith*" (Kant 1996, 31), embracing some variety of religious fundamentalism, new age spirituality, or business-management self-help ideology that gives meaning to our otherwise rudderless lives; or we suppose that nothing can really be known, that every claim to knowledge is a delusion, and that "reality" is just an arbitrary linguistic construction. In this latter case, it scarcely matters whether we celebrate the vertiginous freedom of postmodern indetermination, as some of Derrida's epigones do, or whether, to the contrary, we deplore the "extermination of the real" (Baudrillard) and the "decline of symbolic efficacy" (Žižek). All these approaches share the same basic assumption: that in our highly technologized, thoroughly disenchanted world, metaphysical speculation is no longer possible. It is replaced either by positivist reductionism, by blind faith, or by infinite relativism. In all three cases, metaphysics is over—even if we are ironically condemned, as Derrida suggests, to live out the indefinite postponement of this closure, and never to be done with what is nonetheless already finished.

Whitehead remains cheerfully indifferent to all these alternatives. Instead, he frankly and fully embraces the project of "speculative philosophy" (1929/1978, 3–17). What's more, his speculations issue in a metaphysics that rejects the reductionism of physical science, and yet remains thoroughly and robustly realist. How can this be? It's not that Whitehead is naive, sheltered, or detached; he is fully involved in the great convulsions of early-twentieth-century life, and he recognizes the same uncertainties and instabili-

---

4. The overcoming of metaphysics is the one project that is shared by modernist thinkers as antagonistic to one another as Carnap and Heidegger. The greatest continuity in Wittgenstein's career is that, in both his early and his late thought, he seeks to provide a therapy to cure us of metaphysics, which he conceives as a sort of disease. And the rejection of metaphysics is still the major concern of postmodern thinkers as otherwise different as Derrida and Rorty.

ties as do his contemporaries. In particular, he is acutely aware of the dilemmas that led to the "linguistic turn" of so much twentieth-century philosophy. He knows that "deficiencies of language stand in the way inexorably" of any attempt to get at "metaphysical first principles" (4). Language "breaks down precisely at the task of expressing in explicit form the larger generalities—the very generalities which metaphysics seeks to express." In consequence, no linguistic proposition can ever "refer to the universe in all its detail." But "a proposition can embody partial truth," and to that extent it can still be useful (11). This is why Whitehead rejects Wittgenstein's famous claim that "*the limits of my language* mean the limits of my world" (Wittgenstein 2001, 5.6, 56). Language, as a limited tool, is an empirical part of the world to which it refers, rather than a transcendental condition of that world. And there are other ways, besides the linguistic one, of prehending the world, or more precisely entities in the world.

Whitehead therefore sees the perilous situation of his times as an opportunity, rather than a crisis. Where others feel shock and paralysis when they encounter the modern world, Whitehead finds openness and potentiality. And where others fear that they are staring into the abyss, he simply sees creativity at work. Whitehead does not deny the radical contingency that is inherent to language, and that has become a hallmark of all aspects of modern life. But he suggests that this contingency, this condition of groundlessness, is not a reason to despair. Rather, it should itself be taken as a sort of metaphysical ground. Evanescence, becoming, incessant novelty, and "perpetual perishing" do not make reference and grounding impossible. Rather, these experiences are themselves our fundamental points of reference.

In this way, Whitehead fulfills Brian Cantwell Smith's demand for a metaphysics "that is grounded, simpliciter, without being grounded in α, for any α" (Smith 1996, 370; cf. 83). Creativity is an "ultimate principle" and a universal ground, only because—and precisely because—it is featureless and neutral, entirely "without a character of its own" (Whitehead 1929/1978, 21, 31). Being grounded in creativity may be opposed both to being entirely ungrounded, and to being grounded in anything in particular. As an "ultimate notion of the highest generality" (31), creativity is the one thing that can adequately respond to the absolute singularity—the contingency, novelty, and irreplaceability—of every actual occasion of experience.

The atomistic components of the world are each entirely unique, which is why they can only be characterized by means of a concept that, for its part, is altogether bland and generic. And there can be no intermediate instances between these extremes. To posit a mediation between the "ultimate" and its "accidental embodiments" (7) would be in fact to establish some sort of privileged α, a substance or a category upon which things would be grounded, and in relation to which they could be differentially ranked.

In the absence of a mediating term, no such overall ranking is possible. There is no criterion that can serve as the stable and objective basis for a system of judgments. This is why the only form of valuation, or "graded envisagement" (Whitehead 1929/1978, 189, citing 1925/1967, 176), that Whitehead accepts is an aesthetic one. For aesthetic judgments are singular, unrepeatable, and ungeneralizable. They may be *exemplary*, as Kant suggests; but they cannot provide an actual rule to be followed (Kant 1987, 175, 186–187). Or as Whitehead puts it, "there is not just one ideal 'order' which all actual entities should attain and fail to attain. In each case there is an ideal peculiar to each particular actual entity. . . . The notion of one ideal arises from the disastrous overmoralization of thought under the influence of fanaticism, or pedantry" (1929/1978, 84). Whitehead always opposes the actual to the ideal; but just as actualities are all different, so must the ideals be as well. This is why the only ideals are aesthetic ones. As we have seen, in Whitehead's metaphysics every actual occasion evaluates the world aesthetically, according to the imperatives of "Subjective Harmony" and "Subjective Intensity" (27). Even God only makes singular, aesthetic evaluations, rather than categorical or legislative judgments. His sole goals are the aesthetic ones of intensity (105) and "conceptual harmonization" (346). For Whitehead, the aim of the world—which is to say, the "subjective aim" of every entity within the world, God included—is Beauty, rather than Goodness or Truth (and also rather than Nietzschean will-to-power, or Darwinian self-replication). "Any system of things which in any wide sense is beautiful is to that extent justified in its existence" (Whitehead 1933/1967, 265). Whitehead thus proposes an aesthetics of existence, rather than an ethics; even more, he proposes an aesthetics of the Beautiful, rather than one of the Sublime.

Doubtless this is the aspect of Whitehead's philosophy that we find hardest to accept today. We tend to be suspicious of aesthetic ideals, and we feel called rather to heed the demands of ethics. What's more, Whitehead's own aesthetics of beauty and harmony, with its emphasis on "subjective forms . . . severally and jointly interwoven in patterned contrasts" (1933/1967, 252), has an oddly retrograde, Victorian cast to it, and seems out of touch with the strenuous art of his modernist contemporaries and their successors.[5] Who today would dare to assert that "the teleology of the Universe is dedicated to the production of Beauty" (265)? In sharp contrast with Whitehead, most aesthetic theorists and innovative artists of the twentieth century tend to disparage the very idea of beauty. Modernism shows a marked preference, instead, for the sublime. There are good reasons for this. The sublime is about immensity, excess, and disproportion, whereas the beautiful is about harmony and proportion. The sublime is concerned with questioning the limits of representation and form, whereas the beautiful is entirely contained within, and satisfied with, those limits. The sublime is disruptive, transformative, and potentially redemptive, whereas the beautiful is staid, conservative, and recuperative. As Kant himself puts it, "in presenting the sublime in nature the mind feels *agitated*, while in an aesthetic judgment about the beautiful in nature it is in *restful* contemplation" (1987, 115). All this makes the sublime seem

---

5. Whitehead himself seems to value mostly nineteenth-century art. He devotes an entire chapter of *Science and the Modern World* to the "Romantic reaction" against mechanism and positivism (1925/1967, 75–94). He especially cherishes, and identifies with, Percy Bysshe Shelley, who combines a deep "absorption . . . in scientific ideas" with a rejection of the "abstract materialism of science" in the eighteenth and nineteenth centuries (84–86). But Whitehead offers no comparable discussion of aesthetic modernism in relation to the new physics with which it was contemporaneous. Despite his close contact with Gertrude Stein, he has nothing to say about her work, or that of any other of his own artistic contemporaries.

This is probably why Charles Olson, the twentieth-century poet with the deepest affinities to Whitehead, disparages Whitehead's aesthetics, even while enthusiastically adopting his metaphysics: "he's just the greatest, if you read only his philosophy. If you read him on anything else, especially culture andor [sic] beauty, you realize that old saw, a man can't do everything!" (Olson 1997, 302). My thanks go to Barrett Watten for pointing me to this citation, and more generally to the subject of Olson's interest in Whitehead.

profoundly modern.⁶ The beautiful, on the other hand, seems complacent, conventional, and old-fashioned.

I cannot say that the situation is made any better by a certain recent recuperation of the ideal of beauty (Beckley and Shapiro 1998; Brand 2000). The context of this "return" to beauty is an exceedingly disagreeable one. On the one hand, beauty today has become a mere adjunct of advertising and product design—just as "innovation" has become a managerial buzzword, and creativity has become "a value *in itself*" for the corporate sector (Thrift 2005, 133). There's scarcely a commodity out there that doesn't proclaim its beauty as a selling point, together with its novelty and the degree of creativity that ostensibly went into developing it. Free-market economists like Virginia Postrel (2004) celebrate this state of affairs as the apogee of consumer choice; in the marketplace, she says, we freely express our individual preferences by paying for "aesthetics," or "look and feel."⁷

On the other hand, and at the same time, beauty is exalted as an eternal value, an essential attribute of great art, something that miraculously transcends, and nullifies, all social and political (let alone merely commercial) considerations. Neoconservative art critics like Hilton Kramer (1985) and Roger Kimball (2004) seek to rehabilitate beauty as part of their campaign to purge American culture of diversity, progressivism, and dissent. Beauty in this sense is proclaimed to be absolutely opposed to the marketplace—though it gets marketed nonetheless, in the form of the high prices commanded by art "masterpieces," as well as in the way it serves as a marker of discernment and taste, which is to say of the differentiations of social class (Bourdieu 2007).

In such circumstances, it is hard to disagree with Fredric Jameson when he says that "all beauty today is meretricious and the appeal to it by

---

6. Or even postmodern, at least under certain understandings of postmodernism: most notably, the one proposed by Jean-François Lyotard (1991, 1993). I discuss the modernist preference for the sublime over the beautiful, and propose a Nietzschean "reversal of perspective" that would instead privilege beauty over sublimity, in my article "Beauty Lies in the Eye" (Shaviro 2002).

7. A reflection on this situation is the starting-point for my next book, currently in preparation: *The Age of Aesthetics*.

contemporary pseudo-aestheticism is an ideological manoeuvre and not a creative resource" (1998, 135). For Jameson, the modernist sublime encompassed "art's vocation to reach the Absolute" (84), its endeavor to put forth "truth claims" which are not those of the dominant order (86), and its quest for what Roland Barthes calls bliss, or *jouissance* (Barthes 1975). These ambitions are abjured, Jameson says, by a post- or antimodernist contemporary art practice that is concerned with beauty—in the form of decoration and design—instead of truth, that seeks "pleasure and gratification" instead of *jouissance* (Jameson 1998, 86), and that has been entirely "assimilated into commodity production" (134). Beauty may have had a "subversive role" in the late nineteenth century, when it was "deployed . . . as a political weapon" against the "complacent materialist" pretensions of "a society marred by nascent commodification" (134). But this can no longer be the case today, when "the image is the commodity," without appeal or remainder (135).

If I am to insist upon Whitehead's aestheticism, then I must do so in a manner that takes these developments into account—rather than ignoring them or explaining them away. Whitehead's interest in the beautiful, to the exclusion of the sublime, and his claim that "Beauty is a wider, and more fundamental, notion than Truth" (1933/1967, 265) must be maintained, not in spite of the current capitalist recuperation of the idea of beauty, but precisely *on account of* it—or at least in recognition of it. Now, philosophical concepts like "beauty" and "creativity" are for Whitehead entirely generic notions. That is to say, they apply univocally and indifferently to all entities and to all forms of existence. They do not have any privileged relation to, or any special role to play within, the capitalist mode of production. They are equally valid and important for feudal society, or tribal hunter-gatherer society; or for that matter, for a "society" of bees, or of bacteria, or even one of stones or of neutrinos. No particular political and economic arrangement—indeed, no "society" in Whitehead's expansive use of this term—can claim privileged access to something that is a characteristic of being in general, in all its instances. Whitehead's metaphysics cannot be partisan or politically one-sided, because it is not even especially human-centered in the first place. "No entity can be divorced from the notion of creativity. An entity is at least a particular form capable of infusing its own particularity into creativity. An actual entity, or a phase of an actual entity, is more than that; but, at least, it is that" (Whitehead 1929/1978, 213).

This means that Whitehead's metaphysics cannot be *applied to* particular social and political circumstances. It does not command us, and it does not make ethical demands upon us. It does not make judgments of legitimacy. It certainly does not give us warrant to congratulate ourselves over the crucial role that creativity plays in postmodern marketing, much less to celebrate capitalism for unleashing its continual waves of "creative destruction" (Schumpeter 1962, 81ff.). But also, and by the same logic, Whitehead's metaphysics does not give us any grounds to condemn capitalism—as I would want to do—for purveying a denatured beauty, or for promoting an inauthentic and sadly limited version of creativity. I can only make such a condemnation on my own account, and from my own perspective. For it is only in the singular "decision" of a particular actual entity that "fact is confronted with alternatives" (Whitehead 1929/1978, 189, citing 1925/1967, 176), or that reality is criticized on the basis of "ideal possibilities" (1933/1967, 210). And it is only rarely, in vanishingly few instances of such decision, that "the explicitness of negation, which is the peculiar characteristic of consciousness," comes to the foreground (1929/1978, 273–274).

The critique in which I would like to engage is therefore a matter of *appetition*, rather than one of metaphysical authorization, or of an ethical imperative. There is no appeal beyond the "aversions and adversions" (1929/1978, 32) that are felt in every immediate instance of experience. Whitehead defines "appetition" as the condition of "immediate matter of fact including in itself a principle of unrest, involving realization of what is not and may be" (32). That is to say, appetition is rooted in "stubborn fact," even as it seeks to alter or transform that fact. Appetition is always circumstantial and exceptional, for it is only the striving, or the projection, of one particular entity.[8] Each actual occasion is an endeavor to change the world, in the very process of constituting itself. And each actual occasion does in fact change the world,

---

8. This is even the case when the particular entity in question is God. God's "primordial appetition," Whitehead says, is the "basis of all order" (1929/1978, 347), because it involves "the complete conceptual valuation of all eternal objects" (32). This means that God's appetition is a desire, or a craving, toward the actualization of *all* potentialities, even incompossible ones. But this craving can only be expressed and satisfied in the immediacy of finite actual occasions. Just one potentiality is made actual at a time. "God is completed by the individual,

at least to the extent of adding itself to the world, as something new. This is why appetition must be conceived in terms of an aesthetic of existence, rather than subjected to an ethics of obligation and lack. Appetition is dedicated to creating the "appearance" that "results from the fusion of the ideal with the actual:—The light that never was, on sea or land" (1933/1967, 211).

In contrast to these aesthetic processes of comparison, idealization, and transformation, Whitehead's "generalities," or generic notions, are not subject to negation or exception. They cannot serve as ideals, or as normative criteria. What they *can* do is provide us with a conceptual background, or with a "system of general ideas in terms of which every element of our experience can be interpreted" (1929/1978, 3). That is to say, Whitehead's generic notions can assist us to discern, more fully and more precisely, the shape of the actuality within which we find ourselves. And this actuality also includes the virtuality—the potential for change and difference—that lurks within it, or that haunts it. For every actual entity "really experiences a future which must be actual, although the completed actualities of that future are undetermined" (215). In this way, we can go on to evaluate our actual situation, to praise it or condemn it, to negatively prehend it and seek to change it: not on general metaphysical grounds, but in view of this objective indetermination, and on the more urgent and more immediate grounds provided by our prehensions, our feelings, and our appetitions.

I can put this in more specific terms. Whitehead himself does not offer us any concepts of directly political import. He has nothing in particular to say about capitalism; his politics, though moderately left of center, were certainly not Marxist.[9] He does not contribute in any way to a politico-aesthetic

---

fluent satisfactions of finite fact" (347), in the "immediacy of the concrescent subject . . . constituted by its living aim at its own self-constitution" (244). The "consequent nature of God" is the sum of all these actualizations, as they are preserved in their "objective immortality"; but for this very reason, God is never finished, never total or complete.

9. In some brief "Autobiographical Notes," written late in his life, Whitehead says: "My political opinions were, and are, on the Liberal side, as against the Conservatives. I am now writing in terms of English party divisions. The Liberal Party has now [1941] practically vanished; and in England my vote would be given for the moderate side of the Labour Party" (Whitehead 1951a).

judgment such as the one Jameson makes about the role of the appeal to beauty in late capitalism. But Whitehead *does* provide a "categoreal scheme" (18) within which such a judgment can usefully be framed and articulated. Of course, Jameson himself does not actually invoke this scheme. But it is nevertheless noteworthy that Jameson's critique turns on the question of whether the contemporary invocation of beauty can be mobilized as a "creative resource." Creativity remains a central concern for Jameson, in spite of the way that business and marketing have hijacked the term.

More generally, Whitehead's generic formulations and aesthetic insights might lead us to question the link between creativity and the figure of the entrepreneur—a link so ubiquitous, and so seemingly self-evident, in our society today that even artists (as Andy Warhol foresaw) are now best known as the promoters of their own "brands." These formulations and insights might also help us to take a new look at the way that beauty is commodified and packaged in the postmodern world. The creative process is entirely generic and common, and yet the fruits of this process are appropriated, privatized, and sold under artificially produced conditions of scarcity. At the same time, all the singular actual occasions of creativity are homogenized, through their reduction to the quantitative measure of money as a universal equivalent. These operations are abusive, precisely because they seek to rarify, monopolize, and capitalize on the generic conditions of all existence.

The marketed and branded cultural product that we are so familiar with today is a particular sort of object. It is a "society" that results from specific positive and negative prehensions, bound together by a specific sort of "subjective aim." We can analyze the product of commodity culture in terms of what it takes up and adapts to its own ends, and also in terms of what it refuses and excludes. Whitehead's aesthetics may seem at odds with much of twentieth-century modernism. But such an aesthetics is strikingly relevant to the culture of the present day, which locates creativity almost entirely in practices of sampling, appropriation, and recombination. After all, Whitehead's great topic is precisely the manner in which something radically new can emerge out of the prehension of already existing elements. Innovation is all a matter of " 'subjective form,' which is *how* [a particular] subject prehends [its] datum" (1929/1978, 23). Whitehead's aesthetics, with its intensive focus on this *how*, takes on a special urgency in a culture, such as ours, that is poised on the razor's edge between the corporate ownership, and interminable recycling, of "intellectual property," on the one hand, and the pirating, reworking, and transformation of such alleged "property," often in violation of copyright laws, on the other.

Whitehead warns us that "the chief error in philosophy is overstatement. The aim at generalization is sound, but the estimate of success is exaggerated" (1929/1978, 7). So I do not wish to exaggerate my own claims here. The instances that I have cited do not add up to a focused critique of capitalism, even in the cultural sphere; and I do not mean to suggest that Whitehead ever offers us any such thing.[10] His concerns are as distant from Adorno's as they are from Heidegger's. But at the very least, Whitehead's aestheticism is radical enough that it nudges and cajoles us away from the complacencies and satisfactions of commodity culture. For "progress is founded upon the experience of discordant feelings. The social value of liberty lies in its production of discords" (1933/1967, 257). Whitehead values the experience of "aesthetic destruction" (256) as a corrective to insipid harmonies and perfections.[11] Art

---

10. Aside from Anne Pomeroy's book *Marx and Whitehead* (2004), little work has been done on putting the two thinkers, and their traditions, into contact. (A short bibliography on "Process Thought and Marxism" is available at http://www.ctr4process.org/publications/Biblio/Thematic/Marxism.html). I myself am wary of bringing Whitehead and Marx together, either in terms of how they conceive process and change, or in terms of how they view the relation of philosophical speculation to practice. The divergences in method, in focus of attention, and in the aims they seek to accomplish, are just too great. However, one way of seeing these divergences in terms of "patterned contrast" rather than opposition might be to look at particular conjunctions and resonances, rather than broader comparisons. For instance, Whitehead's generic sense of creativity might usefully be juxtaposed with recent post-Marxist reconceptualizations of class and labor. These would include Michael Hardt and Antonio Negri's recent speculations on affective labor and on the common, and their claim that the creativity that drives the economy today is ubiquitous, and comes from everywhere and everyone (Hardt and Negri 2001); Paolo Virno's closely related speculations on the multitude and general intellect (Virno 2004); and even, much further afield, Alain Badiou's insistence on the paradoxically "generic identity of the working class" (Badiou 2006).

11. Whitehead's praise of "aesthetic destruction" might usefully be compared with Morse Peckham's insistence on "cultural vandalism" as an important prelude to "emergent innovation" and "cultural transcendence" (Peckham 1979, 274ff.).

in particular is important, Whitehead says, because of the way that it offers us an "intensity" that is "divorced from" the "dire necessity" or "compulsion which was its origin" (272). In view of this displacement, "Art can be described as a psychopathic response of the race to the stresses of its existence" (272). And this "psychopathic function of Art" is a necessary one, for it shakes us out of the "feeling of slow relapse into general anaesthesia, or into tameness which is its prelude" (263–264). But even in making declarations of this sort, Whitehead never moves from the terrain of the beautiful into that of the sublime. For he continues to define the goal of art—and even of the art of discords—to be not the rupture of appearances and the emergence of a traumatic "Real," but rather the "purposeful adaptation of Appearance to Reality" (267).

Many of the great thinkers of Western modernity define their goal as a therapeutic one. Spinoza, Nietzsche, Freud, and Wittgenstein all present themselves as diagnosticians and clinicians. They examine symptoms, discern the conditions of our metaphysical malaise, and propose remedies to free us from our enslavement to "passive emotions" (Spinoza), to *ressentiment* (Nietzsche), to traumatic recollections (Freud), or to the "bewitchment of our intelligence by means of language" (Wittgenstein). Therapy in this sense is the modern, secularized and demystified, form of ethics. To my mind, one of the striking things about Whitehead is that he does not make any such therapeutic or ethical claims. He does not say that his metaphysics will cure me, or that it will make me a better person. At best, philosophy and art may awaken me from my torpor, and allow me to subsume the painful experience of a "clash in affective tones" (260) within a wider sense of purpose. Such broadening "increases the dimensions of the experient subject, adds to its ambit" (266). But this is still a rather modest and limited result. At best, philosophy and poetry "seek to express that ultimate good sense which we term civilization" (1938/1968, 174). Granted, Whitehead displays none of Nietzsche's or Freud's justified suspicion regarding the value of "good sense," or of what we call "civilization." But even from the perspective of Whitehead's entirely laudatory use of these terms, he is still only making a deliberately muted and minor claim. We are far from any "exaggerated" promises of a Great Health, of self-transcendence, or of cathartic transformation.

Even in his hyperbolic evocation of "God and the World," in the fifth and final Part of *Process and Reality*, Whitehead does not offer us any prospect to match the "intellectual love of God" exalted by Spinoza in the fifth and final part of the *Ethics*. Whitehead's God, in sharp contrast with Spinoza's, does not know the world *sub specie aeternitatis*. Rather, Whitehead's God is "the poet of the world." This means that he knows the world, not in terms of its first causes, but only through its effects, and only in retrospect. God "saves" the world precisely to the extent, but only to the extent, that he aestheticizes and memorializes it. He *remembers* the world in each and every detail, incorporating all these memories into an overarching "conceptual harmonization" (1929/1978, 346). But if God remembers every experience of every last entity, he does not produce and provide these experiences and memories themselves. That is something that is left for us to do, contingently and unpredictably. Where Spinoza's book ends with the "spiritual contentment" that arises from the comprehension of "eternal necessity," Whitehead's book rather ends by justifying, and throwing us back upon, our "insistent craving" for novelty and adventure (351). That is what it means to write an aesthetics, rather than an ethics.

I can end this book only by attesting to the aesthetic power and splendor of Whitehead's words, by bearing witness to how they have affected me. Whitehead's language is to a great extent "without qualities." The opening sentence of *Process and Reality* characterizes the book as a "course of lectures" (1929/1978, 3); and Whitehead largely conforms to the prosaic, or even pedantic, implications of this description. He descends from an extreme dryness and abstraction only in order to analyze such humdrum phrases as "Socrates is mortal" (11–12; 264–265) and "United Fruit Company" (1933/1967, 182–183). His vocabulary is filled with "technical terms," which he uses despite the "danger" that these terms may either suggest irrelevant associations derived from their common meanings, or else (if they are neologisms) appear insipid, because they are "entirely neutral, devoid of all suggestiveness" (1929/1978, 32–33). This manner of writing is a strategic necessity for Whitehead; it is the only way that he can make statements that are precisely formulated and yet as widely applicable and broadly generic as possible. The result is that I read Whitehead slowly and cautiously, attempting to parse out the details of his argument. But in doing so, I continually read over, or fail to notice, the aphoristic compressions and other "remarkable points" that pepper Whitehead's discourse, and that break out, again and again, from the continuities of his reasoning. It is only when I look at the text with a certain inattentiveness, or when somebody else points out a phrase to me, that I am stopped short—as I finally notice and recognize the brilliance of something that I had already read through a good number of times. It is in this way that Whitehead's own text remains perpetually creative, as it renews the "zest for existence" (351) that so much in our lives tends to annul.

References

Albrecht-Buehler, Guenter (1998). "Cell Intelligence." http://www.basic.northwestern.edu/g<->buehler/cellint0.htm.

Badiou, Alain (2003). *Saint Paul: The Foundation of Universalism*. Trans. Ray Brassier. Stanford: Stanford University Press.

Badiou, Alain (2006). "The Saturated Generic Identity of the Working Class." *InterActivist Info Exchange*, http://info.interactivist.net/node/5400.

Bagemihl, Bruce (1999). *Biological Exuberance: Animal Homosexuality and Natural Diversity*. St. Martin's Press.

Barthes, Roland (1975). *The Pleasure of the Text*. New York: Hill and Wang.

Bataille, Georges (1985). *Visions of Excess*. Trans. Allan Stoekel, with Carl R. Lovitt and Donald M. Leslie, Jr. Minneapolis: University of Minnesota Press.

Bataille, Georges (1988). *The Accursed Share*. Vol. 1. Trans. Robert Hurley. New York: Zone Books.

Bateson, Gregory (2000). *Steps to an Ecology of Mind*. Chicago: University of Chicago Press.

Beckley, Bill, and David Shapiro, eds. (1998). *Uncontrollable Beauty: Toward a New Aesthetics*. New York: Allworth Press.

Ben Jacob, Eshel, Yoash Shapira, and Alfred I. Tauber (2006). "Seeking the Foundations of Cognition in Bacteria: From Schrodinger's Negative Entropy to Latent Information." *Physica A* 359: 495–524.

Bergson, Henri (2005). *Creative Evolution*. New York: Cosimo Classics.

Bloch, Ernst (1986). *The Principle of Hope*. Trans. Neville Plaice, Stephen Plaice, and Paul Knight. Cambridge, Mass.: MIT Press.

Bourdieu, Pierre (2007). *Distinction: A Social Critique of the Judgment of Taste*. Trans. Richard Nice. Cambridge, Mass.: Harvard University Press.

Brand, Peg Zeglin, ed. (2000). *Beauty Matters*. Bloomington: Indiana UniversityPress.

Brassier, Ray (2007). "The Enigma of Realism: On Quentin Meillassoux's *After Finitude.*" In *Collapse: Philosophical Research and Development 2.*

Carter, Angela (1986). *The Infernal Desire Machines of Doctor Hoffman.* New York: Penguin.

Clark, Tim (2002). "A Whiteheadian Chaosmos? Process Philosophy from a Deleuzian Perspective." In *Process and Difference: Between Cosmologicaland Poststructuralist Postmodernisms*, ed. Katherine Keller and Anne Daniell, 191–207. Albany: SUNY Press.

Debaise, Didier (2006). *Un empirisme spéculatif: Lecture de Procès et réalité de Whitehead.* Paris: Vrin.

De Landa, Manuel (2002). *Intensive Science and Virtual Philosophy.* New York: Continuum.

De Landa, Manuel (2006). *A New Philosophy of Society: Assemblage Theory and Social Complexity.* New York: Continuum.

Deleuze, Gilles (1983). *Nietzsche and Philosophy.* Trans. Hugh Tomlinson. New York: Columbia University Press.

Deleuze, Gilles (1984). *Kant's Critical Philosophy.* Trans. Hugh Tomlinson and Barbara Habberjam. Minneapolis: University of Minnesota Press.

Deleuze, Gilles (1986). *Cinema 1: The Movement-Image.* Trans. Hugh Tomlinson and Barbra Habberjam. Minneapolis: University of Minnesota Press.

Deleuze, Gilles (1988). *Spinoza: Practical Philosophy.* Trans. Robert Hurley. San Francisco: City Lights Books.

Deleuze, Gilles (1989). *Cinema 2: The Time-Image.* Trans. Hugh Tomlinson and Robert Galeta. Minneapolis: University of Minnesota Press.

Deleuze, Gilles (1990). *The Logic of Sense.* Trans. Mark Lester. New York: Columbia Universit Press.

Deleuze, Gilles (1991). *Bergsonism.* Trans. Hugh Tomlinson and Barbara Habberjam. New York: Zone Books.

Deleuze, Gilles (1993). *The Fold: Leibniz and the Baroque.* Trans. Tom Conley. Minneapolis: University of Minnesota Press.

Deleuze, Gilles (1994). *Difference and Repetition.* Trans. Paul Patton. New York: Columbia University Press.

Deleuze, Gilles (1997). *Essays Critical and Clinical.* Trans. Daniel Smith and Michael Greco. Minneapolis: University of Minnesota Press.

Deleuze, Gilles (2005). *Francis Bacon: The Logic of Sensation.* Trans. Daniel Smith. Minneapolis: University of Minnesota Press.

Deleuze, Gilles, and Felix Guattari (1983). *Anti-Oedipus: Capitalism and Schizophrenia*. Trans. Robert Hurley, Mark Seem, and Helen R. Lane. Minneapolis: University of Minnesota Press.

Deleuze, Gilles, and Felix Guattari (1987). *A Thousand Plateaus: Capitalism and Schizophrenia*. Trans. Brian Massumi. Minneapolis: University of Minnesota Press.

Deleuze, Gilles, and Felix Guattari (1994). *What Is Philosophy?* Trans. Hugh Tomlinson and Graham Burchell. New York: Columbia University Press.

Deleuze, Gilles, and Claire Parnet (2002). *Dialogues*. 2nd ed. New York: Columbia University Press.

Derrida, Jacques (1994). *Specters of Marx: The State of the Debt, the Work of Mourning, and the New International*. Trans. Peggy Kamuf. New York: Routledge.

de Spinoza, Benedictus (1991). *The Ethics; Treatise on the Emendation of the Intellect; and Selected Letters*. Trans. Samuel Shirley. Indianapolis: Hackett.

Devitt, Susannah Kate (2007). "Bacterial Cognition". In *Philosophy of Memory*, http://mnemosynosis.livejournal.com/10810.html.

Ellis, Warren (2003). *Planetary: Crossing Worlds*. La Jolla: Wildstorm/DC.

Ford, Lewis S. (1984). *The Emergence of Whitehead's Metaphysics: 1925–1929*. Albany: SUNY Press.

Foucault, Michel (1970). *The Order of Things: An Archaeology of the Human Sciences*. New York: Vintage.

Foucault, Michel (1986). *The Use of Pleasure: The History of Sexuality*, vol. 2. New York: Vintage.

Foucault, Michel (1997). *Ethics: Subjectivity and Truth*. Ed. Paul Rabinow. *Essential Works of Foucault*. Vol. 1. Trans. Robert Hurley et al. New York: The New Press.

Foucault, Michel (1998). *Aesthetics, Method, and Epistemology. Essential Works of Foucault*, vol. 2. Trans. Robert Hurley et al. New York: The New Press.

Halewood, Michael (2005). "On Whitehead and Deleuze: The Process of Materiality." In *Configurations* 13.1 (winter): 57–76.

Hardt, Michael, and Antonio Negri (2001). *Empire*. Cambridge, Mass.: Harvard University Press.

Harman, Graham (2007). "On Vicarious Causation." In *Collapse: Philosophical Research and Development 2*.

Hayek, Friedrich (1991). *The Fatal Conceit: The Errors of Socialism*. Chicago: University of Chicago Press.

Hayles, N. Katherine (1999). *How We Became Posthuman: Virtual Bodies in Cybernetics, Literature, and Informatics*. Chicago: University of Chicago Press.

Hegel, G. W. F. (1977). *Hegel's "Phenomenology of Spirit."* Trans. A. V. Miller. New York: Oxford University Press.

Hume, David (1978). *A Treatise of Human Nature*. 2nd ed. New York: Oxford University Press.

Hume, David (1998). *Dialogues Concerning Natural Religion*. 2nd ed. Indianapolis: Hackett.

Investopedia (2008). Economics Basics: Introduction. http://www.investopedia.com/university/economics/default.asp.

James, William (1983). *The Principles of Psychology*. Cambridge, Mass.: Harvard University Press.

James, William (1996). *Essays in Radical Empiricism*. Lincoln: University of Nebraska Press.

Jameson, Fredric (1991). *Postmodernism, Or, The Cultural Logic of Late Capitalism*. Durham: Duke University Press.

Jameson, Fredric (1998). *The Cultural Turn: Selected Writings on the Postmodern, 1983–1998*. New York: Verso.

Kant, Immanuel (1983). *Perpetual Peace and Other Essays*. Trans. Ted Humphrey. Indianapolis: Hackett.

Kant, Immanuel (1987). *Critique of Judgment*. Trans. Werner S. Pluhar. Indianapolis: Hackett.

Kant, Immanuel (1996). *Critique of Pure Reason*. Trans. Werner Pluhar. Indianapolis: Hackett.

Kant, Immanuel (2002). *Critique of Practical Reason*. Trans. Werner Pluhar. Indianapolis: Hackett.

Karatani, Kojin (2003). *Transcritique: On Kant and Marx*. Trans. Sabu Kohso. Cambridge, Mass.: MIT Press.

Kauffman, Stuart (2000). *Investigations*. New York: Oxford University Press.

Kelly, Kevin (1994). *Out of Control: The New Biology of Machines, Social Systems, and the Economic World*. New York: Addison-Wesley.

Kimball, Roger (2004). *The Rape of the Masters: How Political Correctness Sabotages Art*. New York: Encounter Books.

Klossowski, Pierre (1998). *Nietzsche and the Vicious Circle*. Trans. Daniel Smith. Chicago: University of Chicago Press.

Kramer, Hilton (1985). *Revenge of the Philistines*. New York: Free Press.

Lacan, Jacques (1978). *The Four Fundamental Concepts of Psychoanalysis*. Trans. Alan Sheridan. New York: W. W. Norton.

Lapoujade, David (2000). "From Transcendental Empiricism to Worker Nomadism: William James." *Pli* 9: 190–199.

Latour, Bruno (1993). *We Have Never Been Modern*. Trans. Catherine Porter. Cambridge, Mass.: Harvard University Press.

Latour, Bruno (2005). *Reassembling the Social: An Introduction to Actor-Network-Theory*. New York: Oxford University Press.

Lazzarato, Maurizio (2004). *Les Révolutions du Capitalisme*. Paris: Les Empêcheurs de Penser en Rond.

Leibniz, Gottfried Wilhelm (1973). *Philosophical Writings*. Ed. G. H. R. Parkinson. London: Everyman's Library.

Lovelock, James (2000). *Gaia: A New Look at Life on Earth*. New York: Oxford University Press.

Lucas, George R. (1990). *The Rehabilitation of Whitehead: An Analytic and Historical Assessment of Process Philosophy*. Albany: SUNY Press.

Luhmann, Niklas (1996). *Social Systems*. Trans. John Bednarz and Dirk Baecker. Palo Alto: Stanford University Press.

Lyotard, Jean-François (1984). *The Postmodern Condition*. Trans. Brian Massumi. Minneapolis: University of Minnesota Press.

Lyotard, Jean-François (1991). *The Inhuman*. Trans. Geoffrey Bennington and Rachel Bowlby. Stanford: Stanford University Press.

Lyotard, Jean-François (1993). *The Postmodern Explained*. Trans. Julian Pefanis et al. Minneapolis: University of Minnesota Press.

Margulis, Lynn, and Dorion Sagan (2002). *Acquiring Genomes: A Theory of the Origin of Species*. New York: Basic Books.

Marx, Karl (1968). *Selected Works*. New York: International Publishers.

Marx, Karl (1992). *Capital: A Critique of Political Economy*. Vol. 1. Trans. Ben Fowkes. New York: Penguin.

Massumi, Brian (1992). *A User's Guide to Capitalism and Schizophrenia: Deviations from Deleuze and Guattari*. Cambridge, Mass.: MIT Press.

Massumi, Brian (2002). *Parables for the Virtual: Movement, Affect, Sensation*. Durham: Duke University Press.

Maturana, Humberto, and Francisco Varela (1991). *Autopoiesis and Cognition: The Realization of the Living*. Berlin: Springer.

Maye, Alexander, et al. (2007). "Order in Spontaneous Behavior." *PLoS ONE* 2.5 (May): e443. doi:10.1371/journal.pone.0000443.

Meyer, Steven (2005). "Introduction: Whitehead Now." *Configurations* 13.1 (winter): 1–33.

Nakagaki, Toshiyuki, Hiroyasu Yamada, and Agota Toth (2000). "Maze-solving by an Amoeboid Organism." *Nature* 47.6803 (Sept. 28): 470.

Nietzsche, Friedrich (1968). *Twilight of the Idols/The Antichrist*. Trans. R. J. Hollingdale. New York: Penguin.

Olson, Charles (1997). *Collected Prose*. Berkeley: University of California Press.

Oyama, Susan (2000). *The Ontogeny of Information: Developmental Systems and Evolution*. 2nd ed. Durham: Duke University Press.

Peckham, Morse (1979). *Explanation and Power: The Control of Human Behavior*. Minneapolis: University of Minnesota Press.

Pomeroy, Anne Fairchild (2004). *Marx and Whitehead: Process, Dialectics, and the Critique of Capitalism*. Albany: SUNY Press.

Postrel, Virginia (2004). *The Substance of Style: How the Rise of Aesthetic Value Is Remaking Commerce, Culture, and Consciousness*. New York: Perennial.

Pred, Ralph (2005). *Onflow: Dynamics of Consciousness and Experience*. Cambridge, Mass.: MIT Press.

Price, Lucien (2001). *Dialogues of Alfred North Whitehead*. Boston: David R. Godine.

Ranciere, Jacques (2004). *The Politics of Aesthetics*. Trans. Gabriel Rockhill. New York: Continuum.

Robinson, Keith (2005). "Towards a Metaphysics of Complexity." *Interchange* 36.1–2 (Jan.): 159–177.

Robinson, Keith (2006). "The New Whitehead? An Ontology of the Virtual in Whitehead's Metaphysics." *Symposium* 10.1: 69–80.

Robinson, Keith (2007). "Deleuze, Whitehead, and the 'Process Point of View' on Perception." Unpublished essay.

Rorty, Richard (1981). *Philosophy and the Mirror of Nature*. Princeton: Princeton University Press.

Schumpeter, Joseph (1962). *Capitalism, Socialism, and Democracy*. New York: Harper Perennial.

Sha, Xin Wei (2005). "Whitehead's Poetical Mathematics." *Configurations* 13.1 (winter): 77–94.

Shaviro, Steven (2002). "Beauty Lies in the Eye." In *A Shock to Thought: Expression after Deleuze and Guattari*, 9–19, ed. Brian Massumi. New York: Routledge.

Shaviro, Steven (2004). "The Life, After Death, of Postmodern Emotions." *Criticism: A Quarterly for Literature and the Arts* 46.1 (winter): 125–141.

Shaviro, Steven (in preparation). *The Age of Aesthetics.*

Sherburne, Donald (1986). "Decentering Whitehead." *Process Studies* 15.2: 83–94.

Simondon, Gilbert (2005). *L'individuation à la lumière des notions de forme et d'information.* Grenoble: Million.

Smith, Brian Cantwell (1996). *On the Origin of Objects.* Cambridge, Mass.: MIT Press.

Stengers, Isabelle (2002a). "Beyond Conversation: The Risks of Peace." In *Process and Difference: Between Cosmological and Poststructuralist Postmodernisms*, ed. Katherine Keller and Anne Daniell, 235–255. Albany: SUNY Press.

Stengers, Isabelle (2002b). *Penser avec Whitehead: une libre et sauvage création de concepts.* Paris: Seuil.

Stengers, Isabelle (2005). "Whitehead's Account of the Sixth Day." *Configurations* 13.1 (winter): 35–55.

Stengers, Isabelle (2006). *La vierge et le neutrino: les scientifiques dans la tourmente.* Paris: Les Empêcheurs de penser en ronde.

Sylvester, David (1987). *The Brutality of Fact: Interviews with Francis Bacon.* 3rd ed. New York: Thames and Hudson.

Thrift, Nigel (2005). *Knowing Capitalism.* London: Sage Publications.

Toscano, Alberto (2006). *The Theatre of Production: Philosophy and Individuation Between Kant and Deleuze.* New York: Palgrave Macmillan.

Trewavas, Anthony (2005). "Green Plants as Intelligent Organisms." *Trends in Plant Science* 10.9 (Sept): 413–419.

Virno, Paolo (2004). *A Grammar of the Multitude.* Los Angeles and New York: Semiotext(e).

Warhol, Andy (1975). *The Philosophy of Andy Warhol.* New York: Harvest/HBJ.

Whitehead, Alfred North (1920/2004). *The Concept of Nature.* Amherst, N.Y.: Prometheus Books.

Whitehead, Alfred North (1925/1967). *Science and the Modern World.* New York: The Free Press.

Whitehead, Alfred North (1926/1996). *Religion in the Making.* New York: Fordham University Press.

Whitehead, Alfred North (1929/1978). *Process and Reality.* New York: The Free Press.

Whitehead, Alfred North (1933/1967). *Adventures of Ideas.* New York: The Free Press.

Whitehead, Alfred North (1938/1968). *Modes of Thought.* New York: The Free Press.

Whitehead, Alfred North (1951a). "Autobiographical Notes." In *The Philosophy of Alfred North Whitehead*, ed. Paul Arthur Schilpp, 3–14. New York: Tudor Publishing House.

Whitehead, Alfred North (1951b). "Immortality." In *The Philosophy of Alfred North Whitehead*, ed. Paul Arthur Schilpp, 682–700. New York: Tudor Publishing House.

Williams, James (2005). *The Transversal Thought of Gilles Deleuze: Encounters and Influences.* Manchester: Clinamen Press.

Wilson, Edward O. (1999). *Consilience: The Unity of Knowledge.* New York: Vintage.

Wittgenstein, Ludwig (2001). *Tractatus Logico-Philosophicus.* Trans. D. F. Pears and B. F. McGuinness. New York: Routledge.

Žižek, Slavoj (2003). *The Puppet and the Dwarf: The Perverse Core of Christianity.* Cambridge, Mass.: MIT Press.

Žižek, Slavoj (2006). *The Parallax View.* Cambridge, Mass.: MIT Press.

Index

Actual entity or actual occasion, 18–19, 41–43, 110, 143
Actualization, 41–42
Adequacy, 144n
Aesthetic destruction, 159–160
Aesthetic disinterest, 5–7
Aesthetic judgment, 2–3, 13–14, 141, 152
Affective tone, 5, 57
Appetition, 91–92, 94, 131, 156
Aristotle, 105–106, 139
Assemblage, 147, 148n
Autopoiesis, 92, 93, 112n

Bacon, Francis, 6
Baphomet, 120–121, 124
Bataille, Georges, 7n
Bateson, Gregory, 75n
Batman, 117–118, 121
Baudrillard, Jean 150
Beauty, 1–2, 4, 140, 152–155
Beckett, Samuel, 117
Becoming, 19–20
Bergson, Henri, 61, 72, 76, 79n, 113–114n, 130n
Bloch, Ernst, 28n, 113–114n
Body without organs (BwO), 123–130
Borges, Jorge Luis, 114, 117
Brassier, Ray, 78n

Carnap, Rudolf, 150n
Carter, Angela, 124n
Categorical imperative, 8

Categories, 31–32, 51
Causal efficacy, 31
Clark, Tim, 26–27n, 136–137n
Cleopatra's Needle, 17–18, 20–22, 29
Cognition, 94
Coherence, 108–109
Communication, 6
Compossibility/incompossibility, 115–117
Conatus, 20n, 112n
Conceptual reversion, 136–139
Concrescence, 20, 88, 111, 133–135, 137
Connective synthesis, 111–113
Consistency, 108–109
Constructive functioning, 11, 48–50, 111
Contemplation, 13
Contradiction, 115
Creativity, 71–72, 149, 151

Darwin, Charles, 95n
Debaise, Didier, 144n
Decision, 33, 89, 91, 94, 118–119, 135
De Landa, Manuel, 27–28, 35, 109, 109–110n, 148n
Deleuze, Gilles, 6n, 19n, 31–37, 54n, 61n, 101
  on aesthetics, 67–68
  on Kant, 33–37, 76–77, 80–81
  Logic of Sense, 35–36, 85–86, 111, 116n, 125, 125–126n
  The Fold, 17, 26

Deleuze, Gilles, and Guattari, Felix, 2–3, 8n, 48n, 148–149
 Anti-Oedipus, 111–113, 116n, 123–126
Derrida, Jacques, 10n, 145, 150
Desire, 7–8, 111–113
Determination, 42–43, 90–91n, 119, 123
Deterministic chaos, 90
Disjunctive syllogism, 119–123
Disjunctive synthesis, 114–115, 117–119, 121–122

Effects, 36–37, 86
Efficient cause, 86–87, 97
Ellis, Warren, 117
Enduring objects, 30
Eternal objects, 37–43, 130–133, 138
Event, 17–21
Event epochalism, 20n
Excess of subjectivity, 50

Fallacy of misplaced concreteness, 145
Fallacy of simple location, 60, 145
Feeling, 47, 57–63, 66
Final cause, 88–89, 91, 97
Flat ontology, 27–28
Ford, Lewis, 107n, 139n
Foucault, Michel, 45
Freud, Sigmund, 160

Generality, 157
God, 23–26, 69–70, 90n, 99–142, 152, 156–157n, 161
 secularization of, 105
Gombrowicz, Witold, 117

Hardt, Michael, and Negri, Antonio, 127n
Harman, Graham, 78–79n
Hayek, Friedrich, 128n
Hayles, Katherine, 40n
Hegel, G. W. F., 26, 49n, 65n, 115n, 121n, 130n, 139

Heidegger, Martin, 24, 104, 143, 145, 150n
Horkheimer, Max, and Adorno, Theodor, 24
Hume, David, 31, 36, 52–53, 73, 102n
Hylomorphism, 53

Ideas, 9, 33, 43, 117
Individuation, 81, 112n

James, William, 21, 40–41, 58–59, 67
Jameson, Fredric, 154–155, 158
Judgment, 3–4n

Kant, Immanuel, 44–45, 48–50, 72–73, 112, 133–134n, 150
 Copernican revolution, 72–78
 Critique of Judgment, 1–16, 67, 82–84
 Critique of Practical Reason, 79–82, 83–84, 140
 Critique of Pure Reason, 72–73
 doctrine of faculties, 9
 doctrine of time, 76–79
 Transcendental Aesthetic, 52, 55–56, 59–60
 Transcendental Deduction, 33–35
 Transcendental Dialectic, 101–102, 119–123, 131
Karatani, Kojin, 52n
Kauffman, Stuart, 93
Kelly, Kevin, 128n
Klossowski, Pierre, 120–123

Latour, Bruno, 48n
Leibniz, Gottfried Wilhelm, 24–26, 73n, 87, 100–101, 104, 115, 116, 133, 139
Life, 91–93
Locke, John, 12, 24
Lovelock, James, 93

Luhmann, Niklas, 85
Lure for feelings, 2, 5, 15, 143
Lyotard, Jean-Francois, 154n

Margulis, Lynn, 93
Marx, Karl, 96, 126–128, 159n
Massumi, Brian, 47n, 53, 62n, 128n
Meillassoux, Quentin, 78n
Metastability, 81n

Negative prehension, 42
Nexus, 18
Nietzsche, Friedrich, 72, 76n, 95–96n, 100n, 104, 114, 121n, 122, 145, 160
Novelty, 20, 56, 71–72, 135, 142

Objective immortality, 87
Olson, Charles, 153n
Ontological principle, 23–24, 75
Oyama, Susan, 93

Passion, 6–9
Peckham, Morse, 95, 159n
Perpetual perishing, 12, 97–98
Plato, 118
Predicate, 130
Preestablished harmony, 25
Prehension, 28–30, 143
Presentational immediacy, 145
Proposition, 2, 143
Proust, Marcel, 89–90n, 98

Quasi-causality, 37, 85–86, 129

Radical empiricism, 40
Rational idea, 9
Reformed subjectivist principle, 78
Relations, 40
Rhizome, 113
Rorty, Richard, 145, 146, 147n

Satisfaction, 69, 111–112
Selection, 74
Self-enjoyment, 8n, 95, 142n
Self-identity, 30
Self-organization, 84–85
Simondon, Gilbert, 21n, 35, 53–54, 81, 112n
Simulacrum, 118
Singularity, 19, 89–91n, 113
Smith, Adam, 128n
Smith, Brian Cantwell, 151
Society, 18, 143
Specious present, 44
Spinoza, Baruch, 20n, 22–23, 97, 103–104, 142, 160
Stengers, Isabelle, 24, 48n, 106, 146–147n
Stevens, Wallace, 13
Subject and superject, 12, 21, 97
Subjective aim, 74, 89, 137, 140
Subjective form, 55–57, 68, 87–88
Subject–predicate thought, 22–23, 145
Sublime, 153–154
Sufficient reason, 24–25
Synthesis, 110–112. *See also* Conjunctive synthesis; Disjunctive synthesis

Things in themselves, 49
Toscano, Alberto, 82n
Transcendental, 33, 80
Transcendental empiricism, 33–37

Univocity, 21–22, 27, 101

Valuation, 88, 94, 152
Varela, Francesco, 92, 93, 112n
Vector, 62
Virtual, 33–37
Vitalism, 98

Warhol, Andy, 7n, 158
Whitehead, Alfred North, *passim*
  critique of epistemology, 30–31
  critique of Kant, 10–11, 21, 32–33,
    50–54, 64, 74–75, 77, 97, 131–132
  Science and the Modern World, 105–107,
    129, 132, 153n
  The Concept of Nature, 17–18
Wilson, Edward O., 85
Wittgenstein, Ludwig, 145, 151, 160

Žižek, Slavoj, 150